Sermons

of the

𝕮𝖔𝖓𝖋𝖊𝖉𝖊𝖗𝖆𝖈𝖞
1863-1865

edited by

Dr. William G. Peters

CHATTANOOGA:
C. S. Printing Office
2014

Originally published separately in various forms

during the War for Independence

in the

CONFEDERATE STATES OF AMERICA

Edited by

DR. WILLIAM G. PETERS

PRESIDENT

THE CONFEDERATE STATES OF AMERICA, INC.

Copyright © 2014, Dr. William G. Peters, President, THE CONFEDERATE STATES OF AMERICA, INC. — All rights reserved in all media formats under Berne Convention for U.S. and International Copyrights.

Published by the CONFEDERATE STATES PRINTING OFFICE[1],
CONFEDERATE STATES OF AMERICA, INC.

---

[1] A division of the Confederate States of America, Inc. Also designated the C.S. PRINTING OFFICE.

CONTENTS

Foreword i

1863

    Samson's Riddle 1

    Ezra's Dilemma 25

    A Discourse Before the S.C. General Assembly 51

    True Courage — Lt. Gen. Thomas J. Jackson 77

    The Southern Church Justified in its Support of the South 105

    The Blessed Dead are Waiting for Us 137

    A Sermon on the Festival of the Ascension 155

    A Sermon Delivered on the Day of Prayer 179

    True Eminence Founded on Holiness — Lt. Gen. T.J. Jackson ... 197

    The Oath of Allegiance to the U.S., Discussed in its Moral
    and Political Bearings 221

1864

    Vain is the Help of Man 243

    The Devout Soldier 257

    "Power" — A Sermon 275

    Funeral Services of Bp. Leonidas Polk 295

    Sermon Preached Upon the Death of Twenty-Two Deserters 321

1865

    He that Believeth shall not Make Haste 341

Foreword

This work, "Sermons of the Confederacy 1863–1865", is a continuation of the earlier work, "Sermons of the Confederacy 1861–1862."

As I noted in the earlier Foreword, "In this horrific war the United States, ostensibly fighting to "restore the Union", disregarded the recognized rules of war and determined to destroy THE CONFEDERATE STATES by any and all means possible.

This included the destruction of houses and farms, of cities, the raping of women, starving of the populace, deliberately desecrating Southern churches, the killing of prisoners of war through starvation in Yankee concentration camps and withholding of medicines, etc."

THE CONFEDERATE STATES strove through all of this to understand the will of God, to be worthy of God's blessings, and to behave as Christians, even in the face of the brutal Yankee invasion.

These books are a collection of sermons by priests, ministers, bishops, and a rabbi, from 1863 to 1865, as they explained to their congregations the Southern understanding of the causes of the War, their obligations as Confederate citizens, and invoked God's blessings upon the Confederate cause.

They represent men of God looking upon the War and giving their thoughts, prayers and guidance to the citizenry and leadership of THE CONFEDERATE STATES OF AMERICA.

The great war of the Confederacy was fought for freedom and independence, and its defense by Confederate Clergy through the highs and lows of the war, expresses the hope for a real, permanent Republic in North America — THE CONFEDERATE STATES OF AMERICA.

In reading these sermons, the modern reader will find all the problems that we in the 21st Century must face with the

U.S. government are very much the very same problems that the South recognized, sought to separate herself from, and fought so valiantly against.

Gen. Patrick Cleburne warned the South of what was going to happen in defeat:

> "Every man should endeavor to understand the meaning of subjugation before it is too late. We can give but a faint idea when we say that it means the loss of all we not hold most sacred – personal property, lands, homesteads, liberty, justice, safety, pride, manhood.
>
> It means the history of this heroic struggle will be written by the enemy; that our youth will be trained by Northern schoolteachers; will learn from Northern school books their version of the war; will be impressed by the influences of history and education to regard our gallant dead as traitors, and our maimed veterans as fit objects for derision."

It is time for Southerners to realize the truth of the War, and the Clergy are certainly true-speakers of that time of death and destruction which was rained upon THE CONFEDERATE STATES OF AMERICA.

May we, the descendants and citizens of this proud and upright country, which never surrendered, ever remain the custodians of truth, and never fear to speak for our ancestors.

DEO VINDICE!

Dr. William G. Peters
President

THE CONFEDERATE STATES OF AMERICA, INC.

Anno Domini 2014

1863

Samson's Riddle

PREACHED

CHRIST CHURCH, SAVANNAH

ON FRIDAY, MARCH 27th, 1863

BEING THE DAY OF

HUMILIATION, FASTING, AND PRAYER

APPOINTED BY THE

President of the Confederate States

BY THE

RT. REV. STEPHEN ELLIOTT, D.D.

RECTOR OF CHRIST CHURCH, AND BISHOP OF THE DIOCESE OF GEORGIA

"Out of the eater came forth meat, and out of the strong came forth sweetness." — Judges 14:14.

1863

To the Clergy of the Diocese of Georgia

THE PRESIDENT OF THE CONFEDERATE STATES having issued his Proclamation appointing Friday, March 27th inst., as a day of Fasting, Humiliation and Prayer, and inviting the people of the said States "to repair on that day to their usual places of public worship and join in prayer to Almighty God, that he will continue his merciful protection over our cause; that he will scatter our enemies and set at naught their evil designs, and that he will graciously bestow to our beloved country the blessings of Peace and Security."

Now, therefore, I, Stephen Elliott, Bishop of the Protestant Episcopal Church in the Diocese of Georgia, do direct the Clergy of said Diocese to assemble their congregations upon that day, and to keep the Fast with thankful hearts, and with broken and contrite spirits.

Upon the occasion of the Fast, the Clergy will use the following service:

- Morning Prayer as usual to the Psalter.
- Psalms of the day, 3d, 7th, 34th.
- 1. Lesson. Nehemiah, ch. IV.
- 2. Lesson. Matthew, ch. VI.
- Use the whole Litany.

Immediately before the general Thanksgiving, introduce the Confession which precedes the Epistle in the service for Ash-Wednesday and the following prayers:

PRAYER.

O most mighty and gracious God, thy mercy is over all thy works, but in special manner hath been extended towards us, whom thou hast so powerfully and wonderfully defended. Thou hast showed us terrible things that we might see how powerful and gracious a God thou art; how able and ready to help those who trust in thee.

We therefore present ourselves before thy Divine Majesty to offer a sacrifice of praise and thanksgiving, for that thou heardest us when we called in our trouble and didst not cast out our prayer which we made before thee in our past distress. And, we beseech thee, make us truly sensible now of thy mercy as we were then of our danger; and give us hearts always ready to express our thankfulness, not only by words, but also by our lives, in being more obedient to thy holy commandments.

Continue, we beseech thee, this thy goodness to us, that we, whom thou hast saved, may serve thee in holiness and righteousness all the days of our life, through Jesus Christ our Lord and Saviour. Amen.

PRAYER.

O most mighty Lord God, who reignest over all the kingdoms of men; who hast power in thy hand to cast down and to raise up, to save thy servants and rebuke their enemies, let thine ears be now open unto our prayers and thy merciful eyes upon our trouble and our danger.

O Lord, do thou judge our cause in righteousness and mercy, and wherein-soever we have offended against thee, or injured our neighbor, make us truly sensible of it and deeply penitent for it. We humbly confess that we are unworthy of the manifold goodness vouchsafed us in the struggle for our rights, yet we are bold, because of thy long suffering, to pray for the continuance of it and to supplicate thy blessing upon us and our arms.

Cover the heads of our soldiers in the day of battle, and send thy fear before them that our enemies may flee at their presence. Establish us in the rights thou hast given us, in our Government and in our Laws, in our Religion, and in all our holy Ministries.

The race is not to the swift, nor the battle to the strong, but our trust is in the name of the Lord our God. Hear us, O Lord, for the glory of thy name and for thy truth's sake, through Jesus Christ our Lord. Amen.

Given under my hand this twenty-first day of March, A.D., 1863.

STEPHEN ELLIOTT,
Bish. Prot. Epis. Church, Diocese Ga.

Sermon

Judges 14:12-14.

12. "And Samson said unto them: I will now put forth a riddle unto you; if you can certainly declare it me within the seven days of the feast and find it out, then I will give you thirty sheets and thirty change of garments.

13. "But if ye cannot declare it me, then shall ye give me thirty sheets and thirty change of garments. And they said unto him, Put forth thy riddle, that we may hear it.

14. "And he said unto them, Out of the eater came forth meat, and out of the strong came forth sweetness."

There has been for some time past a deep and wide spread yearning for peace. It has exhibited itself in the greediness with which the people of THE CONFEDERATE STATES have listened to every rumor of intervention that has floated across the Atlantic, and in the credulity with which they have believed that the recent political movements in the United States meant anything more than the customary struggle for power. It is a natural yearning, especially in a people unaccustomed as we have been to a state of warfare, for the human mind abhors anxiety and doubtfulness, and shrinks from a condition of things which forces it to live entirely in the present and for the present.

With a war pressing upon us which is continually changing its features and enlarging its proportions — today a war for the Union, and tomorrow a war for emancipation — now waged with the power of an ordinary government, and then with forces almost unprecedented in modern history — there is for us not even a conjectural future. We can form no plans of life, nor look with reasonable probability upon the results of any undertaking. Our households are kept in perpetual agitation — our pursuits are irregular and anomalous — our feelings oscillate between excitement and depression — our affections are ever on the rack of cruel suspense.

Under conditions like these the mind and the heart will both long for peace; for rest from an excitement that is wearing them out; will crave, if only for a little while, a recurrence of those days, when the sound of war was not heard in the land, and when the sun did not cast its setting rays upon fields of blood and carnage.

But this yearning for peace has no smack of submission in it. That has not entered into the thoughts of anybody. It is really nothing more than a natural wish that an useless strife should cease; an earnest desire that a struggle should be ended, which can end but in one way. When the peace which is longed for is embodied in words, it invariably includes the ideas of entire independence and complete nationality — independence from all the bonds, whether political, commercial or social, which have hitherto hindered our development — nationality, with our whole territory preserved to us, and with no entangling alliances binding us for the future.

This is its whole scope and meaning, and is very distinct from any such fainting of the spirit as would precede submission. It is rather the token of a restless energy, which pants to enter untrammeled upon that new career of freedom which it is working out for itself, and which seems to rise before it in brightness and grandeur, and to beckon it onward to glory and happiness.

The courage of THE CONFEDERATE STATES is not failing, but its passive endurance is sorely taxed, and like a beleaguered lion, it chafes against the restraints which keep it from its native haunts, and rages because it cannot at once strike to the earth all the enemies who encompass and goad it, even while they can never either destroy it or make it captive. With a bound and a roar, the Lord of the forest will one day break through the hosts which surround him, but until his opportunity comes, he must bide his time and be satisfied with striking terror into his hunters by the lessons which he may give them, of his fierceness and energy.

But God has thought it best for us that this cruel war should endure yet longer and should be waged with an increased ferocity, if not with augmented forces. Our sins are to be more heavily punished, at the same time that our faith is to be more thoroughly sifted, and our submission to his will made more complete and perfect.

The causes which led to this war — many of the circumstances which have accompanied it and the marvelous manifestations of himself which God has made throughout it — the mighty interests of a moral and religious nature which are bound up in its results — all forbid us from looking upon it as a mere conflict for power.

We must take the Divine will into all our reasonings about it, and our humiliation today must occupy itself in helping us to school ourselves into an acquiescence with his divine arrangements. We may feel sure, seeing how visibly he has fought for us — how strikingly he has supported us through our hours of mortal peril — how he has strengthened us in our weakness, and comforted us in our desolation — that whatever he may order for us in the conduct of this struggle, shall be for our ultimate blessing, and that we ourselves shall one day see it and confess it.

It may be a bitter disappointment to us that the dove has returned to the ark without the olive leaf in her mouth, thus notifying us that the waters of strife have not yet subsided, but the ark is still in safety and under the guidance of Him whose eye never sleepeth and whose love never faileth!

Let us, then, resume our sacred work of stern resistance; let us pray for fortitude, for patience, for endurance, for faith; let us be satisfied that there are lessons of deep moral import which are yet to be evolved from the continuance of this struggle, and we shall discover in God's own time that "out of the eater came forth meat, and out of the strong came forth sweetness."

There is something very delightful in this word Peace. It strikes upon the ear of a tumultuous and ever agitated world with a musical softness that is wonderfully attractive. We associate with its presence, comfort and ease and prosperity and love. All that is brightest in the home and in the heart is wrapped up in it. The pictures of fancy, the dreams of poetry, the richest promises of the gospel are all woven out of its golden hues.

The sequestered valley, with its murmuring stream and its quiet happiness — the cultivated plain, basking in the sunshine and covered all over with the luxuriant harvest — the crowded city, as it lies asleep under the soft moonbeams, its hum of industry stilled by the inexorable decree of nature — the placid waters, reflecting as in a mirror, the softened forms of the huge monsters which, when awakened from their slumbers, are to bear across the ocean the products of the earth — are some of the scenes which we have been accustomed to harmonize with the idea of Peace.

And when we have enlarged the scope of our vision, and risen upon imagination's airy wings, we embrace in the same idea of Peace an interchange of kindly affections among all the nations of the earth, and an universal good will towards men. Philosophy and poetry and prophecy have all combined to body forth its blessings and have alike personified it on earth and in heaven by the mild eye and the gentle murmur of the Holy Dove.

But delightful as is the word, and attractive as are its associations, we should not be seduced by them to yield up either right or truth or justice for its attainment. It would indeed be a great burden rolled from our hearts if we could take our children to our bosoms, and feel that they indeed had a country — if we could look upon our noble sons and rejoice that they were freed with honor from any further conflict with foemen so unworthy of their steel — if we could glance around our hearthstones and be satisfied that no rude trumpet would again disturb their peace, no roar of cannon drive us from their shadow — if we could enter the temples of God and sing the angels song of peace on earth, good will towards men.

But until we can do so with honor and with security, let us banish the idea from our thoughts. Let there be no making haste to find Peace. It will come when God sees that war has accomplished his purposes, and it ought to come no sooner. Unless we follow his guidance in this matter, we shall fall into temptation and a snare, and in grasping at a shadow, lose the substance which we have already gained at the cost of so much precious blood.

We seceded from the Government of which we were once a part, because we felt that under it we no longer had a country. For what is our country? Our country is in its constitution, and its provisions were openly and shamefully violated — our country is in its religion, and its altars were desecrated by infidelity and the vilest fanaticism — our country is in its institutions, and they were threatened with total subversion — our country is in its social life, and that was covered all over with rude abuse and malignant defamation. And shall we, for peace sake, think for a moment of returning to the embrace of such an Union?

God forbid! Let us learn at once the stern truth that we have no country until we make one. We can never go back to that whence we came out. We should not recognize it in its present garb of tyranny. We should not discern that once proud Republic under the mask which it now wears, with the oriental despotism that rules over it, and the oriental submission that kisses its feet. In its delirium it has lost all sense of regulated liberty — it remembers only passion and vengeance.

Closing its eyes against all truth, and shutting its ears against all wisdom, it is striking at man madly in its rage, and it is cursing God who has placed the bit in its mouth, and is saying to it, "Thus far shalt thou go and no further." In quietness and confidence is our strength. Manly fortitude and heroic patience will accomplish for us in due time all that we are contending for. We did not enter upon this conflict in the temper of children, who were quarrelling for some mere point of pique, but with the resolution of men who perceived that every thing which made life tolerable was trembling in the balance.

Let peace come to us, and let us not forget our manhood and go in search of peace. We might find a counterfeit of it among the contrivances of man and meanwhile lose that heaven-descended peace which God will give us, if we will wait his will and abide his discipline. Every thing forbids us to be too solicitous for peace. Our consecrated cause — consecrated by the blood of our children — the aid and comfort it would give our enemies — the permanent welfare of our posterity. If God sends it to us, then welcome, bright-eyed Peace! but woe to us if, for its sake, we sacrifice one jot or one tittle of our duty and of eternal justice!

In the present condition of things such a peace as we ought to accept would be impossible. What have we to offer in exchange for all the territory which the enemy now holds within the borders of the Confederate States, for the half of Tennessee, for the Eastern and Western regions of Virginia, for all our rich sea-coast, for our harbors and forts, for that garden spot of our country, lovely Louisiana?

What have we, at the present moment, to cast in the balance against Maryland and Kentucky and Missouri, whose right to determine their own future destiny, it would be base in us to abandon? Hence is it that foreign mediation would be, at this time, and under our present circumstances, so disastrous to us, and hence is it, I firmly believe, that God has put it into the heart of our enemies to reject it.

What could foreign mediation effect? What could it propose as the basis of settlement, but some such terms as European diplomacy has been conversant about for ages? Would you consent to peace upon the terms of the uti possidetis, each party holding what it possesses? Your own solemn legislative pledges cry out against it.

Virginia would blush for shame at such a proposition, and would weep, as Rachel, for her children, refusing to be comforted. Louisiana would lift her saddened eyes and fettered arms and plead for mercy and deliverance. The home of Jackson would burn with indignation that the ashes of her unconquered hero should be trampled upon by hirelings and slaves. Old ocean would murmur curses against you upon her wailing winds, and would lash your shores in fury at their degradation.

Would you grant to your unscrupulous enemies special commercial advantages and a favored intercourse? This would hold us in as utter vassalage as we have heretofore been held, would ruin our revenues and make us tributary forever to Northern industry.

Would you pay money for peace? At such a thought, the shade of Pinckney would arise from its dust, and bid you remember what Southern spirit was, when he uttered the immortal words, "Millions for defense, but not a cent for tribute." Mediation can do us now no good. It might embarrass us and place us in a false position before the world, but it could not advance us one step towards an honorable peace.

Let us then give thanks this day to God for having so hardened the heart and blinded the eyes of our enemies as to induce them to repel their best and truest friend in his advances for their relief.

But besides mediation, there is another movement of Foreign Powers upon which many have rested their hope for peace, recognition, followed by forcible intervention in our behalf. If such a hope had ever any basis of reality, it is now, in my opinion, forever put at rest by the recent outbreak in Poland and its rumored extension to Hungary. Revolution, and European cabinets will consider our movement to be revolution, has had no friends among the crowned heads of Europe since the convulsions which have swept over their dominions again and again since 1789.

It is an infection which they dread. It rises before them perpetually like a fearful specter, and sits with them at their feasts and troubles their hours of sleep.

They have acquiesced, tis true, from time to time, in changes of dynasty; they have, under very peculiar circumstances, and when the pressure of danger was at their own doors, as in the cases of Belgium and Italy, intervened and saved themselves from internal discord, but the general action of the European powers has been adverse to the early recognition of Governments founded upon revolutionary movements, and especially to any thing like an armed intervention in their favor.

The revolt from Spain of her South-American Colonies began as early as 1810, and although largely assisted by English capital and English muscle, they were not recognized by the government of Great Britain until 1823. Mexico declared her independence in 1813, and it was not until 1825 that she was welcomed into the family of nations. But the most striking example of modern times is that of Greece.

If there was any people whose struggle for independence should have met an instant and enthusiastic response in every court of Europe, whose earliest movements should have caused every heart to bound with joy, and every sword to leap from its scabbard, it was that of the Greeks.

They were the pure descendants of the old Hellenic race, whose history was a household word in every abode of civilized man — whose philosophy had given tone and direction to all the thought of the modern world — whose literature had awakened Europe from its sleep of centuries, and had irradiated its darkness with light and beauty.

Though dead themselves, their voices had been speaking from their graves and animating the nations to a lofty ambition in arms and letters. They were, moreover, Christians, contending against the ancient enemies of the faith, and calling upon the Church of the living God to lift the banner of the Cross once more in conflict with the Crescent.

Hear their own eloquent appeal to the Congress of Verona, made in the second year of their struggle:

"The sentiments of piety, of humanity and of justice by which this assemblage of sovereigns is animated, inspire the Government of Greece with the hope that its just demand will be favorably listened to.

If, contrary to all expectation, the offer of the Government should be rejected, the present declaration must be considered a formal protest which Greece lays this day at the foot of the Throne of Divine Justice — a protest which a Christian people addresses with confidence to Europe and to the great family of Christianity. Weakened and worn out, the Greeks will then place their hope only in the strength of God.

Sustained by his all-powerful hand, they will not bend before tyranny; Christians, persecuted through four centuries for having remained faithful to our Saviour and to God our Sovereign Master, we will defend, even to the last, his Church, our fire-sides and our tombs; happy to descend into them freemen and Christians, or to conquer, as we have hitherto conquered by the alone strength of our Lord Jesus Christ and by his Divine power."

And what was the response of this Congress of Sovereigns? A cold denial even of recognition; an utter refusal to give any countenance to this illustrious people who had sprang, as if awakened by some new Tyrtaes, into the arena of nations, and were fighting upon the very battle fields which Leonidas and Themistocles had made immortal.

It was not, until with a heroism worthy of their race and an endurance which would have illustrated martyrs, they had waded through seven years of the fiercest warfare — through seven years of fire and blood and massacre — through seven years of appalling misery such as we have not yet dreamed of — that the selfish hearts of the nations would listen to their cries, and deliver them from the brutal ferocity of the Mussulman!

Should we, in the face of such examples, lean upon any such hope as foreign intervention? It was well, perhaps, ere we had become conscious of our internal resources, that the public mind should have been flattered with such a delusion. Possibly it encouraged some who might otherwise have fainted in the hour of our weakness, but now, when we have aroused ourselves like a strong man from sleep, and such a reliance is no longer of any consequence to us, it is well to say that we should never have looked for it. Any such expectation was contrary to the lessons of history, and was rested upon grounds which have proved themselves utterly fallacious.

There are but two sources whence we may look for such a peace as we should be willing to accept — a rupture between some great naval power and the United States, which would permit us to recover our sea-coast, together with our cities, harbors, and ports, or a civil war among the remaining States, which would occupy our adversaries at home, and enable us to expel them from our territories.

When either of these contingencies occurs, then may we hope for peace; then may we begin to sing our song of deliverance. But not until then. What the probability is of either of these events, you can judge as well as myself. They are both in God's power to bring about naturally, whenever it pleases Him, and in my opinion he is gradually leading up our enemies to this catastrophe.

The little cloud, like a man's hand, arising out of the sea, is beginning to show itself, and their heavens may soon be black with storm and wind. This is clearly, in my estimation, the next manifestation which God will make of Himself in this conflict.

But, like the prophecies of Scripture, so are these movements upon the stage of the world. We may understand what is the coming event which is to be evolved from the curtained future, but we cannot always reckon the time which that event will consume in its complete development. Time, in God's view, is very different from time in our view.

A thousand years are with Him as one day, and one day as a thousand years. That our enemies are advancing, step by step, to a deep and bitter humiliation, I feel no doubt, and never have felt any; but how long a period may be required by God to bring them into the position, when it shall work upon them the moral discipline it is intended to produce, or for how many years our sins may delay our deliverance, are points which no man can certainly know.

The Israelites were kept forty years in the wilderness, because they needed that discipline. And when I perceive the love of money which is rapidly pervading THE CONFEDERATE STATES — that love of money which the Apostle calls the root of all evil — I tremble lest we shall yet be pierced through with many sorrows. It is sad to think how a noble cause, which should fill the whole heart, and absorb all the energies of our people, is embarrassed and may be sacrificed by a spirit of covetousness, the lowest and meanest of all decent passions, and which God ranks in his holy Scriptures alongside of uncleanness and idolatry.

Is this a time for you, O citizens, when our gallant soldiers are breasting with their indomitable valor the flood of iniquity and desolation which is threatening to involve in one indiscriminate ruin your homes and your altars, to be filling their hearts with anxiety about the loved ones whom they have left behind them? to be reducing, through your unwise speculations and silly competitions, the comforts of your defenders to the very lowest point of subsistence? If you will prey upon one another, for God's sake do not prey upon the soldier.

Let him be an exception to your scale of prices. You satisfy your consciences by whispering to them that the price of everything has risen alike, and that, to protect yourselves, you must sell at extravagant prices, because you buy at extravagant prices. But remember that the pay of the soldier does not increase; that his little pittance remains the same, while your charges upon him are increasing with strides so enormous that imagination can scarce keep pace with them.

And remember, also, that this unnecessary elevation of prices prevents the Government from increasing that pay, because any enlargement of its expenses would only further depreciate the currency, and would ultimately force the Government into a collision with its people, which is most sincerely to be deprecated, or would compel it to give up the struggle in despair.

A country can never be conquered so long as its people are unselfish and self-sacrificing, but when the cause is forgotten in the mad hunt after money, then the eye becomes dim, and the arm falls nerveless. "It becomes," as Isaiah says, "a people of no understanding: therefore, He that made them will not have mercy on them, and He that formed them will show them no favor."

There is no prospect, then, before us, but the prospect of continued war, while God is working out for us our deliverance. Peace cannot come to us now, so far as man can see, save through the course of events which we have just detailed. With God, of course, all things are possible, and He can, if He chooses, produce such a change in the hearts and feelings of our enemies as to cause them at once to desist from their unjust invasion of our homes and firesides.

But as He always acts through natural means; always works out His purposes by a sequence of events which are entirely within the scope of unbelief to consider as customary, we can scarcely hope for such a divine intervention. Nor will our consciences permit us, at this moment, to feel that we deserve it. We must therefore submit to God's will, and become learners once more in the school of war.

We are not morally prepared for peace and prosperity, for as soon as God turned the tide of victory in our favor, we set our hearts upon covetousness, and fell down to worship the golden calf. Let us endeavor, then, to understand the lessons which are wrapped up for us in the experience of this war, so that "out of the eater may come forth meat, and out of the strong sweetness."

War is a great eater, a fierce, terrible, omnivorous eater. It eats out wealth, property, life — it devours cities and nations — it tears to pieces laws and institutions, and scatters their fragments to the winds — it consumes comfort, and happiness and joy — it lacerates the feelings and the affections — it devours religion, and tramples under foot its temples and its altars — it rides in desolation upon the storm of passion and the whirlwind of vengeance.

It is classed by God with famine and pestilence, among His sore judgments, and when He would threaten His people cruelly, He threatens to bring the sword upon them. The blood of man is counted in the Bible as a most mysterious agent, crying from the earth against him that spilleth it, and polluting the land upon whose skirts its drops are sprinkled.

And yet with all this, as God's means of discipline, it has its moral and political lessons, and God is keeping us perchance under its cruel yoke that we may learn them ere we assume our place among the nations of the earth.

Heraclitus, one of the wisest of the Greek philosophers who preceded Socrates, carried this view of the value of war as a teacher and a producer to such an extent, that he advanced it as one of his aphorisms, and left it as a legacy to Greece, that "War was the father of all things"(Πολεμος πατηρ παυτωυ)

— that all things are evolved by the strife of antagonistic forces.

Even under the revelation of God this is a very manifest truth in many particulars, and we can very well understand how one who looked out upon the world — the natural as well as the moral world — without any heavenly light to guide him, or any divine voice to teach him, might consider this strife as the law which God had impressed upon His creation. He perceived everything to be at war — cold with heat — light with darkness — evil with good — conscience with passion — barbarism with civilization — and out of this strife to come all the progress and all the blessing which the world then knew.

Could he have known the sublime truth, of which his contemporaries, the prophets and kings of the Jewish dispensation, had been darkly informed by prophecy, that truth and salvation were to be evolved out of the warfare between Christ and that "archangel ruined," he might well have considered his aphorism as including divine as well as human things. And while I would apply it in a very restricted sense, to the wisdom which may be gained from the warfare of nation with nation, I am satisfied that it is quite as true in that connection, as in its application to physical or moral strife.

Peace is not always the safest condition which a fallen being can enjoy. There may be a cry of peace, peace, when there is no peace; a long prosperity, during which there may creep over us an entire relaxation of moral principle, in which all the energy of virtue may die out, and truth herself be obscured under the sophistry of appearances. Under this condition of things, the wholesome discipline of adversity is the very kindest application which God can make to our necessities, for it at once tears the mask away from things around us, and points us to the stern reality of life.

If we be true at heart — if the corruption has not extended to the core — we may be saved, for the struggle then begins between truth and error, and, by the help of God, the right becomes triumphant, and we attain a wisdom which goes with us through life. And as with the individual, so with nations. A peace without interruption engenders vices which, unless checked, lead rapidly to corruption and decay.

Prosperity follows peace, and wealth prosperity, and luxury wealth, and moral degradation luxury, and thus this greatest blessing of God, if man could rightly use it, is transmuted, through the inevitable alchemy of sin, into its corresponding curse. The civil state needs continual agitation and fresh infusion of virtue from the chastisements of God, just as a lake needs the purifying winds of heaven, and reviving waters from the fresh springs of nature.

Without conflict and chastisement, there is but little exercise for the higher energies of man, whether intellectual or moral, and but little scope for the nobler characteristics of self-denial and self-sacrifice. The old Roman virtue, which has passed into a proverb, and which was certainly the best development of national life which the world had known, before Christian civilization refined and perfected it, was built up out of this continued strife with adverse circumstances, and did not decay until she had conquered the world.

Without this conflict in the formation and growth of a nation, effeminacy creeps in — public virtue becomes enervate — the spirit of a people exhales, even while the forms of its government are preserved. I need not refer you to our own unhappy republic as an illustration of this truth.

The meat which we are bringing forth out of this fierce eater, War, is strong and wholesome, but not always palatable. It is, in some respects, rather humiliating to our conceit, and derogatory to our foresight. But it is well for us to look the truth at once in the face, and to learn as soon as possible our national experience. It will be a most happy circumstance if we can enter upon our career as an independent power upon right principles, and not be compelled to retrace our steps through sorrow and suffering.

If out of the strong wrestlings with adversity we can bring sweetness for our children, we may go to our graves with thankful hearts, and be sure that their blessings will fall thick upon our memories.

At the commencement of our revolution, and for a long time prior to it, we were boasting that we held the civilized nations of the earth, and especially England and France, the leading powers of Europe, in such bonds of dependence upon us, that they could never permit any war which shut them out from our staple productions, to continue for any number of years.

We believed very sincerely that the cotton interest constituted so large a portion of their manufacturing and commercial wealth, that any serious interruption of the supply would create not only great distress in those countries, but would perhaps produce revolution. Under this delusion we continued for eighteen months after our movement began, and it is not yet entirely dissipated.

It will require at least two years more of British endurance to convince us of our mistake, but we are, nevertheless, learning our lesson by degrees. We are finding out that God does not permit, under his Providential arrangements, any one nation to hold in its hand the fate, or even the destiny of other nations, but that climate, soil, labor, staples, are so distributed throughout the world, that if a supply of any necessary article is dried up in one direction, its production can be forced in some other direction.

That we hold great advantages over any other portion of the earth in the growth of our great staples, no one can deny.

We can defy competition, because of the peculiar conditions of our labor and climate, but we cannot rule the world as we once conceived that we could. Indeed, it becomes a serious question whether our blockade is not playing into the hands of British statesmen, who have long desired to be freed from the dependence upon us under which they have writhed for so many years, and which has again and again induced them to submit to aggression on the part of the United States.

They hope, under the stimulus of high prices, and of necessity, to engage other countries, and especially their own colonies, in the culture of cotton, and thus carry to perfection their vast colonial system. We must dismiss this idea, and prepare ourselves to enter heartily and generously into the social life of the world, and give and take as the rest of the nations give and take. And it is a most important lesson for us to learn at once, for it will make us understand the necessity of diversifying our pursuits, and of strengthening ourselves against the domination of foreign powers.

Had we entered upon our career as an independent people without the lessons of this war, we should have been introduced into life with all the coxcombry of youthful conceit, and should have found out in another way, that cotton was not king, and that other nations had weapons more efficacious than staples with which to meet our pretensions.

We shall now, I trust, take our place among the nations of the earth with the manly maturity of experience, fully sensible of the value of our resources, but not flaunting them forever in the face of the world, and properly prepared to defend them with an army and a navy which shall command the respect of the world, while they shall not tempt us to foreign aggression. This is one piece of wholesome, though not palatable meat from the mouth of the eater.

When we entered upon this struggle, all of us were advocates of a system of free trade with the world, which, if adopted, would forever have confined us to agricultural pursuits, as the single channel of our industry. The condition to which tariffs under the old Government had reduced us, produced in us an intolerable aversion to all restrictions upon trade, and drove us, at one period, into forcible resistance to their extension. And this was all right under the circumstances in which we were then placed.

So long as the duties upon imports affected mainly our interests, and the money collected by them was distributed in another section of the Union, it was for us an emasculating process, which was fast exhausting us. We were really nothing more than hewers of wood and drawers of water under the workings of the Government of the United States.

But the pressure of this war is teaching us new ideas upon this subject, and is bidding us beware how we ever permit ourselves to be caught again, as we now are, without clothing, and shoes, and iron, and salt, and the absolute necessaries of life. Free trade is well enough in regard to those articles which are luxuries, but it should never prevail so far as to make us dependent upon other nations for those things which a people must have, under any circumstances, whether of peace or of war.

Luckily for us, this war will force upon us such duties, for revenue sake, in order to preserve the credit of our Government, as will necessarily encourage among us the manufactures that we most need. And still more happily for us, the conduct of foreign governments towards us has put us under no obligations to any of them to arrange our revenue duties otherwise than we shall see to be best for ourselves. We can never be a great or a prosperous people until we change our policy, and combine with agriculture both manufactures and commerce. Entire freedom of trade would be the soundest policy, if the world would only promise to keep at peace forever.

The principles of unrestricted commerce are abstractly true, but they cannot be put into practice without peril, so long as nation will make war against nation, and people will rise up against people. Under the American system of the old Government, which we all so bitterly opposed, our suffering did not arise so much from duties considered abstractly in themselves, as from the fact that they operated almost entirely against the export of our great staples, while the money collected from them was almost all spent elsewhere.

Of the money expended from the period of the adoption of the Federal Constitution until 1828, for all legitimate purposes under the Constitution, such as light-houses, fortifications, &c., fifty-eight millions were expended north of the Potomac, and but eight millions south of it. Such a condition of things could never occur under our new Confederacy, because our pursuits are similar, our population homogeneous, and our interests inseparably united. This is another morsel of meat from the mouth of the eater.

Until within a year after our war began, many of our own people, and almost all the nations outside of us, considered the institution of slavery as resting upon a very insecure basis. They almost universally believed that domestic insurrection would accompany foreign war, and that we should find our slaves rising "en masse," and distracting all our efforts.

Those who had studied this question most thoroughly, and looked at it in the light of philosophy, and especially of the Scriptures, did not fall into this error, and were satisfied from the beginning that the institution would come out of the war stronger than it went into it. Two years of the war have rid every one of any evil anticipations upon this head, and have satisfied the United States government that if these people are to change their condition, it must be changed for them by external force. And while this quiescence on the part of our servants vindicates us from the charges of cruelty and barbarity which have been so industriously circulated against us, it is also teaching us that we can, hereafter, with entire safety, and with most excellent results to ourselves, introduce them gradually to a higher moral and religious life.

They know all that is going on. They are well informed about the proceedings of our enemies, and about their pretended philanthropy, and yet what advantage have they taken of it? When were they ever more quiet, more civil, more useful, more contented than they now are? Ignorance is really our worst enemy amongst them, and I sincerely hope that when this war is over, we shall, in token of their fidelity and good will, render their domestic relations more permanent, and consult more closely their feelings and affections, and thus extract sweetness from the strong mouth of this indiscriminate eater.

Before this war came upon us, the South almost worshipped personal bravery and physical courage. They were considered as the requisite qualities of every gentleman, and whosoever did not possess them, was pitied and despised, even while he was tolerated.

No proper distinction was made between the courage of mere temperament and the moral courage of high principle. The duel was set up as the test of a man's pretension to this quality. And this arose, partly from the natural spirit of our race, but was, likewise, a remnant of feudal usages, which are certainly out of place in our days.

But this war is teaching us what an universal quality personal courage is, and how few men there are who are afraid of death upon the battle-field. How many tens of thousands of soldiers are there who, without any stimulus, save the sense of duty and the impulse of patriotism, march fearlessly up to the cannon's mouth, literally sport with wounds and death, and stand upon the outermost verge of peril, and their check never blanches, and their step never falters.

And is this physical courage, which is so valuable, yet so common, to be estimated above that moral courage, which is so rare — that courage which will not follow a multitude to do evil — which will breast the world in arms for principle — which will restrain the madness of the people at every sacrifice of place, of property, and of life?

What we have needed in our civil affairs in the past has been this moral courage, and now we are learning in this war how much more rare a quality it is than mere personal bravery — such courage as made our gallant Johnson — Sydney in name and Sydney in nature — bear and suffer more than martyrdom, and then lay down in quiet dignity his valued life, that his country's weakness might not be exposed — such courage as led our own heroic Tatnall to disappoint a nation's hopes, and burn his ship rather than sacrifice his brave and trustful men to a selfish and bubble reputation for daring — such courage as has qualified our peerless President to face all calumny, rather than deviate one hair's breadth from his own clear perception of his country's good.

It requires brave men to do these things. No common man can do them. And the longer the war lasts, the more will it develop such characteristics, and moral courage will rise in value, and mere physical courage — that which resolves bravery into brawling and dueling and private rencontres — will sink into merited insignificance.

No people is more brave than the people which can boast of Nelson and Collingwood, of Hill and Wellington, and yet they find nobler employment for their courage than in wasting it upon the field of private revenge. And if we learn this truth, we shall indeed gain another morsel of delicious sweetness from the grasp of the strong.

These are some of the blessings which God is permitting us to take hold of, even in the midst of cruel war; and meanwhile he has not left us without great comfort. In the last ten months, He has granted us an almost uninterrupted series of victories, as if to give us heart and endurance for the conflict which He sees it best for us that we should continue to wage.

Disappointed, as we have been, in our hopes of peace, the Father, who is disciplining us, has not given us over to despair. Peace, with its soft eye and its radiant wing, has not come to us, but victory has! Victory, under circumstances most glorious and unexpected — not only on the land, but upon the sea. His angel has planted one foot on the earth and the other on the ocean, and with his sword of vengeance has smitten this insulting and vain-glorious nation. And what a noble spirit has He infused into the heart of our Confederacy!

How it has warmed anew into fervor Virginia, that old mother of heroes and of statesmen! How grandly she breasts the storm! Under the shadow of the Federal Government she seemed to be sinking into the slumber of death, as one dies under the shade of the poisonous Upas tree. But at the war-cry of her children, "Sic semper Tyrannis," how her rich blood has rushed back upon her heart, and startled her into life! The sound of freedom's cry has disenchanted her, and she has sprung full armed into the arena.

Her noble sons have gathered around her from her hills and from her valleys, from all her fields of historic fame, from the blue waters of the Chesapeake to the dark rushing torrent of the Kanawha — sons worthy of such a mother. All her old energy has come back to her. All her power of self-denial and self-sacrifice has revived within her. Proud, fearless, indomitable, she looks into the very eye of tyranny, and makes it quail before her majesty of right and truth!

The mother of States, she bares her bosom to receive upon it the strokes which are aimed at her children. Hurling defiance in the teeth of her oppressors, she prepares herself to conquer or to die. She hopes, she prays, she struggles for victory, but knowing that everything is in the hands of God, she presses on, uttering the noble words of DeRanville — "If the genius of evil is to prove triumphant, if legitimate government is again to fall, let it at least fall with honor; shame alone has no future."

Ezra's Dilemma

PREACHED IN

CHRIST CHURCH, SAVANNAH

ON FRIDAY, AUGUST 22st, 1863.

BEING THE DAY OF

HUMILIATION, FASTING, AND PRAYER

APPOINTED BY THE

President of the Confederate States

BY THE

RT. REV. STEPHEN ELLIOTT, D.D.
RECTOR OF CHRIST CHURCH, AND BISHOP OF
THE DIOCESE OF GEORGIA

"It is better to trust in the Lord than to put confidence in man." — Ps. 118:8.

SAVANNAH
1863

To the Clergy of the Diocese of Georgia

THE PRESIDENT OF THE CONFEDERATE STATES, having issued his Proclamation, calling upon the people of the Confederacy — "a people who believeth that the Lord reigneth and that his overruling Providence ordereth all things — to unite in prayer and humble submission under his chastening hand, and to beseech his favor on our suffering country," and having appointed Friday, the 21st day of August, as a Day of Fasting, Humiliation and Prayer,

Now therefore I, STEPHEN ELLIOTT, Bishop of the Protestant Episcopal Church in the Diocese of Georgia, do direct the Clergy of said Diocese to call the attention of their respective Congregations to this appointment, on the Sunday preceding the Friday appointed for the Fast, urging upon them, on account of the depressed condition of the country, its observance in all due humiliation of body, mind and spirit.

And I do further direct the Clergy of the Diocese to assemble their Congregations upon the day appointed for the Fast, and to use the following service:

Morning Prayer as usual to the Psalter.

Psalms for the day — the 20th, 44th and 144th.

First Lesson — Deut. chapter 32, verses 26th to 44th.

Second Lesson — Colossians, chapter 3, to verse 18.

Use the whole Litany.

Before the General Thanksgiving introduce the Confession which precedes the Epistle for Ash Wednesday, and the following

PRAYER

O most mighty Lord God, who reignest over all the kingdoms of men; who hast power to cast down and to raise up, to save thy servants and to rebuke their enemies, let thine ears be now open unto our prayers and thy merciful eyes upon our trouble and our danger.

O Lord, do thou judge our cause in righteousness and mercy, and whereinsoever we have sinned against thee, make us truly sensible of it and deeply penitent for it. To us, O Lord, belongeth confusion of face as at this day, yet we are bold, because of thy long suffering and patience towards us, to pray thee to lift up once more the light of thy countenance upon us and to bless us and our arms.

Save us, we humbly beseech thee, from the hand of our enemies, and send thy fear before us, that our enemies may be confounded at thy presence. The race is not to the swift, nor the battle to the strong, but our trust is in the name of the Lord our God. Hear us, O Lord, for the glory of thy name and for thy truth's sake, through Jesus Christ our Lord. AMEN.

STEPHEN ELLIOTT, Bishop of the Diocese of Georgia

A Sermon

EZRA — 8:21-23

21. Then I proclaimed a fast there, at the river of Ahava, that we might afflict ourselves before our God, to seek of him a right way for us, and for our little ones, and for all our substance.

22. For I was ashamed to require of the King a band of soldiers and horsemen to help us against the enemy in the way; because we had spoken unto the King, saying, The hand of our God is upon all them for good that seek him; but his power and his wrath is against all them that forsake him.

23. So we fasted and besought our God for this; and he was entreated of us.

From the beginning of the revolution in which we are yet so sternly engaged, we have boldly assumed the position, that we were fighting under the shield of the Lord of Hosts, of him who "sitteth upon the circle of the earth, and the inhabitants thereof are as grasshoppers." This has been our boast and our consolation. It has supported us under all our sacrifices, and has cheered us through all our days of darkness.

The Psalmist never struck his harp to the animating strain — "The Lord of Hosts is with us, the God of Jacob is our refuge" — in more confident faith than we have re-echoed it. Not only has it been chanted in the sanctuaries of Christianity, but our civil rulers have recognized it in their papers of State, and our great Captains have proclaimed it from the head of their armies in victory as well as under defeat.

The soldier and the statesman, the man of the sword and the man of the gown, has each borne it upon his escutcheon, and our supreme Legislative assembly has engraven it upon our national seal.

All our official documents will go forth in the future, with the sacred inscription **"DEO VINDICE"**, and announce to the world our trust and our strength.

We have not only nurtured this feeling, which seemed to come upon the Confederacy as an inspiration, within our own hearts, hugging it there as a part of our religious life — looking to it, in individual faith, as a light shining in a dark place — but we have blazoned it abroad, and are conspicuous this day before the world as a people who have taken the Lord for their God, caring for nothing so much as "for the good will of him that dwelt in the bush."

We have said not to one King only, but to all Kings within the reach of our voice — not to earthly Kings merely, but to the King of Kings — "The hand of OUR GOD is upon all them for good that seek him; but his power and his wrath is against all them that forsake him." We are bound to this declaration by the most solemn covenants both private and public, and by it must we now stand or fall.

We cannot therefore require of any foreign agency — we should be ashamed to do it — "bands of soldiers and horsemen to help us against the enemy in the way." We have deliberately made our choice. We have taken the Lord of Hosts as our Saviour, and to him must we now turn with fasting and with prayer, and "seek of him the right way for us, and for our little ones, and for all our substance."

This is our only resource. We find ourselves in a condition which calls for a wisdom superior to our own, for a power greater than we can control. A day of darkness and of gloominess has unexpectedly settled down upon us, and without being able to perceive any natural causes sufficient to account for it, we are conscious that "our hands hang down and that our knees are feeble," and that we are in peril of our cause.

It is a consciousness which has come upon us from on high, and which, I firmly believe, cannot be removed by any earthly means. It must be lifted from our hearts, where it rests like a weight of lead, by the hand of the Lord which placed it there. If we look at our Government, it is as stable as ever, directed by the same clear head and sound judgment which have so well guided our affairs. If we turn to our armies, they are, in proportion to those of our enemy, as numerous and as well appointed as they have ever been, and are commanded, with one immortal exception, by the same skilful Captains, who have so often led them to victory.

If we measure our resources, they are greater, in many respects, than they have ever been before. If we examine the field of action, we stand, except in one direction, precisely where we did a year ago. What is it then, which has spread over the Confederate States, so suddenly and without any adequate reason, such a robe of darkness?

Two months ago, and our prospect never looked brighter; our hearts were full of hope, and our watchmen thought that they perceived the dawn of a happier day. The cry of "all's well," had just resounded over the land, when, in a moment, all was in eclipse; dark clouds blotted out the promised light; a day of blood and slaughter and captivity rose upon us; the sound of lamentation was heard through the land; our hearts sank within us under the shock and grew as insensible as stone. Nothing like it had occurred even in the worst moments of the past.

Twice before had we been defeated and depressed, but we had risen from those disasters chastened yet defiant. From this recent shock we have not rallied as we should have done, had we been stricken by the hand of man alone. We still continue most unaccountably paralyzed, as inactive as if we were courting the condition of slaves.

It is a visitation from God, to teach us our own weakness; it is the hiding of his countenance from our rulers, from our armies and from our people to make us understand that present victory and final success depend altogether upon his presence and his favor.

We are placed in the like dilemma in which Ezra found himself and his people. We have assumed a very grand but a very solemn position, and we cannot, without utter shame and confusion of face, abandon it, and confess that we have been trusting in vain and unfounded expectations.

We are compelled to acknowledge this day, supposing our despon-dency to have any proper foundation, either that we ourselves have been deceived in supposing that God was on our side, fighting for us against our enemies, or we must declare him to be a Being in whom no reliance can be placed — fickle and faithless — favoring today and abandoning tomorrow — puffing up with hope in the beginning, only the more surely to destroy in the end.

Let us examine both these positions, and determine whether it is really necessary to lodge ourselves upon either horn of this dilemma; whether God may not be on our side, even while we are suffering defeat and disaster; whether he may not be firm in his purposes and persistent in his good will, even while we are provoking him to anger and forcing him to hide his face from us and from our cause.

A review of the grounds upon which we claimed, for so long, the presence of God with us in our conflict, may restore our confidence, and a consideration of the reasons why he is dealing harshly with us, may lead us to repentance and a happier condition.

We believed, when we began this conflict, that the hand of God was with us, because we had the right and the true upon our side under every aspect in which we could view the case between us and our adversaries. We could not think, and we cannot yet think, that he who rules in righteousness would permit the injured and the oppressed to be overwhelmed by the tyranny of brute force, and consigned to degradation and infamy.

He might try severely our fortitude — he might chasten heavily our sins — he might keep us long in the furnace of affliction, but in the end, he would deliver us and justify our trust in him. "He is the Rock, his work is perfect; for all his ways are judgment; a God of truth, and without iniquity, just and right is he."

The question of right in our movement upon general principles is settled, as between us and those who are trying to subjugate us, by that charter which was adopted by our forefathers as a declaration of civil rights, and to the observance of whose principles they pledged their lives, their fortunes and their sacred honor. This charter was not meant only for their times — it was put forth for all the world, and for all times.

It has been held up continually before the nations by our orators — it has been shaken defiantly in the face of the old governments of Europe by our statesmen — it has overturned thrones and broken up dynasties. It belongs to us today as fully as it belonged to our ancestors, and upon it, if we intended to be true to them and to their principles, we were bound to plant ourselves.

This declaration laid it down as a fundamental principle, "that whenever any form of government becomes destructive of the ends for which governments were instituted among men, it is the right of the people to alter or to abolish it, and to institute a new government, laying its foundation on such principles and organizing its powers in such form, as to them shall seem most likely to effect their safety and happiness."

Upon this principle, the colonies of Great Britain, then existing upon this continent, considered themselves justified in declaring themselves independent of the mother country, and they declared it with nothing like the show of right which we exhibited when we followed their example. They were colonies, and assumed their independence through the right of revolution.

We were sovereign States, and asserted ours by simply resuming our rightful sovereignty. They flew to arms before any legislative action had given color to their violence, and thus their proceedings had a smack of rebellion in them. We dissolved our connection with our sister States, not after war had already dipped its foot in blood, but through Conventions, constitutionally assembled, chosen freely by the people, whose ordinances were afterwards ratified by the same people.

They rushed into their conflict with the mother country with quite a half of their fellow citizens against them. We seceded with an unanimity unparalleled in such a revolution. They fought through the war of independence with many of the very best people of the Colonies against them. We have, up to this time, conducted our conflict with our people firm, determined and united.

If our forefathers were right in their action, then are we right, our enemies themselves being the judges, for they had very much less to complain of than we. The wrongs of the government of Great Britain affected only their civil rights; the wrongs inflicted upon us, threatened our whole social condition.

Beginning with the Missouri question we bore, I cannot say patiently, but still we bore, for forty years, wrong upon wrong, and never pronounced for separation at all hazards, until we perceived that every barrier which kept back the angry floods of fanaticism and infidelity had been broken down. All the lessons we had learned from our forefathers not only justified our action, but pointed out to us our duty. Whatever other nations may say of us, the month of our present adversaries is stopped upon every principle of justice and truth.

If we pass from the Declaration of Independence, from the general principles upon which our forefathers justified a change of government, to the Constitution which united us for certain specific and limited purposes, to our sister States, we shall find that we have ever kept the right upon our side.

We have never encroached upon the privileges which that Constitution guaranteed to our partners in the Union. We have always been, confessedly, the strict constructionists. We have asked no more than that the Constitution should be observed to its very letter. With a liberality which really amounted to weakness, and which received no return, we yielded point after point, and gave up territory after territory, rather than break up the government under which we had lived at least in safety.

We generously stripped ourselves of our rightful heritage, to give our adversaries the means of expansion upon their own principles. Those States which are now persecuting us most implacably, were formed out of territory ceded to the government by the State of Virginia. When by our arms new domain was conquered, the acts which partitioned them into Territories and incorporated them with the United States, were clogged with provisos which excluded us from them as settlers, unless we would consent to sever the ties which bound us to our households.

Liberty bills covered the statute books of the Northern States, intended to wrest our property — property most distinctly recognized and guaranteed by the Constitution — from us, if we dared to carry it beyond a certain line. Should we be prudent enough not to carry it, societies were formed, receiving the patronage and encouragement of many of the best people of the North, whose business it was, through secret agents sent among us and living upon our trustful hospitality, to entice our slaves away from their homes, and to receive and protect them until they could be placed beyond the reach of their masters.

An armed raid was arranged and carried out against us, which was expected to be accompanied by insurrection and murder and rapine. When its leaders were punished, their memories were held sacred, and their ashes glorified. Against all this we used every constitutional mode of resistance. We appealed to the promises of their forefathers, to the memories of the past, to the better feelings of the present. All was in vain.

The conservative portion of the North either could not or would not restrain these aggressions. At last we determined to strike for our homes and for our firesides, but not until a party had been organized and was triumphant, which threatened to overturn our whole domestic and social life.

Which party was right in all this? The Northern States in their persistent aggressions, or we in our resistance? Can any man, with any sense of justice, hesitate how to decide? What else could we do? Could we permit every thing that made life valuable to be torn from us, and we the while stand mute and impassive? We did what every high-minded people would have done, transferred the question from the courts of Earth to the courts of Heaven, and committed our cause to him who reigneth in righteousness.

If we go yet a step further, we shall see, that as between us and our adversaries, even admitting all their positions, we still had the right with us. Supposing slavery (for I argue now upon the hypothesis of our adversaries) to have been a wrong to the slave and an evil to the country, I would ask, who did the wrong and who bears the evil? Where did these slaves come from and who brought them here?

They came from their native haunts, brought here by the forefathers either of those very men who are fighting this battle with us, or of those who are standing coldly by, seeing us cut each other's throats.

These slaves were imposed upon us — imposed upon us, in many cases, against our wills — imposed upon us just so long as it was profitable for those hypocrites to bring them here.

And now when they have become interwoven with our whole social life, forming a part of our representation, of our prosperity, of our habits, of our manners, of our affections, all these ties are to be rudely broken asunder, not at our will or in our own time, but at the will and in the appointed time of those who forced this evil upon us.

Were our people required, upon any principle of equity, to submit to be the shuttle-cocks of these contemptible gamesters? to be the tools of such mock philanthropy and such real wickedness? Was this our breeding? Was this the spirit which Burke foreshadowed as the temper of the slaveholder?

Have they who committed the wrong and took money for it — aye, received their full bond, flesh and all — the right, whether in the sight of man or God, to dictate to us, who have paid the bond and rescued the poor savages from their greedy and bloody grasp and made men and Christians of them?

And who bears the evil, as they have been pleased to term it? We bear it, and have borne it, and have endeavored to turn it into a blessing, and have many of us been martyrs in its cause. At that day of terrible judgment, when the secrets of all hearts shall be disclosed, many will stand before God, who shall be able to show that they have sacrificed feelings dearer than life itself for the benefit of these very slaves, who have spent days of toil and nights of prayer to understand what was best for their temporal and eternal state.

Many, very many, I know, have been insensible to their duty and have neglected the great trust committed to their charge, and for this, punishment has fallen upon us, but many have acquitted their consciences before God. Let their increase attest their general comfort! Let their change from the tattooed savage to the well-bred courteous menial, bear witness to their culture!

Let their quiet subordination thro' all this fierce conflict speak trumpet tongued to the world of their treatment. Let the numbers who flock to the table of the Lord attest to the nations the missionary work which is going on amongst them. Here we are, engaged in one of the bloodiest wars on record, pressed on every hand, with the enemy at our very doors, inviting them, alluring them, tempting them, deceiving them, and yet who wait upon us morning and night?

Who keep the keys of our houses and who nurse and tend upon our children? Who cook the food we eat and minister to all our necessary wants? These very slaves!

And does the head of any one of us rest less easily upon his pillow? Does any one tremble as he sees his little ones, dearer to him than life, nestled in their bosoms and sung to sleep with their lullabies? Does any one require a taster of his food, an analyzer of his drink?

What does all this mean? How does it harmonize with the ground assumed by our enemies, that we are inflicting upon these people a great natural and moral wrong?

It means, that upon the score of humanity, there is no reason for this cruel invasion. It means that we are guiltless of the insulting and calumnious charges which have been laid at our doors. It means that we have been not only masters to these people, but so far as circumstances have permitted us, that we have been friends and instructors.

It means that all the blood which has been shed — that all the misery which has been endured — that all the desolation which has been visited upon our land — that all the curse which is laid up in the future, whether for the white race or the black race, is upon our enemies, and that God will require it at their hands.

But besides having reasons like these, depending upon the righteousness of our cause, to believe that God was with us, we had, likewise, another ground of hope arising out of the character and motives of those who were warring against us.

We had said in the words which Ezra put into the mouth of his people, not only that "the hand of God is upon all them for good that seek him," but "his power and wrath is against all them that forsake him," and we felt no doubt that the party, which had formed and was directing this crusade against us, had grown up out of elements un-Christian and really atheistic.

Pretending to a peculiar philanthropy, it was a philanthropy opposed alike to the word and the will of God. Instead of believing in the curse of God upon sin, which curse manifested itself in poverty, in suffering, in slavery, in a thousand forms which made the world as miserable as it is, they determined that human effort could remove them all.

Instead of bowing before the word of God, which said "the poor shall never cease out of the land;" instead of submitting to the Divine decree imposed upon Adam and his posterity, "Cursed is the ground for thy sake; in sorrow shalt thou eat of it all the days of thy life;" instead of acquiescing in the triple curse upon the descendants of Ham, "And he said, cursed be Canaan, a servant of servants shall he be unto his brethren. And he said, Blessed be the Lord God of Shem; and Canaan shall be his servant. God shall enlarge Japheth, and he shall dwell in the tents of Shem; and Canaan shall be his servant," they turned their rage against the word of God, and covered it all over with ridicule and with abuse.

Catching the echo of the French revolution, they set up liberty, equality, fraternity, as their idols, and virtually dethroned the God of the Bible. They did not work that the evils of social life might fade out quietly under the influence of Christianity, but they defied God, because there were any social evils at all.

They were ready, in their fanatical worship of these terrible delusions — delusions made more terrible than ever because of the immense developments of physical science and material prosperity — to blot out all the records of Divine inspiration, should they be found in opposition to their human conclusions.

It was not Truth which led them on, it was Passion. It was not the path of pure morality which they were treading; it was the track of a lawless licentiousness, which led over the ruins and ashes of the altar and the fireside.

At home, its fruits have been fraud, corruption, unbelief, falsehood, free love. Abroad, wherever their arms have been victorious, those fruits have been theft, rapine, cruelty, fornication, desolation. The face of this party was for a time covered with a silver veil, but the veil has been lifted and lo, the hideous features of the false Prophet!

It carried, for a time, the semblance of wisdom, for it developed immense material prosperity, but has proved itself to be "the wisdom which descendeth not from above, but is earthly, sensual, devilish." Can God be with a cause, engendered out of such materials, led on by such Prophets and Apostles?

Will he permit crime, falsehood, wickedness, unmercifulness, to be triumphant in the end? Will his power be with those who have forsaken him, and trampled upon his word and his immutable morality? Impossible; he is only biding his time while he chastens us for our sins and tries our faith, and while he ripens them for slaughter and vengeance.

Did any of us ever doubt, in the first years of this conflict, that God was on our side? Did not the whole land resound with one universal shout of thanksgiving and of praise, as event after event plainly indicated God's presence with us? Did we not, in solemn festival, send up our acknowledgement of gratitude, of devotion, of unswerving faith? Did we not proclaim it from the house tops, that our God was manifesting himself to us almost as palpably was he had done to his own chosen people?

The remarkable unanimity with which the seceding States came out of the Union — the harmony with which a new and permanent Constitution was adopted — the skill with which vexed questions were avoided, and discordant elements brought into combination — the recognition of God as our Lord in the face of all the world, were assumed, on all hands, as tokens of the presence of his Spirit in our Councils and of his good will towards the rising Government. And as with our civil affairs so with our military affairs.

The first victory at Manassas, when God smote that proud army with His fear, and gave us time to gather our resources and discipline our armies for the future — the capture of Norfolk, which supplied us with heavy artillery, while we were preparing to manufacture it for ourselves. —

The supplies of arms and of ammunition, which came in from abroad, often at the most propitious moment, to enable us to sustain the struggle, until we could procure them for ourselves — the unaccountable delays in the movements of our enemies, when promptness and decision might have overwhelmed us — the frequent changes of their Generals at times the most critical for us — the expiration of the term of service of their troops, happening often when their armies most needed their presence. —

The marvelous successes of our little Navy, coming to us just when our hearts were most in want of comfort and hope — all these and a thousand minuter circumstances which were deeply felt when they occurred, were all taken to our bosoms and hugged there as precious proofs that God was with us of a truth.

They were to us what the miracles at the Red Sea and in the wilderness were to the Israelites. Have we forgotten all these things? Have they faded from our hearts and from our memories because of a few reverses? Are we faithless the moment that God withdraws himself for a little while from us?

O fools and slow of heart to believe! "God is not a man, that he should lie, neither the son of man, that he should repent: Hath he said and shall He not do it? or hath He spoken and shall He not make it good?" And how could He more plainly have spoken, than by the acts of his Spirit and of his Providence which we have just recalled to your minds.

Even while he was threatening judgment against the Israelites, his comforting words were "For I am the Lord, I change not; therefore ye sons of Jacob are not consumed."

Why then, you will ask, if God is so clearly on our side, are we so sorely pressed and made to bleed at every pore? Why do our enemies triumph over us, and spoil our homes and desolate our hearth stones? Why are our young men smitten and our houses filled with lamentation? Why does the widow send up her wail before the Lord and why does the orphan weep because he is fatherless? Why are all faces filled with anxiety and every brow with care? My hearers, it requires no research, nor any ingenuity to answer this question.

Our Bibles answer it very directly and very plainly. What you suppose hard of reconcilement, was asked by the people of Israel thousands of years ago, and has been asked ever since by the people of God under whatever dispensation and in whatever condition.

Did not Moses say, when he was recapitulating to the Israelites the wonders of God in their behalf, "For what nation is there so great, who hath God so nigh unto them as the Lord your God is in all things that we call upon him for?"

And yet this did not hinder but that the Israelites were discomfited in battle, were slain by the sword, were visited with pestilence, were often reduced to very great straits and extremities. Those of whom God is intending to make a nation to do his work upon earth, are precisely those whom he tries most severely.

His purpose is to give them not merely victory, but character; not only independence, but righteousness; not peace alone, but the will to do good, after peace shall have been established.

His plan, when his hand is upon a people for good, is to discipline as well as to support — to support through discipline, for moral discipline, like military discipline, gives strength and power. His severity goes along with his goodness; he so intermingles them that the one may temper the other and keep down effeminacy and presumption.

If you suppose, because God is with you, that you are to run on from victory to victory, without any regard to their moral effect upon you, you will bring upon yourselves much bitter disappointment.

The law which God has established for nations as well as for individuals, that any high standard of virtue — virtue which may be relied upon to withstand temptation and to resist corruption — must be gained through the discipline of suffering, is always inflexibly worked out.

When we assume the ground that God has taken us, in spite of our sins, under his especial care and guardianship, we must prepare ourselves to carry on this struggle under the conditions which this sacred relationship involves. We have made our choice before the world, boasting that the Lord is our God — not only boasting of it, but until lately rejoicing in it — and we believe that he has graciously accepted our proffered allegiance.

We have said "The hand of the Lord our God is upon all them for good that seek him," and shall we faint and be bewildered, and know not where to turn, the instant we encounter difficulties in the way? Shall we be looking to the right hand and to the left, with trembling limbs and countenances of dismay, when we have boasted to the world that we have such an ally as the Lord of Hosts?

Ezra was ashamed, when he had made such an utterance to Artaxerxes, to require of him a band of soldiers and horsemen to help him and his against the enemy in the way. What did he? He proclaimed a fast at the river of Ahava, that he and his might afflict themselves before their God to seek of him a right way for them, and for their little ones, and for all their substance.

That was his course; a faithful and a consistent one, and it had its reward, as faithfulness and consistency always will, of entire success. The Lord turned his face once more upon them and showed them that right way which they sought after. "So we fasted," is his simple and beautiful language, "and besought our God for this; and he was entreated of us."

Most surely do we need, my hearers, at this moment, to have the right way pointed out to us — "the right way for us, and for our little ones, and for all our substance." We are sadly out of the way. We have lost sight of the landmarks which directed us so safely upon our first setting out. We seem to have forgotten the resolution with which we entered upon this journey towards the promised land of our national independence — the resolution to suffer anything and to lose everything rather than fail in our purpose.

We appear to have abated the enthusiasm which swept everything before it in the outset — which hurried our sons to the field, our wives and daughters to the hospitals, ourselves to any and every work which we could undertake for the advancement of the cause. We have grown apathetic, if not indifferent.

We are murmuring and complaining, and some are beginning to ask of our leaders "And wherefore hath the Lord brought us unto this land, to fall by the sword, that our wives and our children should be a prey? were it not better for us to return into Egypt?"

What shall we do? How are we once again to regain our lost devotedness and to string ourselves afresh for the duties and the sacrifices which are before us? We must follow the example of Ezra. We must afflict ourselves before our God — we must fast and beseech the Lord to give us true repentance and grace to do the first works.

"In the early history of the Roman Republic, there yawned in the centre of the Forum a deep and dark abyss — an abyss that had opened of its own accord, and had hourly grown wider and wider and threatened to engulf all Rome. The Chief Augur, upon secret consultation with the Senate, uttered these solemn words:

"People of Rome! a heavy doom hangs over our beloved city! The wrath of the Gods has been kindled against you; and in that black abyss you behold its token. See! it gapes with greedy jaws to swallow Rome, and each hour that it remains unclosed, will it become wider and wider, till domestic hearth, sacred altar, Senate house, Capitol, all shall be engulfed."

"Yet may the doom be averted by a fitting oblation. The angry Deities demand a sacrifice — a sacrifice of that, whatsoever it be, which is the most precious of sublunary things. They have not intimated to us what is the sacrifice they demand; that is left to your own judgment and your own faith.

"Choose ye that which ye deem most valuable, and cast it unreluctantly into this gulf. If the sacrifice be acceptable, the chasm will close; if it continues open, seek ye, by a further offering to propitiate the Deities.

"Is there one, O Romans, who would hesitate a moment to give his best, his most valued, nay all he possesses for his fellow citizens and his country?

"Shall Rome pass away ere she is out of her infancy, because ye selfishly love aught more than Rome? Or shall she Endeavour to fulfill a glorious destiny, purchased by the generous sacrifice of her sons?"

"The augur had scarcely ceased, when he was answered by an unanimous and animated shout — Rome! Rome!! let her be perpetual."

"Down into the abyss were poured showers of glittering coin, the hoarded wealth of the citizens. But the abyss closed not; money was too cheap a sacrifice for such a blessing."

"Next advanced the matrons of Rome in regular order, each bearing the caskets in which were contained her most valued ornaments and her most precious jewels. And as they passed, they sang a solemn chant and cast into the abyss their sparkling gems. One flash of light and they were gone. But the abyss closed not; Gems were too cheap a sacrifice for such a blessing."

"There was a dead silence, and a troubled eye was fixed upon that greedy abyss, that had received so much and yet demanded more."

"Suddenly a shout arose upon the outskirts of the crowd. The tramp of a steed was heard; the throng gave way and a noble warrior dashed towards the abyss, reined up his steed and with a motion of his spear commanded silence."

"Romans," said Curtius, "ye have offered sacrifice of your possessions, of your treasures, of your affections, but who has offered the sacrifice of self? Trust me, Romans, it is the sacrifice of self that is the most precious."

"With these words, rider and steed plunged into the unfathomable abyss. There was a moment of dreadful feeling — a moment that seemed an age. Slowly the abyss closed; the self sacrifice was received, and Rome was delivered."

Has not this legend of ancient Rome, thus graphically described by an English writer, a deep and rich moral for us at this critical moment! We have freely cast into the black abyss of this war our wealth, our treasures, our children, but have we sacrificed self? Have we determined to give up everything, if need be, for the cause of our country; to lay down upon its altar our private and personal griefs; to overcome our prejudices, to forget our enmities, to put under foot our jealousies?

Have we resolved to bear all things from man or God, neglect, humiliation, suffering, rather than be a hindrance in the way of success? It is far easier to cast into this gulf such things as property, money, treasures, gems, and even sons, than it is to strip ourselves of vanity, of self-conceit, of pride of opinion, of ambition, of evil habits, of those things which make up our identity. SELF! SELF!! in how many subtle, deceitful guises does it dress itself! under how many high sounding names does it mask itself!

How terrible it is to think that the like features of a noble nature, the deep earnestness, the heroic self-denial, the labor night and day, the intense concentration, can arise from impulses so opposite, and that patriotism, one of the noblest, and selfishness one of the meanest motives, have but the same machinery to work with. And yet so it is.

The impulse which would make a man a hero, a martyr, a being to live in his country's heart forever, is as wide apart from that which makes him a selfish creature, living within himself and for himself, with no aspirations higher than his own interests or his own wants, as is inspiration from Heaven and cunning from earth, and yet the instruments of their work are strikingly alike, so strikingly as to make not only others, but ourselves, unable to distinguish them.

It is very often by their fruits only — the one reaping in the end honor, admiration, the world's immortality; the other, the ashes of all their expectations — that we can finally separate the wheat from the chaff, the pure gold from the worthless dross.

In turning ourselves, therefore to God in fasting and prayer, let us truly humble ourselves and beseech Him to show us our own hearts and to convict us especially of those sins which are offensive to him and which have placed us in the wrong way. There should be great searchings of heart today.

From THE PRESIDENT OF THE CONFEDERATE STATES, who now occupies, for a time, the most responsible position in the world, to the humblest person who is involved in their destiny, each one of us should examine himself and find out, if possible, wherein he has offended God and turned away his face from us. Let us not be looking at and criticizing others; let each one look at himself.

We shall find sins enough in ourselves to mourn over, without laying all the blame upon our neighbor's doings. Let the spirit of the Publican — "God be merciful to me a sinner" be with us rather than that of the Pharisee which is now so common; "I thank thee, O God, that I am not as other men are, extortioners, unjust, adulterers, or even as this Publican." My pride of opinion, if I be one in authority, may be doing as much harm to the cause, both with man and God, as another man's covetousness.

My vanity and self-conceit may work as much mischief, if I be in a position to make them felt, as your love of ease or your indifference to the cause. It is the aggregate of sinfulness that is working our ruin; that is eating out the heart and spirit of the cause, eating it out naturally and consequentially, for one sin leads inevitably to another. The confidence which grew out of continued victory led to presumption and presumption led to security and the feeling of security begat within the community the desire of wealth, which circumstances seemed to place within every man's grasp.

And this making haste to be rich took rapid possession of the minds and hearts of the whole people. Commencing with those who were legitimately engaged in commerce and trade, it soon extended to the farming interests of the country and from them was communicated to the soldier in the camp and the officer in the garrison. Every man became anxious to take part in this game which was to enrich himself, without seeing that it would, most certainly, ruin his country.

Men were seen skulking in every way to avoid service in the army, not from cowardice, not from any doubt about the value of the conflict or the certainty of its success, but that they might be at liberty to mingle in this mad hunt after money.

Feeble substitutes were put in the place of able bodied men; hundreds sought exemption upon pleas which they would never have dreamed to offer except under the influence of this all-pervading madness, and the soldier, who had retained his early enthusiasm and was ready to sacrifice every thing for the cause, grew dissatisfied when he perceived that he was to bear and to suffer, while others, as able-bodied as himself and as deeply interested in the struggle, remained at home to speculate and grow rich upon his endurance and his sufferings.

Just as victory was foreshadowed at the beginning in the earnestness of every heart, in the devotion of every spirit, in the one concentrated idea of victory and independence, so was defeat just as plainly foreshadowed in the distraction of the public mind, in the struggle which rapidly grew up between the administration and the people, in the complaining and the murmuring against the inefficiency of the armies, which was but the natural result of the demoralization of the country. And man could not arrest it. He might force the body, but he could not give the spirit. He might carry the man to the camp, but he could not impart the dash which distinguishes him whose heart is in the work.

What we should now ask of God is, that he would revive within us those qualities of mind and of heart — so near akin to the graces of the spirit — which qualify us for carrying on our conflict successfully, earnestness, singleness of purpose, honesty, integrity. The whole people need to be aroused and the government should take the lead, under God, in doing it. The chord of sympathy which vibrated so harmoniously in the past, must be touched anew.

This is not a warfare which can be coldly left to the Government and the army; it is the cause, emphatically, of the whole nation — of every man, woman and child in the Confederacy. In vain are conscriptions and impressments; in vain are proclamations and fastings, unless after we shall have fasted and prayed, we use means to rekindle the sacred fire of patriotism which burned so vividly in the outburst of this revolution.

Where is the orator? Where is the statesman? Where are the voices which, like a trumpet's blast, led on the soldier to the field of glory — of glory, because the field of duty? They are all mute; some silent in death, some wrapped in inglorious ease. Is this the time for him who has the divine gift of eloquence to keep it pent within his own burning bosom? Is this an hour when any man, who can sway his fellow men, who can enkindle his hope with lips touched with a live coal from off the altar, or excite his fears with the dark shadows of coming events, should leave his country and his country's hopes to drift to ruin without one effort to arrest the misery?

Where are the people themselves? Where is that influence of the multitude which is so terrible for evil, so powerful for good? Where is the low sweet voice of woman which has mingled so harmoniously thro' all this tumult with the clangor of the trumpet and the clash of arms? Why is it unheard? Has grief frozen it within her bosom or has terror hushed it into silence?

Awake to the reality of things and arouse yourselves, children of the sun, or God's hand will not be with you. "Wherefore criest thou unto me," said the Lord to Moses, when he and his people were hedged up among the mountains, with the fierce Egyptians in their rear, and the deep waters of the red sea before them, "speak unto the children of Israel that they go forward."

Forward, my hearers, forward, with our shields locked and our trust in God, is our only movement now. It is too late even to go backward. We might have gone backward a year ago, when our armies were victoriously thundering at the gates of Washington and were keeping at successful bay the Hessians of the West, had we been content to bear humiliation for ourselves and degradation for our children. But even that is no longer left us.

It is now victory or unconditional submission; submission not to the conservative and Christian people of the North, but to a party of infidel fanatics, with an army of needy and greedy soldiers at their backs. Who shall be able to restrain them in their hour of victory?

When that moment approaches, when the danger shall seem to be over and the spoils are ready to be divided, every outlaw will rush to fill their ranks, every adventurer will hasten to swell their legions, and they will sweep down upon the South as the hosts of Attila did upon the fertile fields of Italy. And shall you find in defeat that mercy which you did not find in victory?

You may slumber now, but you will awake to a fearful reality. You may lie upon your beds of ease and dream that when it is all over, you will be welcomed back to all the privileges and immunities of greasy citizens, but how terrible will be your disappointment! Yon will have an ignoble home, overrun by hordes of insolent slaves and rapacious soldiers. You will wear the badge of a conquered race, Pariahs among your fellow creatures, yourselves degraded, your delicate wives and gentle children thrust down to menial service, insulted perhaps dishonored.

Think you that these victorious hordes, made up in large part of the sweepings of Europe, will leave you any thing? As well might the lamb expect mercy from the wolf. Power, which is checked and fettered by a doubtful contest, is very different from power victorious, triumphant and irresponsible. The friends whom you have known and loved at the North; who have sympathized with you in your trials and to whom you might have looked for comfort and protection, will have enough to do then to take care of themselves. The surges that sweep over us, will carry them away in its refluent tide.

Oh! for the tongue of a Prophet to paint for you what is before you, unless you repent and turn to the Lord and realize that "His hand is upon all them for good that seek him." The language of Scripture is alone adequate to describe it — "The earth mourneth and languisheth: Lebanon is ashamed and hewn down: Sharon is like a wilderness. They that did feed delicately are desolate in the streets: they that were brought up in scarlet embrace dunghills.

They ravished the women in Zion and the maids in the cities of Judah. They took the young men to grind, and the children fell under the wood. The joy of our heart is ceased; our dance is turned into mourning. The crown is fallen from our head: woe unto us that we have sinned."

Let us turn then this day to the Lord our God with all our heart and soul and mind, believing that His hand is upon all them for good that seek him, trusting that He will show us the right way for us and for our little ones, and for all our substance. Let our prayer be that which Milton offered against the enemies of his country — "Let them all take counsel together and let it come to naught; let them decree and do thou cancel it; let them gather themselves and be scattered; let them embattle themselves and be broken; let them embattle and be broken, for thou art with us."

A DISCOURSE

BEFORE THE

GENERAL ASSEMBLY

OF

SOUTH CAROLINA

ON DECEMBER 10, 1863

APPOINTED BY THE LEGISLATURE

AS A DAY OF
FASTING, HUMILIATION AND PRAYER
BY

B. M. PALMER, D. D.
Southern Methodist Episcopal Church
OF NEW ORLEANS, LA.

1863

DISCOURSE

Psalm 60:1-4.

"O! God, thou hast cast us off; thou hast scattered us; thou has been displeased: O! turn thyself to us again. Thou hast made the earth to tremble; thou hast broken it: heal the breaches thereof, for it shaketh. Thou hast showed thy people hard things; thou hast made us to drink the wine of astonishment; thou has given a banner to them that feared thee, that it may be displayed because of the truth."

There is a deep significance in this assemblage, and in the manner of its convocation. The supreme legislative authority of a sovereign State has set apart this day as a sabbath to the Lord. The Representatives of a free people arrest the work of legislation in an hour of public peril, that they may lead their constituency in an act of solemn worship to Almighty God, humbly imploring Him to withdraw the chastening hand that has fallen so severely upon our common country.

It is the nearest approach which can be made to an act of worship by the State, as such. We reject the shallow nominalism which makes the State a dead abstraction. It is more than an aggregation of individuals. It is an incorporated society, and possesses a unity of life resembling the individuality of a single being. It can deliberate and concur in common conclusions which are carried out in a joint action, analogous to the powers of thought and will in a single mind.

It stands in definite moral relations, not only to the individuals who are subject to its authority, but to other societies similarly constituted — giving rise to a code of public morality, and to the law of nations by which their mutual intercourse is regulated. It is this principle which lends significance to these religious solemnities; — that the State is, in some clear sense, a sort of person before God, girded with responsibilities which draw it within His comprehensive government, capable of executing a trust, and distinctly recognizing both its obligations and its rights.

Thus, to-day, this venerable Commonwealth, through her constituted authorities, legislative and executive, bends the knee before the God of Heaven, acknowledging her dependence upon Him who "ruleth in the kingdom of men, and giveth it to whomsoever He will."

A sacred awe steals upon me in placing upon your lips, Senators and Representatives, the words of the Hebrew monarch, uttered three thousand years ago, yet so apposite to our own times. You remember the circumstances under which David came to the Jewish throne, and with what difficulty the succession was transferred from the house of Saul.

Through seven years a fearful schism had rent the tribes of Israel; during which the retainers of the feeble Ishbosheth disputed the supremacy of him whom the prophet of the Lord had, by solemn unction, prefigured to the throne. The nation was still rocking beneath the ground-swell of these political troubles, at the time the text was penned. No sooner, too, did David grasp an undisputed sceptre, than he was called to enter upon that series of conquests by which the prophetic limits of the Hebrew empire should be attained.

Upon comparing, however, the title of the sixtieth Psalm with the corresponding events in the national chronicles, we derive the immediate occasion of its composition. A formidable and successful expedition had been sent against Syria — not only that portion lying between the Tigris and Euphrates, but that also lying towards the more distant Orontes. Whilst the military strength of the country was thus withdrawn, the Edomites, the hereditary enemies of Palestine, took advantage of its defenseless condition to make a bold and sudden invasion.

The tide of war swept with unrebuked severity over the land, until it threatened to extinguish the national existence — a catastrophe only averted by the seasonable return of the conquerors of the East, who overthrew the barbarous marauders with dreadful slaughter in the Valley of Salt, upon the south of the Dead Sea.

The issue of these sanguinary conflicts is familiar to all readers of the Sacred books. The power of David became more firmly consolidated; his enemies from within and from without were overthrown; and he continued to reign over an undivided empire, the greatest military chieftain of his times, transmitting at length a peaceful sceptre to his illustrious son. But in the midst of these perilous adventures, when the fate of the realm was trembling upon the balance, the monarch bard penned these mournful lines, so descriptive of the dangers which invoke this day's prayer on the part of our afflicted State.

Truly, the wine of astonishment is given us to drink! The throes of a stupendous revolution shake the land as with the terrors of an earthquake; and the burning crust upon which our people tread threatens at every step to part asunder and to swallow them up in the yawning abyss. Thou, O God, hast made the earth to tremble; and thou alone canst heal the breaches under which it shaketh! O thou, who hast scattered us in thy displeasure, hear the prayer of thy people this day, and turn thyself to us again!

But whilst we address our supplications to the most high God, let it be remembered that the language of true prayer is never the cry of supine imbecility, nor the wail of craven despondency. It is always the languages of hope and of expectation.

It is the utterance of a strong and brave heart, struggling with its difficulties, and casting itself with sublime faith upon the power of an omnipotent arm. In its very cry for help, it gives the pledge of a resolved purpose to fulfill whatever obligations are imposed by the dangers which surround it, or which are involved in its own expectation of deliverance.

The man does not truly pray, whose heart is paralyzed with fear; his despair stifles the petition in its utterance; and the feeble whisper, which breathes forth the enervated appeal, confesses in the cowardice of its distrust the falsehood of its plea. He alone prays, who pledges his endeavor to do and to endure all that is comprehended in the answer to his petition.

Piety, therefore, combines with prudence, and both unite with a lofty courage, in calmly surveying the perils which surround us; that we may deduce the solemn duties which spring from the bosom of our trials, and which bind the consciences of a people who have undertaken to lift up to God the voice of hopeful and confiding prayer.

During the progress of this relentless war, our enemies have wrested from us the great river of the west, which once bore upon its waters the commerce of half a continent; and though its possession has proved nearly valueless to them, its loss to us severs the connection between portions of the Confederacy, and renders active cooperation betwixt them almost impossible.

They have placed the heel of oppression upon the queenly city which, within the embraces of this imperial stream, once filled her horn with plenty, and danced gaily to the sound of the viol and harp. They have trodden down and defiled other noble towns and cities, once the abodes of affluence, the seats of learning and science, whose ancient families handed down from father to son a proud, ancestral name.

Their mailed ships beleaguer our coast, and seek to seal our ports against the commerce of the world. They have massed their numerous armies and driven them, like a wedge, nearer and nearer to the heart of the land; exulting in the hope of speedily riving it in sunder, as the axeman of the forest rives the gigantic but fallen oak.

They have stirred up the resentment of the civilized world against our social organization, and pointed their prejudices, like poisoned spears, against our cause, that our strength may dry up within our bones in this state of dreadful seclusion. In all history there is nothing more grandly sublime than the perfect isolation in which the Southern Confederacy is now battling for those rights which are so dear to the human heart.

The nations of the earth have no eye of pity for our distress, no tear of sympathy for our wrongs. They turn away in cold indifference, and leave us to grapple with a superior foe, whose malice feeds upon the memories of past brotherhood, and can be satiated only by drinking the life of a people to whom they were once bound by the most sacred of covenants. Yet all alone, this young nation, strong only in her consciousness of right, girds herself for the mighty struggle.

Like the fabled Antoeus, she gathers strength from the very reverses which bring her to the ground, and rises with new energy to the conflict. She drops a tear over the tombs of her martyrs, and then goes patiently again under her baptism of blood. All alone, she lifts an eye of faith to Heaven above, and beneath the shadow of Jehovah's throne, strikes again for liberty and life.

All alone, with God for her avenger, she treads danger beneath her feet, and moves forward to the triumph which an assured faith reveals steadily to her gaze. Like David in the text, she stands upon the trembling earth, and whilst drinking the wine of astonishment mingled in her cup, she recognizes a commission from the God of Heaven which binds her to duty in the face of trial, and receives at His hands a banner which she must display because of the truth.

Let us, my hearers, read the inscriptions upon this banner; and then throw its folds anew to the breeze, in testimony of the principles which we are called this day to confess before the nations of the world.

I. In the first place, a banner is given us to be displayed in defense of republican institutions upon this continent. Among the issues involved in this conflict, this certainly is not the least. The imagination may, perhaps, be more impressed with the physical dimensions of the war, with the hundreds of thousands in armed array upon the field of battle, with the ponderous artillery hurling its deadly missiles against our beleaguered fortresses.

But the moral grandeur of the struggle lies in the immortal principles which are at stake, and which will give to it its true place in the history that shall hereafter be written. Schlegel has well remarked, in his Philosophy of History, that "in the whole circumference of the globe there is only a certain number of nations that occupy an important and really historic place in the annals of civilization."

In a comparatively narrow belt, extending from the southeast of Asia to the northern and western extremities of Europe, he finds the only historical and highly civilized countries who have made any substantive contribution to the general progress of mankind. Without pausing now to inquire whether his classification is complete, or whether since his day additions should not be made to the fifteen nations embraced within his "land chart of civilization," his discrimination between the historic and unhistoric races must be allowed as just.

It is unquestionable, moreover, that every historic people is marked by characteristics which render it strictly individual. Egypt, for example, from the moment she lay in her cradle of bulrushes upon the banks of the Nile, has exhibited a character purely and intensely Egyptian. The Hebrew and the Persian differ as clearly from the Roman and the Greek, as those in turn differ from the English and the Spaniard, and these again from the Russian and the Turk.

Nor can it be denied that in the comprehensive scheme of Divine providence, all such nations have an assigned work, and are preserved in being till that work is done. Thus, Greece was perpetuated until she had carried the arts of sculpture and painting, of poetry, eloquence and song, to a perfection which has never been surpassed; and when she could do no more in philosophy and science, she was trodden in the dust beneath the iron-heeled legions of Rome.

When Rome, too, had built up an empire as wide as the world, and could do no more by her systems of jurisprudence and state-craft, she slid into a military despotism; until at length her mighty framework gave way, under the pressure of barbarian hordes, that from her ruins might spring the present Congress of European nations.

It is not, then, aside from the purposes of this day, to consider what may be the task which the great Ruler of the earth has set our people to accomplish, and how far its successful issue may be bound up in the history of the present struggle. The grand problem undertaken to be solved by our forefathers was the establishment of a free government under republican forms, in which the exercise of sovereign power should be lodged in representatives chosen by the people.

The possibility of such a government, and of its continuance to remote posterity, is the question now submitted to the arbitrament of the sword between the North and the South. It is our clear conviction that the same grave in which this Confederacy shall be buried, will prove the sepulchre of republicanism upon this continent.

During the progress of this fearful strife, expressions of doubt as to the feasibility and value of such a government have fallen from many lips — and sometimes the preference has been openly avowed for a constitutional and limited monarchy. Too much importance should not be attached to utterances, which are probably the language of impatience, wrung out by disappointment and suffering, rather than of matured and sober reflection.

It is, however, a weakness to shrink from the discipline to which all nations are subjected in working out their allotted destiny. No grand experiment in the science of legislation can be achieved without trial and conflict; for in the clashing interests and passions of men, causes of insecurity will ever be found, and constant modification of existing institutions will be required to adapt them to the changes of outward circumstances.

When, therefore, a stable government, like that of England, is enviously cited in contrast with the fluctuations of our own, it is overlooked that this great boon was not purchased except at the cost of seven hundred years of conflict.

We have but to look into the brilliant pages of Macaulay to learn how long and bitter was the struggle between prerogative on the one hand, and privilege on the other, before these two poles of the English constitution were adjusted in even tolerable harmony. It is far too early for us to abandon the experiment commenced by our fathers, and unmanly to succumb beneath the first difficulties encountered in our historic probation. Rather let us, with the patience and moderation of our British ancestors, amend by gradual changes what experience shows to be defective in our institutions, without capriciously changing the foundation of the government under which we were born.

But be the abstract preferences of men what they may, it should be borne steadily in mind, that governments at last are not made, but grow. The philosopher may sketch, in the seclusion of his closet, the Utopia which charms his fancy; but the statesman must accept that form of government which the antecedent conditions of society may impose.

Despite all the artifices of a speculative legislation, it will crystallize according to a fixed law, in precisely that shape which the exigencies of the times and the character of the people shall determine. We, at this day, must work out the problem bequeathed to us according to the conditions in which we find it, as did our fathers before us.

The republican form of government was adopted by them, not through original choice, but as a simple necessity. The controversy with England was not begun for republicanism, though it ended in it. With them monarchy was not so much repudiated, as liberty was sought: and if any branch of the royal family had resided here, and had sympathized with the passionate struggle of a young nation to be both great and free, the conservative spirit of our forefathers would have led to the establishment of monarchy upon these republican shores.

But there was no titled class, having the prestige of nobility and rank, from which a monarch could be chosen; and the statesmen of this period dwelt too much in the light of past history not to know the impossibility of lifting a single family, from the uniform level of society, to permanent presidency over the rest. They were too well skilled in political science not to be aware that the wide interval between the commonalty and the throne must be filled with an intermediate class, who should render the ascent less abrupt and precipitous.

These conditions of monarchy failing, our fathers evinced their practical wisdom in striking the golden mean between the radicalism which overturns only for the sake of remodeling, and that fatal conservatism which, in its blind attachment to inheritance and prescription, resists the progress it should aim to guide.

The actual sovereignty of the people was accordingly recognized; but the country was saved from the savage rule of unlicensed democracy by the establishment of a Confederate republic, with its written constitution, and all the checks and balances which can be furnished by two deliberative chambers, the presidential veto and state sovereignty.

A little reflection should convince every mind that the same difficulties which interdicted monarchy in 1776, exist in even stronger force in our own day. Nothing consequently is left us but to accept our problem exactly as we find it, and to solve it, if we can, under the smiles of a benignant Providence. It is the dream of the Radical to change our whole political fabric from turret to foundation stone; but true wisdom dictates that such modifications shall be gradually admitted as time and experience shall hereafter suggest.

The maintenance of republican institutions being then at once a duty and necessity, no proposition seems clearer, than that these are bound up in the fate of our own Confederacy — which conviction gives us assurance of the ultimate and complete triumph of our cause.

The Northern people, from the commencement of American history, have failed to seize the true idea of a republic. They have confounded it with democracy, from which it is as generically distinct as from monarchy itself. Republicanism, with them, is only democracy writ small, a merely mechanical device for condensing the masses, and rendering practicable the government of the mob.

They have pushed the doctrine to the verge of ungodliness and atheism, in making the voice of the people the voice of God; in exalting the will of a numerical majority above the force of constitution and covenants, and creating in the despotism of the mob the vilest and most irresponsible tyranny known in the annals of mankind.

Not, however, to insist upon their fundamental misconception of the very nature of republicanism, which has worked out its legitimate result in the total prostration of civil liberty, and in the ignominious surrender of all its safeguards, a fatal defect is patent in the very structure of their society, which renders them utterly incompetent to achieve what our forefathers had commenced. I allude to the fact that no class exists with them, which stands forth the representative and guardian of the conservative element in human society.

This is sufficient to explain the rupture between the two portions of the old confederation. The conservative element existed only at the South. Long and patiently it battled against the usurpations of an aggressive and unprincipled democracy; but overpowered at length, its only resource was separation from a lawless power, which could not even be held in check.

This withdrawal leaves the North hopelessly destitute of that conservative influence, which must always be proportioned with the aggressive forces at work — or the nation drives recklessly forward to its own destruction. Individuals may, doubtless, be found in their ranks, of sound and conservative views; but these are not grouped and consolidated in a class holding the balance of power in the nation: and the singular ease with which all moderate views have been swept away by the stormy clamors of the populace, too mournfully attests how feeble is the breastwork against vulgar fanaticism presented by insulated individuals.

In the South, however, whatever odium may attach to her social organization through a perverted and unscriptural philanthropy, this capital advantage accrues: that the dominant race, by the force of its position towards an inferior and servile class, is rendered conservative in the highest degree. All their interests are bound up in the perpetuation of the prevailing institutions of the land; and the class, whose tendencies might be to change, has no share whatever in the administration of public affairs.

It matters not whether slaves be actually owned by many or by few: it is enough that one simply belongs to the superior and ruling race, to secure consideration and respect. So that, without a hereditary and privileged nobility, inconsistent with the simplicity of republican taste, all the political benefit which springs from the existence of such an order, lodges with the entire population who have any control over the land.

But whatever may be thought of the relative competency of the North and the South to perpetuate republican principles, it is perfectly clear that the subjugation of the latter closes the door of hope against both.

The South, sunk into the condition of a dependent province, will have lost the opportunity of realizing in external form any of her most cherished opinions; while the conquering North, in the very fact of her triumph, will have extinguished the last vestige of that government which she now wages war professedly to maintain.

Holding her conquest only by military force, she can never hope to construct anew the old Confederacy, whose elementary and pervading idea was the free consent of all the parties. Constrained by her very success to become a despot, her standing armies, levied for the suppression of revolt, will soon tread beneath their feet the last poor remains of civil liberty — and the history of ancient Rome's subjection to the Praetorian guards, will be reenacted, amidst the scorn and derision of all mankind.

Say I not well, that the banner given us to be displayed is in defense of a pure republican government upon this American continent? It is my unwavering conviction that God has rent the old nation by this terrible schism, not only because it had grown too great to be good, and to prevent its becoming the scourge and pest of the world, but also to afford in this Confederacy, a last asylum for the genius of republicanism to work out, if possible, its promised blessings to the nations of the earth.

II. In the second place, a solemn duty is imposed upon us to protect the slave, peculiarly dependent upon our guardianship, from the schemes of a false philanthropy which threaten his early and inevitable extermination.

It is not my purpose here to discuss the institution of domestic servitude existing amongst us. The argument has long since been exhausted upon both sides of this disputed topic; and those who have given it their attention have long since reached, upon the one side or the other, probably an unchangeable conviction. Some facts have, however, been grievously overlooked by the fanatical assailants of slavery, which, it seems to us, have much to do with a correct interpretation of God's providence in reference to this entire subject.

The negro race, for example, has never in any period of history been able to lift itself above its native condition of fetishism and barbarism; and except as it has indirectly contributed by servile labor to human progress, might well be discounted, according to Schlegel's view, in the general estimate of the world's inhabitants.

Often as they have been brought in contact with other and superior races, they have never been stimulated to become a self-supporting people, under well regulated institutions and laws; but have invariably relapsed from a partial civilization into their original state of degradation and imbecility.

It is moreover notoriously true that the highest type of character, ever developed among them, has been in the condition of servitude; and that, in the fairest portions of the earth, after the advantage of a long discipline to systematic toil, emancipation has converted them instantly from productive laborers into the most indolent and squalid wretches to be found upon the globe.

Whilst too, as by the force of a universal law, an inferior race melts away in the presence of a superior civilization, a few thousand Africans have expanded under this system of domestic slavery into four millions of people; constituting, at this moment, the best conditioned, the happiest, and I will add, in the essential import of the word, the freest operative class to be found in Christendom.

It is also beyond dispute that a larger number of slaves at the South are in the communion of the Church of Christ, and have been made partakers of the blessings of the gospel, than is furnished in the returns of missionary labor by all the branches of the Christian church taken together, over the whole surface of the globe.

And last of all, one of the most significant facts in this entire series, is, that whilst slavery has existed in every variety of form through the whole tract of human history, it has been reserved to our times to beat up a crusade against it under precisely that patriarchal form in which it is sanctioned in the word of God, and in which it has never been found since the overthrow of the Hebrew empire, until now.

My individual belief is, that servitude, in some one of its forms, is the allotted destiny of this race, and that the form most beneficial to the negro himself is precisely that which obtains with us; where, either as born in the house, or bought with our money, he is a regular member of the household, and is protected alike by the affection and by the interest of the master.

I am not in the least appalled by the apparent unanimity with which the voice of Christendom protests against the lawfulness of slavery, and pronounces it both a heresy and a crime. It is the fashion of the world to go periodically mad upon some wild scheme, which contrives to enlist in its support a misdirected religious zeal. This is far from being the first instance where a religious fanaticism has stirred the depths of the human heart, and brought the world in fearful collision with the grand and fixed purposes of Almighty God.

Medieval Europe, with all the fervor of religious consecration, poured forth her armed myriads to rescue the Holy Land from the polluting tread of the Saracen. It shocked the conscience of that superstitious age that the sepulchre of our blessed Lord should be in possession of the Infidel. Under the passionate appeals of vagrant monks, a sustained fanaticism, surviving a thousand disasters, held Christendom to the visionary enterprise through a period far longer than that which attests the folly and superstition of the age in which we now live.

But as the gathering tides of ocean dash in vain against the continents by which the Creator bounds their fury, so this wild fanaticism, after a frightful waste of treasure and of life, broke into spray against the decree of God: and Europe's proud chivalry returned from the vain conflict, to learn at home the lesson of submission to the behests of Heaven.

Perhaps one of the results of this grand struggle will be to correct the error of the world as to this whole matter of domestic slavery — to teach mankind that the allotment of God, in the original distribution of destinies to the sons of Noah, must continue, despite the ravings of a spurious and sentimental philanthropy — to illustrate the riches of his grace, and the workings of a beneficent gospel, through the relation of master and servant, not less than through that of parent and child, and all the other permanent relations in which man stands to his fellow man.

On this point, however, I do not wish to be misunderstood; and having said so much, I desire to say a little more. Whilst rebuking the presumption of those who clamor for the emancipation of those whom God has manifestly placed under the yoke, I would not fall into the same condemnation, by insisting upon the perpetual bondage of those whom it may please Him finally to release.

Being firmly persuaded that the relation of master and servant is clearly ordained of God, and that there is no more sin intrinsically in it than in the subordination of parent and child, I feel no compunction of conscience in the holding of slaves. But if it be the Divine purpose to elevate them into a condition of freedom, I believe our people will be the last to rebel against the decrees of Providence, and not a feeling of their hearts will rise in opposition to that advancement. I confess frankly that I have no expectation of such a result.

From all the attributes of the negro character, from the whole history of God's dealings towards him, and from all the light shed upon his destiny from the sacred Scriptures, I judge his true normal position to be that of "a servant of servants," and that his own interests are best subserved in this condition of subordination and dependence. But the decision of all this I am willing to remit to that future to which it belongs.

If the day shall ever arrive when the slave ought to be free, God will sufficiently indicate it by evincing his aptitude for a new and independent career, and by making it the interest of the master to dissolve the relation hitherto sustained. We agree, with all our hearts, to leave the solution of this intricate problem to the generation which shall be called to decide upon it; in the assured conviction that, if emancipation be brought about at all, it will be in God's own sublime way, by the silent operation of secret but efficient causes: and to the Divine will, clearly indicated through the unfoldings of His providence, we respond from the depths our hearts a most cheerful amen.

But we do protest against the impertinent obtrusion of men into the counsels of Almighty God, and their insolent attempt to dictate the policy of His administration of human affairs, and to dig the channels in which the current of His providence must be made artificially to flow.

We do insist further, that in the present posture of the two races, the African cannot cease to be a bondman without bringing utter ruin upon both: and especially that our subjugation, in the present struggle, will be the signal for the extirpation of the negro, now cast by God upon the protection of the white master. The truth of this, alas! there is no room to doubt.

All history attests the impossibility of two unequal races living side by side with mutual advantage. The inferior gives way before the energy and resources of the superior; nor would it be difficult to trace the causes which necessitate the direful catastrophe. Does any one dream that the fairest portion of this continent will be abandoned to the fate of the West India islands, and suffered to grow up into a wilderness merely to furnish a home for a lot of indolent barbarians?

The lean and hungry vandals, now hoping to appropriate our broad and fertile fields, will be restrained by no such romantic sentiment from swarming upon the land which their own arms have subjugated. Beneath that fearful invasion the negro will be buried. Mocked with a delusive freedom which exists for him only in name, task-masters, more unrelenting than those of Egypt, will exact for scanty wages a degree of toil which the bondman never knew. Precisely here his ruin will begin.

Among the proofs of the negro's fitness for servitude is the striking fact that he cannot easily be over tasked. The white man may be induced to labor beyond his power of endurance, until nature gives way beneath the protracted effort. But the negro reaches his natural limit, and becomes at once incapable of toil, which no compulsion will prompt him to achieve.

What hope has he of competing with the hardy and aggressive race who shall then be masters of the soil? Can he thrive as the slave of capital, which has no bowels of mercy for the aching limbs and overstrained nerves which are bending and breaking beneath the scourge of starvation? Yielding to his constitutional revulsion from undue labor, and emancipated from that mild constraint which now exacts of him a moderate industry, he will sink back into his native indolence — melting away at last through filth, disease and vice, until not a vestige of his existence will remain.

If this be the doom to which he is reserved, then is the mystery of that providence insoluble, which first brought him to our shores; and which has advanced him from a savage to the dignity of a man, and made him a member of the household of faith through a blessed gospel, which here in bondage he has been taught to embrace.

Whatever the nature and extent of our crimes, which have drawn upon us the avenging judgments of Heaven, with what does this poor feeble race stand charged, that they should be led to the shambles by the inhuman butchers who, during the progress of this war, have already destroyed one half the victims seduced into their power? It cannot be that a benignant providence has allotted to them such a destiny as this: and the presence of the helpless African is to us a sign of the Divine protection and blessing.

With his fate bound up so entirely with our own, I believe that for his sake at least we shall be preserved: and while he spreads forth his hands in mute appeals to us for guardianship, the banner of defense must be unfurled, beneath whose righteous folds both the master and the slave may boldly rally. I cannot doubt that one of the compensations of this bitter conflict will be to sanctify, and to endear, the tie by which these two races are linked together.

The timid amongst ourselves will be reassured, when they discover this relation, regarded by many so unstable, unshaken by the rockings of this terrific tempest: and in the sweeping away of these groundless fears, the way will be prepared for the more faithful discharge of all the duties which slavery involves.

Relieved of those embarrassments which a hypocritical fanaticism has interposed, we shall be able, with greater freedom, to give them God's blessed word, to protect their persons against the abuses of capricious power, and to throw the shield of a stronger guardianship around their domestic relations.

It may be for this that our people are now passing under the severe discipline of this protracted war — on the one hand to chasten us for past shortcomings, and on the other to enlarge our power to protect and bless the race committed to our trust.

III. The contest in which we are embarked is a struggle for existence, in which defeat means simple destruction. Our enemies profess indeed to fight only to restore the Union, and to maintain the integrity of the nation: but the pretext is too hollow to deceive those who have watched their aggressions during the past.

Through more than forty years the North has striven, by a partial and discriminating legislation, to reduce the South into a state of political vassalage. They have systematically drained her wealth to enrich themselves, and have thrown upon her the chief burden of sustaining the common government; whilst, with a refinement of cruelty, they have persistently sought to cripple her resources, and with suicidal madness to overthrow her domestic economy, upon which the welfare of both depended.

The ferocity of the present war cannot be explained, except as the culmination of a studied jealousy which has been cultivated through the life of an entire generation. No hatred is so intense as that which glows in the bosom of him who inflicts a wrong, and which can justify itself only by its implacability for existing at all.

To suppose the enmity of the North appeased just at the moment it is tasting the sweetness of revenge, is to give it credit for a generosity which would have forbidden it ever to arise. Nor will the prize for which a parliamentary conflict has been waged through half a century be relinquished, just as it is within the grasp.

Nothing is less desired by the dominant party of the North, than the reconstruction of the old Union, if the South shall ever lie at its feet a helpless prey, to be devoured at its will.

Nor, on the other hand, can the seceded States yield again a free consent to reenter the old Confederation; which consent the Declaration of Independence assumes to be the corner-stone upon which all just governments must rest. An experience through half a century of the perfidy of the North, interposes an insuperable bar to all reconstruction.

The utter recklessness of truth on the part of our foes is one of the most appalling developments of the present war; and I believe all history may be vainly searched for a parallel instance of the abandonment of all truthfulness by an entire people. It is a degree of profligacy not reached by a single leap. Rapid as may be the deterioration in morals of an individual or of a class, there are stages in the declension; and it is a fearful education which conducts at last to the lowest deep.

At an early period, the people of the North commenced to tamper with their religious symbols, until the very creeds of the Church became the nests of heresy and deceit. The Bible fell next before this fell spirit of apostasy; its dogmatic authority was overthrown, or else ridiculed as an idle and obsolete superstition; and its sacred language perverted into a sanction for all the utterances of an infidel philosophy.

The transition was easy to a perverse criticism which should eviscerate the Constitution of all its meaning, or to a "higher law," which should summarily dispense with the obligation of oaths and covenants. It needs no argument of mine to show that treaties and compacts depend at last upon the good faith and honor of the parties contracting; and that where truth has lost its sanctity, the last bond between man and man is severed, and society dissolves in universal anarchy and chaos.

Suppose then that, with inconceivable generosity, the North should offer to the subjugated South the liberty of reentering the Union she has abandoned, what guaranties can be proposed more sacred than those which have been already trampled profanely underfoot? And what security can the South have of the fulfillment of promises by a people who have proclaimed, with unblushing profligacy, their insensibility to honor and to truth?

Besides all this, an impassable gulf now yawns between the North and South; a sea of blood rolls its deep, dark tide betwixt them, which never can be crossed; and over the graves of our dead, it will be impossible to shake hands in amity and love. History will perpetuate the memory of this heroic struggle, and our most distant posterity will kindle with a just resentment at the story of our wrongs. No, my hearers, there is no going back — the past is an abyss.

The South may possibly be subjugated, if such be the stern decree of Heaven, and may henceforward be held as a conquered province, to be impoverished and crushed beneath the heel of a bitter and relentless foe; but as equal members in a just and faithful alliance, it is not written in the book of fate that South Carolina and Massachusetts shall sit side by side as in days of yore.

The dream of reconstruction can be cherished only by a madman, who is heedless of the most solemn lessons taught us by the past, and who knows nothing of the fury of those passions set loose by this war to devour the helpless and the innocent. Imagination sickens at the horrors to be enacted, should the South fail in this great struggle for independence.

The last act in the fearful drama will be one of terror and of blood. The brave and noble of our land, who stand forth the representatives of Southern manliness and pride, will bend their necks to the executioner, and expiate the crime of daring to be free. When the weary headsman rests from his ignominious toil, proscription and banishment will follow with all their lingering torture.

Our gallant people will be poured forth, in forced or voluntary exile, to mingle their blood with other races, or else to melt away like the drifting snow upon the unfriendly earth. The hungry agrarian of the North will abandon his rocky glebe to carve for himself a kinder fortune upon our vacant lands. The miserable remnant of our people that shall remain to weep amid the tombs of their fathers, will bow beneath a servitude which daily insult will render as humiliating as it is oppressive.

Suspicion will dog them at every step; with a picket at every corner, and a spy in every house, bullied and badgered by insolent ruffians at every turn, they will find a prison in their homes, and live as culprits in the land of their birth. This gloomy picture I hold up, not as a prophecy of the fate we are doomed to incur, but only as descriptive of what the term subjugation unquestionably imports.

I thank God that, in the darkest hour, I have never despaired of the Republic. I have an abiding faith in the righteousness of our cause, as well as in the constancy and patriotism of our people; and a faith stronger still in the wisdom and goodness of that Providence which has watched over us thus far in our momentous struggle. With God's blessing upon our strong arms and willing hearts, we shall yet be free, and fulfill a glorious destiny among the nations of the earth.

It is well, however, to consider the fate which awaits every conquered people, that we may resolve to escape it. If self-preservation be the first law of nature, let us write upon our banner that we have a right to live; and enter anew upon the conflict, as those whose very existence is at stake. Better, infinitely better, if fall at last we must, to fall with the brave upon the field of battle, with our face to the foe, a nation of martyrs; than as slaves, to be consumed by lingering decay, the shame and the scorn of history.

IV. A far more solemn and august view of our struggle remains to be presented, for the banner which waves over us bears upon its folds this inscription — God's right to rule the world.

There is no attribute of the Divine Being guarded with more jealousy than His own sovereignty; and history is read to little purpose if we do not discover, in all its grand epochs, a special vindication of God's supremacy. "The Lord hath prepared his throne in the heavens, and his kingdom ruleth over all."

"His dominion is an everlasting dominion, and his kingdom is from generation to generation — all the inhabitants of the earth are reputed as nothing, and he doeth according to his will in the army of Heaven, and among the inhabitants of the earth; and none can stay his hand, or say unto Him, what doest thou?"

Yet, with this very interrogatory in its most profane spirit, the North has, for more than a generation, challenged the most High God. Claiming for themselves a purity superior to his own, they have presumptuously pronounced against the Divine administration from the beginning of time. Though slavery has existed through all the past, and though it is sanctioned and regulated in the scriptures of the Old and of the New Testaments, they arraign before their bar the Providence which has ordained and perpetuated it until now.

Nay more: not content with impeaching the Divine morality, and hurling their impious accusations against the integrity of God's rule, they proceed, in all the madness of fanaticism, to rectify the errors of His administration, and to shape the providence which shall henceforth guide and govern the world.

Unabashed by the sublime patience with which "God's eternal thought moves on his undisturbed affairs," and with whom one day is as a thousand years, and a thousand years as one day, these fierce zealots would quicken the Divine activity in the accomplishment of their puny reforms.

Though the universe should lie in ruins at his feet, nothing must retard their glowing ambition to make the world more perfect than God would have it to be — and the sun must be swept from the face of the sky, because their telescope has revealed a spot upon his disc.

It is this spirit of arrogant dictation, finding its climax in the pretensions of "a higher law," which has involved the North in the guilt of perjury, and has broken the holiest political covenant ever sworn between man and man.

It is this which has since lifted up the sword to butcher those who will not bend to a merciless proscription. It is the same spirit, mounting to frenzy, which has seized upon wise and venerable ministers of the Church — who have turned away from the gospel of God, to hound on this war of exterminating and bitter revenge.

And this it is, which stamps with ungodliness and atheism this effort of our foes to lay waste our land with fire and sword. Under this aspect, our struggle rises from the heroic into the awful and sublime. We strike not only for country and for home, for the altars of our worship and for the graves of our dead; but we strike for the prerogatives of God, and for His kingly supremacy over the earth.

The question at issue simply is, whether He who has created the world shall rule it by his wisdom, or abdicate his power at the bidding of a lawless fanaticism: whether his robust justice shall continue to administer human affairs, or yield to the sickly fancies of a sentimental and insane philanthropy.

We are thus summoned to stand as sentinels around Jehovah's throne, and to vindicate the honesty of his reign against those who have assailed the one and impugned the other. The preeminent grandeur of this war is found in the fact that it centers upon a religious idea.

On the one hand is a wicked infidelity, lifting its rebellious arm against the Ruler of the universe; and on the other, humble loyalty, receiving the blow, and offering itself a sacrifice to His insulted majesty. Patriotism is sanctified by religion, which from her sacred horn pours upon it the oil of consecration.

Can we doubt the issue of such a conflict? By virtue of its relation to the cause of God, we can see why the instruments of His glory should be purged with trial upon trial; but history and the Bible unite their testimony, that in the end the wicked will be trampled in His fury, and those who wait for His salvation shall rejoice in their deliverance.

I utter these sentences with due consideration; for here, I judge, is the pivot upon which our triumph will turn. At the precise juncture when independent nations are to dwell side by side, and the principle of a balance of power is introduced upon this western continent, it is suitable that God should practically demonstrate His lordship over the earth, and compel the admission that He "ruleth in the kingdom of men."

As soon, therefore, as this truth shall be imbedded in the convictions of our people, and prepare us to be candid confessors of the Divine supremacy, then, and not till then, will He overthrow our enemies and establish us in the land.

In the firm belief that He will assert our liberties in the assertion of His rights, we are certain of ultimate triumph, since the battle is not ours, but His. We lay the nation beneath the shadow of His throne, and bide His arbitration through the fearful ordeal of battle.

Such, Senators and Representatives, is "the banner given us to be displayed because of the truth." For myself, I solemnly and reverently accept it from the hands of Almighty God, willing in life and in death to confess the principles inscribed upon its folds.

Do you this day, on behalf of a noble constituency, accept it with a like devotion? Then send forth the utterance, whose echo rebounding from our mountain sides, shall mingle with the deep, hoarse murmurs of the sea, and be borne by the winds of heaven to the distant nations who have left us alone with our fate and with our God. Here to-day, at the Capital of this ancient and venerable Commonwealth, let us "in the name of our God set up our banner."

It is for you, the representatives of a suffering and heroic people, to reflect the spirit of martyrdom which reigns in the hearts of your constituency. Our sons have gone forth, girdling the Confederacy with a living wall: at whose foot is heard the sullen roar of the invading tide, rolling up in the madness of its rage, and dashing into idle foam.

Our martyrs are upon the battle plain, undergoing the fearful baptism of blood: and when the electric wires convey to every home the tidings of death, pale and silent mourners are there, undergoing the equal baptism of grief. Wife and mother press the hand upon their breaking hearts, and plead with God to accept the sacrifice which the strongest human love has not wished to withdraw from the altar.

Beside that altar you have now summoned the priest to stand, and with the holy offices of religion to sanctify the oblation. The offering which patriotism renders to country, a sovereign State, on bended knee, with sacramental fervor, dedicates to God. Lift up the right hand to Heaven, as the grand oath rolls up above the stars, that you are prepared for death, but not for infamy — that the sacred rights, for which we are now contending, shall never be extinguished, but in the blood of an exterminated race.

The vow is registered: and He, who sits enthroned beneath the emerald rainbow, smiles upon us from out the dark cloud, as he writes against it the hour of deliverance. Let us but do, and endure, till the hand upon the dial-plate touches the last second of the appointed time, and sounds forth the note of our redemption.

Patiently submitting to that righteous discipline by which He prepares us for greatness and for glory; trusting in that

Almighty arm which is pledged to strike down the haughty and the proud; humbling ourselves in penitence and shame for our private and our public sins; piously accepting every trust which His sovereign will imposes; and consolidated by the sufferings which He calls us to endure; we wait the fullness of the time when we shall once more rejoice in the blessings of liberty and of peace. Oh Israel, "there is none like unto the God of Jeshurun, who rideth upon the heaven in thy help, and in His excellency on the sky.

The eternal God is thy refuge, and underneath thee are the everlasting arms; and He shall thrust out the enemy from before thee, and shall say, destroy them. Israel then, shall dwell in safety alone; the fountain of Jacob shall be upon a land of corn and wine; also His heavens shall drop dew. Happy art thou, O! Israel: who is like unto thee, O! people saved by the Lord, the shield of thy help, and who is the sword of thy excellency! and thine enemies shall be found liars unto thee, and thou shalt tread upon their high places."

TRUE COURAGE

A DISCOURSE COMMEMORATIVE

OF

Lieut. General Thomas J. Jackson

BY

REV. R. L. DABNEY, D. D.

PROFESSOR IN UNION THEOLOGICAL SEMINARY,
VA.

1863

TRUE COURAGE

"Be not afraid of them that kill the body, and after that, have no more that they can do. But I will forewarn you whom ye shall fear: Fear him which, after he hath killed, hath power to cast into hell; yea, I say unto you, fear him." — Luke 12:4,5.

A little wisdom and experience will teach us to be very modest, in interpreting God's purposes by his providences. "It is the glory of the Lord to conceal a thing." His designs are too vast and complex for our puny minds to infer them, from the fragments of his ways which fall under our eyes. Yet, it is evident, that he intends us to learn instruction from the events which occur before us under the regulation of his holy will.

The profane are more than once rebuked by Him (as Is. 5: 12.) because "they regard not the work of the Lord, neither consider the operation of his hands." And our Saviour sharply chides the Jewish Pharisees: "O ye hypocrites! ye can discern the face of the sky; but can ye not discern the signs of the times?" (Matt. 16:3) We are not therefore to refuse the lessons of those events which Providence evolves, because caution and humility are required in learning them.

We have a guide, which will conduct us securely to the understanding of so much of them as God intends us to study: That guide is the Holy Scriptures. Among the several principles which they lay down for the explanation of God's dealings, it is sufficient for our present task, to declare this one: That the characters of his children, which exhibit the scriptural model, are given as examples, to be studied and imitated by us. He would thus teach us more than those abstract conceptions of Christian excellence, which are conveyed by general definitions of duty; he would give us a living picture and concrete idea.

He thus aims to stimulate our aspirations and efforts, by showing us that the attainments of holiness are within human reach. He enstamps the moral likeness on the imitative soul by the warmth of admiration and love. That such is the use God intends us to make of noble examples, the Apostle James teaches us, (5:10.) — "Take, my brethren, the prophets, who have spoken in the name of the Lord, for an example of suffering affliction and of patience;" and the Epistle to the Hebrews, (6:12.) when it desires us to "be followers of them who, through faith and patience, inherit the promises."

Common sense teaches us then, from these texts, that the lesson is important and impressive, in proportion as the example given us was illustrious. By this rule, God addresses to us instruction of solemn emphasis, in the character, and the death, which we have now met to commemorate.

Our dead hero is God's sermon to us. His embodied admonition, His incorporate discourse, to inculcate upon us the virtues with which he was adorned by the Holy Ghost; and especially those traits of the citizen, the Christian, and the soldier, now most essential to the times. He calls us, not to exhaust the occasion in useless sensibilities, but to come and learn the beauty of holiness, by the light of a shining example; and to let our passionate love and grief burn in upon the plastic heart, the impress of his principles.

Happy shall I be, if I can so conceive and execute my humble task, as to permit this character to speak its own high lesson to your hearts. The only reason which makes you think this task appropriate to me, is doubtless this: that I had the privilege of his friendship, and an opportunity for intimately observing, his character, during the most brilliant part of his career.

The expectations which you form from this fact, must be my justification from the charge of egotism, if I should allude to my own observations of him, in exemplifying these instructions. But I must also forewarn you, that should there be any expectation of mere anecdote to gratify an idle curiosity, or of any disclosures of confidential intercourse, now doubly sanctified by the seal of the tomb, it will not be gratified.

And let it be added, that however the heart may prompt encomiums on the departed, these are not the direct object, but only the incidental result, of this discourse. I stand here, as God's herald, in God's sanctuary, on this holy day, by his authority. My business is, not to praise any man, however beloved and bewailed, but only to unfold God's message through his life and death. Among that circle of virtues which his symmetrical character displayed, since time would fail me to do justice to all, I propose more especially, to select one, for our consideration, his Christian courage.

Courage is the opposite of fear. But fear may be described either as a feeling and appreciation of existing danger, or an undue yielding to that feeling. It is in the latter sense, that it is unworthy. In the former, it is the necessary result of the natural desire for well-being, in a creature endued with reflection and forecast. Hence a true courage implies the existence of fear in the form of sense, that is, of a feeling of danger. For courage is but the overcoming of that feeling by a worthier motive.

A danger unfelt is as though it did not exist. No man could be called brave for advancing coolly upon a risk of which he was totally unconscious. It is only where there is an exertion of fortitude in bearing up against the consciousness of peril, that true courage has place. If there is any man who can literally say that "he knows no fear;" then he deserves, no credit for his composure. True, a generous fortitude, in resisting the consciousness of danger, will partly extinguish it; so that a sensibility to it, over-sensitive and prominent among the emotions, an indication of a mean self-love.

There are three emotions which claim the name of courage. The first is animal courage. This is but the ferment of animal passions and blind sympathies, combined with an irrational thoughtlessness. The man is courageous, only because he refuses to reflect; bold because he is blind. — This animal hardihood, according to the obvious truths explained above, does not deserve the name of true courage; because there is no rational fortitude in resisting the consciousness of danger.

And it is little worthy of trust; for having no foundation in a reasoning self command, a sudden, vivid perception of the evil hitherto unnoted, may, at any moment, supplant it with a panic, as unreasoning and intense as the previous fury.

The second species of courage is that prompted by the spirit of personal honor. There is a consciousness of risk; but it is manfully controlled by the sentiment of pride, the keener fear of reproach, and the desire of applause. This kind of fortitude is more worthy of the name of courage, because it exhibits self-command. But after all, the motive is personal and selfish; and therefore the sentiment does not rise to the level of a virtue.

The third species is the moral courage of him who fears God, and, for that reason, fears nothing else. There is an intelligent apprehension of danger; there is the natural instinct of self-love desiring to preserve its own well-being; but it is curbed and governed by the sense of duty, and desire for the approbation of God. This alone is true courage; true virtue; for it is rational, and its motive is moral and unselfish.

It is a true Christian grace, when found in its purest forms, a grace whose highest exemplar, and whose source, is the Divine Redeemer; whose principle is that parent grace of the soul, faith. "David and Samuel, and the prophets, through faith subdued kingdoms, waxed valiant in fight, turned to flight the armies of the aliens." (Heb. 11: 33,34.) Trust in God, in his faithfulness, his approbation, his reward, his command to brave the risks allotted to them, was their motive. But "Christ dwelleth in our hearts by faith." (Eph. 3:17.)

This is the principle by which the soul of the believer is brought into, living union with Christ; and the heart, otherwise sapless and withered, is penetrated by the vital sap of his holy Spirit. He is the head; men of faith his members; he the stock; they the branches; his divine principles circulate from him into their souls, and assimilate them to him. But the whole mission of Jesus Christ on earth is a divine exemplification of moral courage.

What was it, save the unselfish sentiment of duty, overruling the anticipations of personal evil which made him declare, in prospect of all the woes of his incarnation, "Lo I come, in the volume of the book it is written unto me; I delight to do thy will Oh my God?"

What else caused him to press forward with eager, hungering haste, through the toils and obloquy of his persecuted life, to that baptism of blood, which awaited him at Jerusalem?

What else nerved him, when deserted, betrayed, and destined to death, desolate, and fainting, amidst a pitiless flood of enemies, one word of disclaimer might have rescued him, to refuse that word and assert his rightful kingship over Zion, with a tenacity more indomitable than the grave?

Jesus Christ is the Divine Pattern and Fountain of heroism. Earth's true heroes are they who derive their courage from him.

Yet it is true, the three kinds of bravery which have been defied, may be mixed in many breasts. Some who have true moral courage may also have animal hardihood; and others of the truly brave may lack it. No Christian courage, perhaps, exists without a union of that which the spirit of personal honor, in its innocent phase inspires; and many men of honor have perhaps some shade of the pure sentiment of duty, mingled with the pride and self-glorifying, which chiefly nerve their fortitude.

But he is the bravest man, who is the best Christian. It is he who truly fears God, who is entitled to fear nothing else.

I. He whose conduct is governed by the fear of God, is brave, because the powers of his soul are in harmony. — There is no mutiny or war within, of fear against shame, of duty against safety, of conscience and evil desire, by which the bad man has his heart unnerved.

All the nobler capacities of the soul combine their strength, and especially, that master power, of which the wicked are compelled to sing: "It is conscience that makes cowards of us all," invigorates the soul with her plaudits. In conscious rectitude there is strength.

This strength General Jackson eminently possessed. He walked in the fear of God, with a perfect heart, keeping all his commandments and ordinances, blameless. Never has it been my happiness to know one of greater purity of life, or more regular and devout habits of prayer. As ever in his great task-master's eye, he seemed to devote every hour to the sentiment of duty, and only to live to fulfill his charge as a servant of God.

Of this be assured, that all his eminence and success as a great and brave soldier were based on his eminence and sanctity as a Christian. Thus, every power of his soul was brought to move in sweet accord, under the guidance of an enlightened and honest conscience. How could such a soul fail to be courageous, for the right?

But especially did he derive firmness and decision, from the peculiar strength of his conviction concerning the righteousness and necessity of this war.

Had he not sought the light of the Holy Scriptures, in thorough examination and prayer, had his pure and honest conscience not justified the act, even in the eye of that Searcher of hearts, whose fear was his ever-present, ruling principle, never would he have drawn his sword in this great quarrel, at the prompting of any sectional pride, or ambition, or interest, or anger, or dread of obloquy.

But having judged for himself, in all sincerity, he decided, with a force of conviction as fixed as the everlasting hills, that our enemies were the aggressors, that they assailed vital, essential rights, and that resistance unto death was our right and duty.

On the correctness of that decision, reached through fervent prayer, under the teachings of the sure word of Scripture, through the light of the Holy Spirit, which he was assured God vouchsafed to him, he stood prepared to risk, not only earthly prospects and estate, but an immortal soul; and to venture, without one quiver of doubt or fear, before the irrevocable bar of God the Judge.

The great question: "What if I die in this quarrel," was deliberately settled; so deliberately, so maturely, that he was ready to venture his everlasting all upon the belief that this was the path of duty.

And so, we may assert, it is with all the best of our land. Just in proportion to the integrity of men's principles, to their magnanimity, to their incorruptible love of right and truth, to their fear of God, have been their decision and zeal in the cause of the Confederate States.

Our mothers, wives and sisters, with their disinterested and generous instincts; our most honored and venerable citizens and jurists; the most saintly and reverend pastors in the Church of Christ; have been foremost to justify our defense. If there have been any to dissent, they have been found usually among the ignorant, the mercenary, and the base. This is our answer to the slanderers, who denounced our revolution as a scheme of wicked politicians, an artifice of the ambitious and factious few.

II. The second reason which makes the man of faith brave, is stated in the context:

"Are not five sparrows sold for two farthings, and not one of them is forgotten before God? But even the very hairs of your head are all numbered: Fear not therefore; ye are of more value than many sparrows."

God's special providence is over all his creatures, and all their actions; it is over them that fear Him; for their good only. By that almighty and omniscient providence, all events are either produced; or at least permitted, limited, and overruled. There is no creature so great as to resist its power, none so minute as to evade its wisdom.

Each particular act among the most multitudinous which confound our attention by their number, or the most fortuitous, which entirely baffle our inquiry into their cause, is regulated by this intelligent purpose of God.

Even when the thousand missiles of death, invisible to mortal sight, and sent forth aimless by those who launched them, shoot in inexplicable confusion over the battle-field,

His eye gives each one an aim and a purpose according to the plan of his wisdom. Thus teacheth our Saviour.

Now, the child of God is not taught what is the special will of God as to himself; he has no revelation as to the security of his person. Nor does he presume to predict what particular dispensation God will grant to the cause in which he is embarked. But he knows that, be it what it may, it will be wise, and right, and good.

Whether the arrows of death shall smite him or pass him by, he knows no more than the unbelieving sinner; but he knows that neither event can happen him without the purpose and will of his Heavenly Father. And that will, be it whichever it may, is guided by Divine wisdom and love.

Should the event prove a revelation of God's decision, that this was the place, and this the hour, for life to end; then he accepts it with calm submission; for are not the time and place chosen for him by the All-wise, who loves him from eternity?

Him who walks in the true fear of God, God loves. — He hath adopted him as his son forever; through his faith on the righteousness of the Redeemer. The Divine anger is forever extinguished by the atonement of the Lamb of God, and the unchangeable love of God is conciliated to him by the spotless righteousness of his Substitute.

The preciousness of the unspeakable gift which God, gave for his redemption, even the life of the Only-begotten, and the earnest of the Holy Ghost, bestowed upon him at first while a guilty sinner, are the arguments to this believer, of the richness and strength of God's love to him.

He knows that a love so eternal, so free, so strong, in the breast of such a God and Saviour, can leave nothing unbestowed, which divine wisdom perceives to be for his true good. — "He that spared not his own Son, but delivered him up for us all, how shall he not with him also freely give us all things." (Rom. 8:32). And this love has enlisted for his safeguard, all the attributes of God, which are the security of His own blessedness.

Why dwelleth the Divine mind in ineffable, perpetual peace? Not because there are none to assail it; but because God is conscious in himself of infinite resources, for defense and victory; of a knowledge which no cunning can deceive; of a power which no combination can fatigue. Well, these same attributes, which support the stability of Jehovah's throne, surround the weakest child of God, with all the zeal of redeeming love. "The eternal God is his refuge; and underneath him are the everlasting arms." (Deut. 33:27.)

Therefore saith the Apostle, that the believer hath "his heart and mind garrisoned by the peace of God which passeth all understanding." (Phil. 4:7.) And therefore our Saviour saith, with a literal emphasis of which our faint hearts are slow to take in the full glory: "Peace I leave with you; my peace I give unto you." (John 14:27.)

In proportion as God's children have faith to embrace the love of God to them, are they lifted in spirit to his very throne and can look down upon the rage of battle, and the tumult of the people, with some of the holy disdain, the ineffable security, which constitutes the blessedness of God. "Their life is hid with Christ in God."

It has been said that Gen. Jackson was a fatalist, by those who knew not whereof they affirmed. He was a strong believer in the special providence of God. The doctrine of a Fate is, that all events are fixed by an immanent, physical necessity in the series of causes and effects themselves; a necessity as blind and unreasoning as the tendency of the stone towards the earth, when unsupported from beneath; a necessity as much controlling the intelligence and will of God as of creatures; a necessity which admits no modification of results through the agency of second causes, but renders them inoperative and non-essential, save as the mere, passive stepping stones in the inevitable progression.

The doctrine of a Providence teaches that the regular, natural agency of second causes is sustained, preserved, and regulated by the power and intelligence of God; and that in and through that agency, every event is directed by his most wise and holy will, according to His plan, and the laws of nature which He has ordained.

Fatalism tends to apathy, to absolute inaction: a belief in the providence of the Scriptures, to intelligent and hopeful effort. It does not overthrow, but rather establish the agency of second causes, because it teaches us that God's purpose to effectuate events only through them (save in the case of miracles,) is as steadfast, as his purpose to carry out his eternal plan. Hence it produces a combination of courageous serenity, — with cheerful diligence in the use of means.

My illustrious leader was as laborious as he was trustful; and laborious precisely because he was trustful. Every thing that self-sacrificing care, and preparation, and forecast, and toil, could do, to prepare and to earn success he did. And therefore it was, that God, without whom "the watchman waketh but in vain," usually bestowed success. So likewise, his belief in the superintendence of the Almighty was a most strong and living conviction.

In every Order, or Dispatch, announcing a victory, he was prompt to ascribe the result to the Lord of Hosts; and those simple, emphatic, devout ascriptions were with him no unmeaning formalities. In the very flush of triumph, he has been known to seize the juncture for the earnest inculcation of this truth upon the minds of his subordinates.

On the momentous morning of Friday, June 27th, 1862, as the different corps of the patriot army were moving to their respective posts, to fill their parts in the mighty combination of their chief, after Jackson had held his final interview with him, and resumed his march for his position at Cold Harbor, his command was misled, by a misconception of his guides, and seemed about to mingle with, and confuse, another part of our forces.

More than an hour of seemingly precious time was expended in rectifying this mistake; while the booming of cannon in the front told us that the struggle had begun, and made our breasts thrill with an agony of suspense, lest the irreparable hour should be lost by our delay; for we had still many miles to march.

When this anxious fear was suggested privately to Jackson, he answered, with a calm and assured countenance: "No; let us trust that the providence of our God will so overrule it, that no mischief shall result." And verily; no mischief did result. Providence brought us precisely into conjunction with the bodies with which we were to cooperate; the battle was joined at the right juncture and by the time the stars appeared, the right wing of the enemy, with which he was appointed to deal, was hurled in utter rout, across the river.

More than once, when sent to bring one of his old fighting brigades into action, I had noticed him sitting motionless upon his horse with his right hand uplifted, while the war worn column poured in stern silence close by his side. At first it did not appear whether it was mere abstraction of thought, or a posture to relieve his fatigue. But at Port Republic, I saw it again; and watching him more narrowly, was convinced by his closed eyes and moving lips, that he was wrestling in silent prayer.

I thought that I could surmise what was then passing through his fervent soul; the sovereignty of that Providence which worketh all things after the counsel of his own will, and giveth the battle not to the strong, nor the race to the swift: his own fearful responsibility, and need of that counsel and sound wisdom, which God alone can give; the crisis of his beloved country, and the balance trembling between defeat and victory; the precious lives of his veterans, which the inexorable necessities of war compelled him to jeopardize; the immortal souls passing to their account, perhaps unprepared; the widowhood and orphanage which might result from the orders he had just been compelled to issue. —

And as his beloved men swept by him to the front, into the storm of shot, doubtless his great heart, as tender as it was resolute, yearned over them in unutterable longings and intercessions, that "the Almighty would cover them with his feathers, and that his truth might be their shield and buckler."

Surely the moral grandeur of this scene was akin to that, when Moses stood upon the Mount of God, and lifted up his hands, while Israel prevailed against Amalek! And what soldier would not desire to have the shield of such prayers, under which to fight? Were they not a more powerful element of success than the artillery, or the bayonets of the Stonewall Brigade?

III. The true fear of God ensures the safety of the immortal soul. United to Christ by faith, adopted into the unchanging favor of God, and heir of an inheritance in the skies which is as secure as the throne of God, the believing soul, is lifted above the reach of bodily dangers.

But the soul is the true man, the true self, the part which alone feels or knows, desires or fears, sorrows or rejoices, and which lives forever. It is its fate which is irrevocable. If it be lost, all is lost; and finally lost; if it be secure, all other losses are secondary, yea, in comparison trivial. To the child of God, the rage of enemies, mortal weapons, and pestilence are impotent. True, he has no assurance that they may not reach his body, but they reach his body only, and,

>"If the plague come nigh,
>And sweep the wicked down to hell,
>T'will raise the saints on high."

This is our Saviour's argument, "Be not afraid of them that kill the body; and after that have no more that they can do." Pagan fable perhaps intended to overshadow this glorious truth, when it described its hero with a body made invulnerable by its bath in the divine river, and therefore insensible to fear, and indifferent to the weapons of death.

But the spiritual reality of the allegory is found only in the Christian, who has washed his soul from the stain of sin, (which alone causes its death,) in the Redeemer's blood. He is the invulnerable man.

"The arrow cannot make him flee; darts are counted as stubble; he laugheth at the shaking of a spear." He shares, indeed the natural affections and instincts which make life sweet to every man and bodily pain and death formidable. But these emotions of his sensuous being are counteracted by his faith, which gives to his soul a substantial, inward sense of heavenly life, as more real and satisfying than the carnal.

The clearer the faith of the Christian, the more complete is this victory over natural fears. To the mere unbeliever, this mortal life is his all-in-all, bodily death is utter extinction, pain is the master evil, and the grave is covered by a horror of great darkness unrelieved by one ray of hope or light. — And Christians of a weaker type, in their weaker moments cannot shake off the shuddering of nature in the presence of these, the supreme evils of the natural man.

But as faith brightens, that tremor is quieted; the more substantial the grasp of faith on eternal realities, the more does the giant death dwindle in his proportions, the less mortal does his sword appear, the narrower and more trivial seems the gap which he makes between this life and the higher; because that better life is brought nearer to the apprehension of the soul.

Does the eagle lament to see the wolf ravage its deserted nest, as it betakes itself to its destined skies, and nerves its young pinions and fires its eyes in the beams of the king of day? The believer knows also, that should his body be smitten into the grave, the resurrection day will repair all the ravages of the sword, and restore the poor tenement to his occupancy, "fashioned like unto Christ's glorious body."

He can adopt the boast of inspiration: "God is our refuge and strength; a very present help in trouble. Therefore will not we fear though the earth be removed, and though the mountains be carried into the midst of the sea." (Ps. 46:1,2.) Amidst the storm of battle, and even the wreck of defeat, his steadfast heart knows no fear.

But that the enemy of God should have courage in battle, is incomprehensible to me. It can only be explained by thoughtlessness. When the danger which assails the body reaches the soul also, when the weapon that lays the body in the dust, will plunge the soul into everlasting and intolerable torments, by what philosophy can a reasoning being brace himself to meet it?

He who has not God for his friend, has no right to be brave. But we should be far from inferring thence, that the citizen who is conscious of his enmity to God, is therefore justified in shunning the exposure to this risk, at the expense of duty and honor. — This would be but to add sin to sin, and folly to folly. If safety is not found in the path of duty, still more surely it will not be found when out of it.

He is in the greatest danger, who is disobeying God; and infinite wisdom and power can never be at a loss for means to strike their enemy, however far removed wounds and weapons of war may be. To refuse a recognized duty is the surest way to alienate the mercy of God, and to grieve that Holy Ghost, on whom we depend for faith and repentance.

The only safe or rational course therefore, for the ungodly soldier, is to make his peace with God at once; and thus advance with well-grounded confidence in the path of his duty, and of all men, the soldier has the strongest reasons to become a Christian!

Such was the foundation of the courage of Jackson. He walked with God, in conscious integrity; and he embraced with all his heart "the righteousness of God which is by the faith of Jesus Christ." His soul, I believe, dwelt habitually in the full assurance that God was his God, and his portion forever.

His manly and vigorous faith brought heaven so near, that death had slight terrors for him. — While it would be unjust to charge him with rashness in exposure to danger, yet whenever his sense of duty prompted it, he seemed to risk his person with an absolute indifference to fear. The sense of his responsibilities to his country, and the heat of his mighty spirit in the crisis of battle, might sometimes agitate him vehemently; but never was the most imminent personal peril seen to disturb his equanimity for one moment.

It is a striking trait of the impression which he has made upon his countrymen, that while no man could possibly be farther from boasting, it always became the first article of the belief of those subject to his command, that he was of course, a man of perfect courage.

But courage alone does not explain the position which he held in the hearts of his people. In this land of heroic memories, and brave men, others besides Jackson have displayed true courage. God did not endow him with several of those native gifts which are supposed to allure the idolatry of mankind towards their heroes. He affected no kingly mien nor martial pomp; but always bore himself with the modest propriety of the Christian.

Nor did he ever study or practice those arts, by which a Buonaparte or an Alexander kindled the enthusiasm of their followers. The only manifestation which ever he made of himself was in the simple and diligent performance of the duties of his office. His port on the battle field was usually rather suggestive of the zeal and industry of the faithful servant, than of the contagious exaltation of a master-spirit.

Nature had not given to him even the corporeal gift of the trumpet tones, with which other leaders are said to have roused the divine frenzy in their followers. It was only at times that his modest and feeble voice was lifted up to his hosts; and then, as he shouted his favorite call: "Press forward," the fiery energy of his will, thrilled through his rapid utterance, rather like the deadly clang of the rifle, than the sonorous peal of the clarion.

His was a master-spirit; but it was too simply grand to study dramatic sensations. It impressed its might upon the souls of his countrymen, not through deportment, but through deeds. Its discourses were toilsome marches and battles joined, its perorations were the thunder-claps of defeat hurled upon the enemies of his country. It revealed itself to us only through the purity and force of his action; and therefore the intensity of the effect he has produced.

This may help us to explain the enigma of his reputation. How is it that this man, of all others least accustomed to exercise his own fancy, or address that of others, has stimulated the imagination, not only of his countrymen, but of the civilized world, above all the sons of genius among us?

How has he, the most unromantic of great men, become the hero of a living romance, the ideal of an inflamed fancy in every mind, even before his life had passed into history! —

How did that calm eye kindle the fire of so passionate a love and admiration in the heart of his people?

He was brave, but not the only brave. He revealed transcendent military talent; but the diadem of his country now glows with a galaxy of such talent. He was successful; but we have more than one captain, whose banner never trailed before an enemy.

I will tell you the solution. It was, chiefly the singleness, purity, and elevation of his aims. Every one who observed him was as thoroughly convinced of his unselfish devotion to duty as of his courage; as certain that no thought of personal advancement, of ambition or applause, ever for one instant divided the homage of his heart with his great cause, and that "all the ends he aimed at were his country's, his God's, and truth's," as that he was brave.

The love of his countrymen is the spontaneous testimony of the common conscience, to the beauty of holiness. It is the confession of our nature that the virtue of the Sacred Scriptures, which is a virtue purer and loftier than that of philosophy, is the true greatness, grander than knowledge, talent, courage, or success.

Here, then, as I believe, is God's chief lesson in his life and death, (and the belief encourages auspicious hopes concerning God's designs towards us.) He would teach us the beauty and power of pure Christianity, as an element of our social life, of our national career.

Therefore he took an exemplar of Christian sincerity, as near perfection as the infirmities of our nature would permit, formed and trained in an honorable retirement; he set it in the furnace of trial, at an hour when great events and dangers had awakened the popular heart to most intense action; he illustrated it with that species of distinction which above all others, attracts the popular gaze, military glory; and held it up to the admiring inspection of a country grateful for the deliverances it had wrought for us.

Thus he has taught us, how good a thing his fear is. He has made all men see and acknowledge that, in this man, his

Christianity was the fountain head of the virtues and talents, which they so rapturously applauded; that it was the fear of God which made him so fearless of all else; that it was the love of God which animated his energies; that it was the singleness of his aims which caused his whole body to be so full of light, that the unerring decisions of his judgment, suggested to the unthinking, the belief in his actual inspiration; and that the lofty chivalry of his nature was but the reflex of the Spirit of Christ.

Do not even the profane admit this explanation of his character? Here then, is God's lesson, in this life, to these Confederate States: "It is righteousness that exalteth." — Hear it ye young men, ye soldiers, ye magistrates, ye law-givers; that "he that exalteth himself shall be abased; but he that humbleth himself shall be exalted."

But what would he teach us by his death, to our view so untimely? To this question human reason can only answer, that God's judgments are far above us, and past our finding out.

One lovely Sabbath, riding alone with me to a religious service in a camp, Gen. Jackson was talking of the general prospects of the war, hopefully, as he ever did. But at the close, he assumed an air of intense seriousness, and said: "I do not mean to convey the impression that I have not as much to live for as any man, and that life is not as sweet. But I do not desire to survive the independence of my country."

Can this death be the answer to that wish? — Can the solution be, that having tried us, and found us unworthy of such a deliverer, he has hid his favorite in the grave, in the brightness of his hopes, and before his blooming honors received any blight from disaster, from the calamities which our sins are about to bring upon us?

Nay; we will not believe that the legacy of Jackson's prayers was all expended by us, when he died; they will yet avail for us all the more, that they are now sealed by his blood. The deliverance of the Jews did not end with the untimely end of Judas Maccabee. The death of William of Orange was not the death of the Dutch Republic. The lamented fall of John Hampden was not the fall of the liberties of England.

And, if we may reverently associate another instance with these, the crucifixion of Jesus of Nazareth, was, contrary to the fears of his disciples, but the beginning of the sect of the Nazarenes. So, let us hope, the tree of our liberties will flourish but the more for the precious blood by which it is watered.

May it not be, that God, after enabling him to render all the service which was essential to our deliverance, and showing us in him, the brightest example of the glory of Christianity, has bid him enter into the joy of his Lord, at this juncture, in order to warn us against our incipient idolatry, and make us say: "It is better to trust in the Lord, than to put confidence in princes?"

No man would more strongly depreciate this idolatry of human instruments, than Jackson, and never so strongly, as when addressed to himself. None can declare more emphatically than would he, if he spoke to us from the skies, that while man is mortal, the cause is immortal. Away then, with unmanly discouragements, God lives, though our hero is dead.

That he should have toiled so hard for the independence of his country, and so ardently desired it; and then at last, be forbidden to hail the day of our final deliverance, or to receive the grateful honors which his fellow-citizens were preparing for him; this has saddened every heart with a pang both tender and pungent. The medicine to this pain, my brethren is to remember, that he has entered into a triumph and peace, so much more glorious than that which he bled to achieve for his country.

It would have been sweet to us, to hail him returning from his last victory to a delivered and enfranchised country; sweet to see and sympathize with the joy with which he hung up his sword, and paid the sacrifices of thanksgiving in the courts of the Lord's house; sweet to witness, with reverent respect, the domestic bliss of the home for which he so much sighed, solacing him for his long fatigues.

That happiness we have lost; but he has lost nothing. He has laid down his sword at the footstool of his Father God; he now sings his thanksgiving song in a nobler sanctuary than the earthly one he loved so much; he "bathes his weary soul in seas of heavenly rest."

We who loved him, while we bewail our own loss, should not forget the circumstances which alleviate the grief of his death. Surely, it was no ill-chosen time for God to call him to his rest, when his powers were in their undimmed prime, and his military glory at its zenith; when his greatest victory had just been won; and the last sounds of earth which reached him were the thanksgivings and blessings of a nation in raptures for his achievements; in tears for his sufferings.

I love to remember too, that his martyr-life had just been gladdened by the gratification of those affections which were in him so sweet and strong, and which yet, he sacrificed, so patiently, for his country.

Still more do we thank God that it was practicable, as it might not have been at an earlier, or a later period, for him to enjoy those ministrations of love, in his last days, which were the dearest solace of his sufferings. Into the sacredness of those last communings, and of the grief which survives them in his widowed home, we may not allow even our thoughts to intrude.

And yet, may not a mourning nation venture to utter their blessing on the mourning heart which blessed him with its love; and to pray, that the breast which so magnanimously calmed its tumult, to make a quiet pillow for the dying head of their hero, may be visited by God, with the most healing balm of heavenly consolation? Will not all the people say: Amen?

Nor will they forget the tender flower, sole off-shoot of the parent stock, born to bloom amidst the wintry storms of war, which he would fain have forbidden the summer breeze to visit too roughly. The giant tree which would have shielded it with pride so loving, lies prone before the blast. But His God will be its God; and as long as the most rugged breast of his hardy comrades is warm, it will not lack for a parent's tenderness.

And now, with one more lesson, I leave you to the teachings of the mighty dead. If there was one trait which was eminent in him above the rest, it was determination. This was the power, before whose steady and ardent heat obstacles melted away. This was the force, which caused his battalions to breast the onsets of the enemy like ramparts of stone, or else launched them irresistibly upon their shivered lines; "the unconquerable will, the purpose never to submit or yield!"

Every one who was near him felt that defeat was a result wholly excluded from his contemplation. Let us imbibe this spirit. As we visit the soil which drank his blood! or the grave where his body rests in the bosom of his beloved valley, we will adopt them as new seals to our pledge to be free or to die. Let us resolve that as the solemn mountain peaks keep their everlasting watch around the home and the tomb of Jackson, even so immovably will we guard the rights for which he died.

APPENDIX

Sketch of the Life of Lieut. Gen. T. J. Jackson.

A few facts in regard to the life and death of Gen. Jackson may not be inappropriate, as an appendix to the foregoing discourse. The following sketch appeared in the Richmond Sentinel, from the pen of an intimate friend of the illustrious dead:

"Thomas J. Jackson was born on the 21st day of January, 1824, in Clarksburg, Harrison county, Va. His great grandfather, John Jackson, and his great grandmother were of English birth.

They emigrated to this country at an early day, and settled on the South branch of the Potomac. Subsequently, they removed to what is now Lewis county, in Northwestern

Virginia. Their son, Edward, (grand-father of Thomas J.,) was surveyor in Harrison county for many years, and subsequently represented the county of Lewis in the Legislature for several years.

Jonathan Jackson, the father of Gen. Jackson, studied law under Judge John G. Jackson, in Clarksburg; and thence commenced its practice, acquiring some reputation. He became embarrassed as security for his friends, and all his property was swept away before his death, which took place in 1827.

He left four children, of whom Thomas was the youngest, was but three years old. An uncle, then residing in Lewis county, took the little orphan to live with him. Here Thomas, by going to school three months in the winter, and laboring on the farm the residue of the year, as was the custom with the farmers' sons in Western Virginia, acquired the rudiment of a plain English education. About the age of seventeen he was appointed to a Cadetship at West Point. He here graduated with high distinction.

Gen. Jackson entered the military service under Gen. Zachary Taylor, with the rank of Brevet Lieutenant. — When Gen. Scott was ordered to Mexico, Lieut. Jackson joined him at Vera Cruz. In the short but sanguinary and brilliant campaign that followed, resulting in the capture of the city of Mexico, Lieut. Jackson, by successive promotion for his gallantry and merit, became Brevet Major. — Perhaps none who started even with him attained so high.

After the Mexican war was over Major Jackson left the army because of impaired health, and accepted a Professorship at the Virginia Military Institute.

When the present troubles commenced, he repaired at once to Richmond, where he was commissioned Colonel by Governor Letcher, and ordered to take command at Harper's Ferry. He arrived there May 2d, 1861, and the next day entered upon his duties. From that day to the fatal 3rd of May, 1863, just after midnight, when he received his disabling wounds, he was never absent from the first day of duty.

Gen. Jackson was twice married. The first time to a daughter of Rev. Dr. Junkin. Her children all died. His widow was Miss Morrison, of North Carolina, who, with an infant daughter of five months, now survives him."

We need not speak of his brilliant military career, beginning with the masterly defense of Harper's Ferry, and continued through the Napoleonic campaign in the Valley, and ending with the glorious but mournful field of Chancellorsville. The impression produced by it abroad, may be inferred from some extracts from English papers. The London Post (Government organ,) of May 5th, speaking of him says:

"Whilst his religion taught him humility and dependence upon the Creator, it did not lead him to confound the true nature of the objects for which he and his followers were striving, and to suppose that because their ends were noble, that therefore, they were the champions of God. If he was occasionally a preacher in the camp, he was skillful and also a gallant general in the field; and it is not surprising that those who had so frequently followed him to victory should have considered him as specially favored by Providence, and have regarded him with feelings akin to devotion.

As a soldier he will hold probably the foremost place in the history of the great American civil war. His name is indelibly associated with the most brilliant achievements of the Confederate armies; for those achievements, by his genius and his courage, he more than any one else specially contributed. — Strategic ability is the most valuable qualification a General can possess; but it is not always that consummate military tacticians command the confidence of their followers, or insure the success of the operations they conduct.

It was, however, the good fortune of General Jackson, to lead men who, whilst their courage was exalted in an extraordinary degree by the conviction that nothing could be worse than defeat, were inspired with an unshaken faith in the genius and ability of their General. To follow Jackson they knew was to march to certain victory; and, if it was necessary that success should be purchased at the cost of many lives, that reflection did not dispirit them, for the cause in which they were fighting stripped death of all its terrors."

The *London Herald* (Derby organ,) of the 27th says:

"He was animated by the spirit which rendered the soldiers of the Commonwealth irresistible in fight — which carried Havelock through incredible dangers to the gates of Lucknow in triumph.

The Northern Republic has produced no heroes of the stamp of Jackson. One such man might be the salvation of them yet. Blatant demagogues at home, bragging imbeciles in the field, afford a spectacle so absurd, and yet so painful, that Europe knows not whether to laugh or weep at the degradation of her children. — The Northerners want a man to do a man's work.

The only great men of the war have been developed in the South. — It is very difficult to explain this. Some may call it a fatality, some a providential arrangement. That it is a fact is at present enough for us."

An impression exists in many minds that his religion was of a stern and austere type. But this is a mistake. He was stern in discharging his duty, but his religion was of a sunny and hopeful character. A little incident illustrates this.

It was habit, when camp duties permitted, to gather his staff in his tent on Sabbath evening to sing hymns. When asked what hymns should be sung his usual reply was, we will begin with "How happy are they, who their Saviour obey." and the fact that this joyous, exulting hymn was his favorite is a sufficient key to the general tone of his religious character.

It had that blended tenderness, hopefulness and firmness that constituted his natural character, and made him the remarkable man he was. Two other incidents recorded in the papers from authentic sources illustrate this fine combination of characteristics:

"Previous to the first battle of Manassas, when the troops under the command of Stonewall Jackson had made a forced march, on halting at night they fell on the ground exhausted and faint. The hour arrived for setting the watch for the night. The officer of the day went to the General's tent, and said —

"General, the men are all wearied, and there is not one but is asleep. Shall I wake them?"

"No," said the noble Jackson, "let them sleep, and I will watch the camp to-night."

And all night long he rode around that lonely camp, the one lone sentinel for that brave but weary and silent body of Virginia heroes. And when glorious morning broke, the soldiers woke refreshed and ready for action, all unconscious of the noble vigils kept over their slumber.

The night preceding that on which he received his wounds, Gen. Jackson and his staff were in the open air without tents. One of his aids prevailed on the General to accept of him a light covering. In the night, however, when all was wrapped in deep sleep, Jackson arose, and gently laying the covering over the young aid, he lay down again and slept without any protection whatever. In the morning he awoke with a cold, which brought on the attack, eventually causing his death from pneumonia."

As soon as it was ascertained that he was wounded, Gen. Lee sent him the following note, as noble a tribute to the writer as it was to the hero to whom it was addressed:

"Chancellorsville, May 4th.

GENERAL: — I have just received your note informing me that you were wounded. I cannot express my regret at the occurrence. Could I have directed events I should have chosen, for the good of the country, to have been disabled in your stead.

I congratulate you upon the victory which is due to your skill and energy.

Most truly yours,

(signed)
R. E. Lee, General.

Lieut. Gen. J. T. Jackson."

On hearing this, he was deeply affected by the generous tribute of his chief, but humbly remarked, that the glory of the victory was due to God alone.

When he saw the anxiety of those around him concerning his wounds, he said that he esteemed them great blessings, that they were all right and would work together for good to him.

It was a special kindness of God to him that his wife and child, whom he had seen so little during the war, were allowed to reach him soon after he was wounded, to soothe and cheer his closing days. When he saw the irrepressible grief of his beloved wife, he tried to cheer her saying, "I know you would gladly give your life for me, but do not be sad. I hope still to recover. Pray for me, but always remember to say, "Thy will be done."

When speaking of the probability of his death, he advised her to make her home with her "kind and good father," as he termed him; but he added no one is so "kind and good as your Heavenly Father."

When told that his old Stonewall Brigade had gone into battle with the watchword, "charge, and remember Jackson," and inspired by it had swept the enemy before them in resistless triumph, he was moved, and remarked "it was just like them, they are a noble body of men."

His thoughts ran much on the Bible, and he made many inquiries about it from theologians around him, which elicited some characteristic remarks about what he called "the headquarters" of Christianity and its first preachers. He inquired whether any of those persons healed by Jesus ever had a return of their disease, declaring that to him this seemed impossible, so great was the power exerted, "that the poor paralytic could never again tremble with the palsy," and exclaimed once, "Oh for this infinite power."

As his end drew near, he was told that he had but two hours to live. He calmly replied, "it will then be infinite gain to be translated to heaven, and be with Jesus." When his unconscious babe was brought to him for a last farewell, he gazed tenderly on her, and said, "how sweet it would be to live for this dear babe," then looking up serenely he added, "No, it is better to depart and be at peace."

His wanderings of mind were on his duty. He was again at the head of his fiery columns, the light of battle in his eye, and its thunder in his ear, and he ordered one officer to prepare for action, another to "bring the infantry to the front," and another to have provisions brought to the men. At last he faintly whispered, "all right," as if his heroic spirit heard the shout of victory, and was ready for its rest.

He had always desired to die on the Sabbath, and this wish was kindly gratified. And during the morning when his thoughts were not wandering, he made special inquiry about the arrangements for preaching, and was not satisfied until assured that the men should be supplied with religious services, he seemed to sink into a calm repose of both body and mind, from which he never fully rallied.

As his thoughts were wandering on some scene, earthly or heavenly, he was heard to murmur "let us pass over the river and rest under the trees," as if the bright unfading scenes on the other side of Jordan were dawning to his gaze; and before the shadows had grown long on that bright Sabbath noon, his noble and holy spirit had passed over the river, and was walking in brightness beneath the trees that fringe the banks of the crystal stream, and had entered upon that rest that remaineth for the people of God.

> "Servant of God, well done!
> Rest from thy loved employ,
> The battle fought, the victory won,
> Enter thy Master's joy."

The Southern Church Justified in its support of the South in the present War

A LECTURE

DELIVERED BEFORE THE

YOUNG MEN'S CHRISTIAN ASSOCIATION

OF RICHMOND

ON THE 21st MAY, 1863

BY

HON. JOHN RANDOLPH TUCKER

1863

LECTURE

A Committee of the YOUNG MEN'S CHRISTIAN ASSOCIATION of Richmond, was appointed some time since, to prepare an address to Christians throughout the world, in respect to the principles, which controlled their action in the bloody and wasteful war, in which these States are engaged: The suggestion has given occasion for the present address, in which it is proposed to present the grounds of justification of the attitude, which the Southern church holds to the present war.

Certain preliminary considerations are proper before proceeding to the special discussion proposed.

The divorce of Church and State is accepted as an axiom in this discussion. The union of Church and State, we think, in this country, at least, is fraught with great evils; and, though attractive in its outward form, to a superficial observer, tends, inevitably to injure the cause of pure religion by its corrupting contact with politics, and to do no ,good to political action, from its merely formal connection with religion. That union is fatal to both. It engenders hypocrisy in the State, and formalism in the Church.

But while all this is true, it is equally so, that Church and State deal with the same subjects of influence: the one in matters spiritual, the other in matters, social and political. It is obvious, therefore, that the action of the State, within its sphere, must, to a large extent, effect the progress and success of the Church. Social and political changes, may, therefore, produce good or evil results on the cause of religion — and may greatly advance, or retard the progress of Christianity.

The Church, therefore, can never be indifferent to political action: and where it is such as to impair or destroy its efficiency in the accomplishment of its great work, it is bound by the highest obligations of duty, to throw its influence against State policy, so disastrous to the kingdom of God.

Especially is this true, where a policy is proposed which upturns society, and threatens to array in fatal opposition, the classes composing it — those very classes, which are component elements in the organization of the Church: for the conflict once raised in society, will find its way into the peaceful fold of the Church, acid thus rend its unity, and destroy the Christian harmony, so essential to its well-being and progress.

But there is a still more important view of the interest, which the Church must ever feel in political action.

The great Apostle has enjoined upon the Church to pray"for all that are in authority, that we," (that is, the Christian Church) "may lead a quiet and peaceable life in all godliness and honesty."

The Church is deeply involved in having good government — where right will be maintained — where justice will be administered — where Liberty under law will prevail. It is false to its duty, if it fails to throw its lawful influence on the side of good, and against bad, government. It is in as grievous error, where it takes the part of despotism against liberty — as where it sustains licentiousness against rightful authority.

The Church cannot ignore the civil rights of its members, or be indifferent to the oppression to which they may be subjected by unconstitutional power. Religion cannot prosper — men cannot be brought under its benign influence, when despotism is destroying the liberty and trampling on the rights of the people for men in such circumstances will be diverted from their religious to their civil interests, and will postpone spiritual concerns, for the attainment of present temporal benefits.

God has ordained the State Power, as the shield of His Church and it is the right and the duty of the Church, entrusted with the interests of His religion, to sustain the State Power, when it is a shield against wrong — and to oppose it when it is a sword wielded for outrage and oppression.

But there is a still deeper view proper to be presented.

Civil and religious liberty are intimately related. Religious liberty is essential to the progress of Christianity. Freedom to think on religion, is vital to its existence. *Personal* responsibility requires freedom of mind to think and act under religious conviction, Interference and intrusion here is, therefore, fatal to true religion. The State that dares to mediate between the soul and its God, is a traitor to God — and the church is bound to aid in its overthrow.

"There is one God, and *One* Mediator between God and men — the man Christ Jesus:" This is *the Constitution* of the Church. The Church cannot, dare not, permit its subversion. The State, which substitutes itself for the "One Mediator" between the Church and its Maker, commits sacrilege; puts its unhallowed hand upon the Ark of God, and must be smitten down! There is no alternative.

But the history of the world has shown a wonderful gravitation between the civil and religious power. Civil power, (especially if despotic,) seeks the aid of religion to uphold its influence with its subjects. Thus, civil liberty has been achieved, where religious liberty, to the same degree, has not been obtained — but I think history furnishes no instance, where religious liberty has survived the destruction of civil liberty!

A most mournful evidence of the truth of this, is at hand — and will be hereafter adverted to — where a despotism which destroys civil liberty by a revival of the Star Chamber, stifles prayer and religious utterance by the bayonets of its soldiery!

It is thus evident, that the Church in its freedom of religious thought — in its access to its God, through the Divine Mediator — is imperiled by the destruction of civil liberty — for, if religious cannot survive civil liberty, it follows that the overthrow of the one is involved in that of the other.

When power, therefore, seeks, without lawful authority to destroy civil liberty, the Church, charged with the protection of its religious freedom, is bound to take its part with liberty against usurped power — and to struggle, under God, for civil rights, as the defensive outworks, which, if carried, must expose religious liberty to the assault of despotism.

These general views will be sufficient to show how far the Church is involved in the social and political questions which may convulse the world — and that occasions may arise, when duty may call it to the exertion of its energy, for the protection of civil institutions, menaced by usurpation.

I come now to the special consideration of the proper relation of-the Church in the South to the present war: a war of *defense — not of aggression.*

War is not to be sought for aggression upon the rights of others — but it is not to be tamely avoided, when outrage and wrong threaten the heritage of liberty and right, which a kind God has granted to a people. War in defense of such an heritage, becomes stern and religious duty. It is the defensive holding of a talent, lent to promote the Divine glory — which cannot be surrendered without breach of faith and loss of character.

In such a war, the Confederate States are engaged. We vindicate its rightfulness. We neither sought, nor provoked it. We stood upon our right in the peace of God; and met war, when pressed against us, upon our very hearthstones, by the violator of that right. We had no alternative, but to surrender our heritage to the wrong-doer, or to defend it to the death.

In the fear of God, we decided to protect our birth right, assailed by war. For two years we have poured out an oblation of blood for the deliverance of our native land: and we will struggle, even to the end, for our national independence; and never — never — survive its loss!

In all this, we feel we are right in the sight of a just God. The facts which influence, and the principles which guide our decision, have been misrepresented or misunderstood. To have a conscience void of offence towards God and men is the highest and best support of a Christian people.

It is an inferior, but a desirable blessing, that the Christian world should respect our conscience, and acknowledge the rectitude of our decision — that those, united with us, as members of the Great Head of the Church, should recognize the purity of our motives, and the justice of our action As a Christian people, we appeal to them — nor shall our appeal be in vain

The *occasion* (but *not* the *cause)* of this war, was secession. The *cause* of *secession,* the CAUSE OF THE WAR, was outrage perpetrated, and threatened, upon the constitutional rights of these States, and a violation of the charter, which bound. all the States together in the late Federal Union.

In the providence of God, this union of thirty-three commonwealths, had grown up under, and upon the terms of, the Constitution of the United States. Up to the moment of its adoption, the separate sovereignty and independence of each of the original States was expressly retained and reserved by the old Articles of Confederation.

In forming the Federal union, this State and others, expressly declared in their several acts of ratification of the Constitution, that the powers thereby granted "may be resumed by them, whensoever the same shall be perverted to their injury and oppression;" "that every power not granted thereby, remains with them and at their will;" and, by an express article of compact, it was declared, that all powers not delegated, were reserved to the States respectively, or to the people.

These Constituted the charter under which the Federal Government was established. The union was formed upon the basis of the Constitution, as a compact between sovereign States. The reserved rights of the States were as essential to be maintained and defended, as the delegated powers vested in the union. The *two* together constituted "the Powers that be," which were ordained of God.

We were as *religiously* bound to *defend* the one, as to *obey* the other. The preservation in proper equilibrium of the granted powers and the reserved rights; was the law of life to the union.

The test question of our national being always was, whether the powers exercised had been really delegated. If exercised, when not granted, it was pure usurpation upon the reserved rights of the States — a disturbance of the equilibrium; an overthrow of the system. This, we were bound to oppose and resist, where the usurpation was fatal, by all the means in our power.

The right of judgment and final decision as to such usurpation, was not in the Government — but, by reservation, remained with the States; for it is obvious, that if the right, finally to decide such an issue, resided in the Government exercising the disputed power, its delegated authority would become unlimited, and despotic, which was never intended; and would have made the reservation of all ungranted power, an empty form, and of no effect.

These abstract questions, so little understood by foreigners, became intensely practical, in our early history, and so continued, by reason of the difference in the structure of society, North and South.

By the hand of God, four millions of Africans had come to form the substratum of Southern society; the upper stratum being composed of the Caucasian race, to the number of eight millions.

These Africans constituted the labor of the South — and being adapted to rural industry, made the South chiefly a planting section. The North was chiefly commercial and manufacturing. The two sections were diverse, and even, antagonistic, *industrially*.

The presence of the African race, incapable of amalgamation with the white race, by natural law, fixed and unalterable: incapable of political or civil equality with the white race, by original inferiority, and the debasement of centuries; incapable of freedom, except to be licentious and brutal and savage, and only fit to be enslaved, if order and security were to be conserved; their deportation impracticable, and cruel to the African himself; the presence of this race, with these incapacities, raised questions of vital importance to the good order, to the moral character, and to the social security of the Southern States.

But with all these incapacities, there was one great Providential compensation. The presence of an inferior race with such a *status* fixed upon it, by necessary law, solved some political questions which have convulsed so-called free societies. It made the political institutions of the South more stable; its action less liable to the turbulence of free Democracies; and elevated the tone of political principle beyond the too ready influence of designing demagogues. It banished the "Isms" and political empiricism of the free States from our borders; and radicalism was, very slowly, introduced, and only from imitation, into the creed of the Statesmen of the South.

It did more. It secured the South from the curse of all countries, where this race, in slavery, does not constitute the laboring class. It saved us from the grinding conflict between capital and labor Elsewhere these classes are in antagonism — here, they are, happily, at one!

It is obvious, without further suggestion, that the presence of this race in the South, presented subjects of momentous interest to us — questions of industry — of social order — of political stability — of moral and religious character.

The relation of Master and Slave race, where kindness to the slave is the rule, and cruelty the exception; under which the master has been elevated, by discipline, for the high duty of guardianship to an inferior race in its state of pupilage; under which, the African has been civilized and Christianized to a greater extent, than under any other educational process to which he has ever been, or can be, subjected — this was the relation, we, of this generation, found in existence, which we could not change with safety — and proposed to control under the law of Him, whose Providence ordained it for us, and who never condemned it, but prescribed regulations for it, as he did for all other lawful relations in life!

This relation was our social necessity Its disturbance would be a social disaster — might be our social ruin. We could not surrender its control to any other than ourselves —

especially to those who could not, or would not understand it — and, *more* especially, to those who were not only ignorant of the nature of the relation, but who religiously and fanatically detested it, and politically and socially antagonized us, on account of it. A government ignorant of the relations it assumes to control, is a mighty evil — but one, as hostile as it is ignorant, is absolutely fatal.

When, therefore, the North became, in all departments of the Federal Government, the controlling power, it was natural, that the South, in its hopeless minority, should jealously watch any attempt of the dominant section, to disturb this keystone in the arch of our social structure.

Let this Sampson majority once lay hold upon these Ebon pillars of Southern society, and its ruin would be inevitable. The South saw this for fifty years, and strove honestly to prevent it. It felt, when Federal usurpation, grievous as it had been, but not yet intolerable, seized upon this question, the Union must be dissolved, or the South must perish!

But this question of slavery presented a serious aspect also, in matters of religion.

For more than half a century, the Northern mind had been deeply imbued with a hostile sentiment towards slavery. Fanaticism had seized the pulpit, the press, the hustings, the school. Professing Christian men saw slaveholding to be the most heinous sin. Preachers ceased to denounce the sin of unbelief in Christ, and preached perdition as the slaveholder's doom. Churches were disordered by the schismatic dogma, that slavery, *per se,* was sin. To hold a slave, was to hold damning heresy.

In vain did the Christian slaveholder quote the Old and New Scriptures — the language of Peter, of Paul, and of Christ — in vain, did he point to the slaveholding centurion, as the Saviour's exemplar of a faith unattained by his chosen people — in vain, did he claim that the apostolic injunction of justice from the master to his slave, and of obedience from the slave to his master, was inconsistent with the doctrine of the inherent sinfulness of the relation between them.

The answer of Abolition was simple: "If the Bible sanctions slavery, it is not from God! If Christ tolerated slavery, he is not a divine teacher!" Thus, antislavery became anti-Christ! and Abolition became Infidelity and Atheism!

The Southern Christian was denounced in the convention, the conferenee and the assembly of his church. He was virtually excommunicated — or so stigmatized, that he felt he was useless in union with those, who so abhorred him. Within the fold of the Southern Church, were "believing masters" and "believing slaves," who sat as brethren at the same communion, and worshipped the same Master in Heaven.

The teachings of the Northern Church tended to rend this Christian unity; to make the master severe from suspicions of the fidelity of his slave, and the slave discontented and rebellious, from the idea of the outrage upon his rights by his master, which Abolition so loudly proclaimed. The Southern Church was reviled for not preaching, Abolition — and thus its progress was retarded, its unity was rent, its peace was destroyed.

The Christian slaveholder found his duty to his slave enjoined in the Bible; taught him the way of eternal life.; made him a Christian man; loved him, tended him in sickness, and promoted his well being and his happiness.

The church, of which he was a member, denounced him, and pilloried him before the world as the greatest of sinners, as the enemy of the cross of Christ. His conscience was condemned, and not respected. His usefulness in the church was gone. Bound to seek peace and to pursue it, he found his only course as a Christian, was in separation — in Secession.

Several denominations, containing large numbers of masters and slaves; more Christian slaves in communion with their Christian masters, than there were of the African race, in all the world besides, many fold — divided on this question. Thousands of Southern Christians separated from Northern churches, as Abraham from Lot, and founded new churches, which have prospered, in the unity of the Spirit, in the bond of peace, and in righteousness of life.

Let Christendom, therefore, remember what it either does not know, or is prone to forget, that Abolition rent in twain the church, before it divided the States — and that Southern Christians were constrained for the sake of peace and safety, to secede from Northern Christians, years before Secession dissolved the union of the old United States.

Other churches avoided like schism by simply ignoring the question. But the sentiment of antagonism, though smothered and concealed; was as real, and not less dangerous to the peace of the Church and the progress of religion.

'We assert, therefore, that the antagonism between the North and south, was founded, in a large degree, upon. their diverse convictions on a question of conscience — upon a religious issue.

This being so, it is obvious, that the religious conviction of the church member, would largely control his action as a citizen. The Southern conscience, which had been goaded to rend a church upon the relations of the domicile; which stood upon its humble threshold, under the sanction of the Divine Master, to protest prayerfully, but bravely, for the integrity of the social tie between master and slave, against a reckless fanaticism, sowing the seeds of hate amid the scenes of a peaceful home.

That Southern conscience, when State power assailed it by law, violating civil right, and inciting to insurrection, rapine and murder, was ready to rise. in the deep sense of religions duty, to break the base bonds of a prostituted union, and to hurl back the invader of its peace, with the stern defiance of war!

The views thus presented, suffice to show, that the causes of variance between the North and South, tending to Secession, were both secular and religious.

The danger to property in slaves, and to all property, valuable because of slavery; the peril to the white race, from the insubordination of the African, under the impulse of Abolition agitation and law; the overthrow of Southern society and the destruction of Southern civilization, by the action of ignorant and fanatical enemies.

The submergence of all the hopes for progress of eight millions of civilized men, by the tide of empirical legislation upon our social and political institutions; the subjection of all the interests of the South to the absolute control of an alien and hating majority; these made up the *secular element,* which drove the Southern people to disunion, as the only hope of safety, for their property, their homes, their liberties, their civilization.

The *religious element* arose from other views.

When the white race, possessed of the refinement and Christian civilization of the best nations, looked upon the *four millions* of semi-barbarians, entrusted to their keeping by the hand of Providence, they felt a deep and growing responsibility for their improvement in character for time and for eternity The immortal interests of such a mass of savage life, pressed hard upon the conscience of Southern masters. Nor had they wholly failed to meet it.

Out of this large number of the descendants of heathen, in less than two centuries, *half a million are professing members of evangelical churches.* This fact is worth a thousand theories as to the savage nature of slavery The home of the slave is the only spot, whence, as yet, Ethiopia has stretched out its hands unto God. Missionary effort elsewhere fails to point to such a triumph of Christianity among the sons of Africa, as the Southern Church can justly claim in behalf of Christian slaveholders

Emancipation, wherever tried, has proved fruitless of Christianizing influence upon this race. In the West Indies, at the North, in the South, the proportion of Christians among the freed Africans, is far less than among the slaves. The reason is obvious. Freedom to a savage or semi-civilized race, is only freedom to be idle and depraved. Such races need guardianship.

They are in the infancy of their development — and must be kept in a state of pupilage to a better race. This is the philosophy of the relation of master and slave, based on experience and facts. All other philosophy based on theory, in ignorance of the facts, is vain and frivolous, and in practice, must be vicious.

Northern churches insisted upon emancipation, as a present imperative duty of the slaveholder. They disturbed the relation, and thus prevented the best practicable discipline and education of the slave. They interfered with the conscience of the master in meeting the obligations of duty imposed upon him.

They agitated to make the races hate, instead of love and trust each other They sowed seeds of discord in the Church and made religious instruction difficult and even dangerous. If the master taught his slave to read the Bible, the Abolition emissary used this attainment, as a means of instilling hatred and revenge against his master, and placed an appeal in his hands, for arson, murder and rebellion.

The Church was bound, as a Christian duty, to repel this interference — to protect its fold from the incursions of the wolf — and to preserve the threatened unity of its communion. Religion in the South, for the white and black, must inevitably perish, if the work of Abolition was left unobstructed. The Church, as the guardian of religion, was, therefore, constrained to oppose Abolitions by every lawful means.

Such were the secular and religious elements in the South, which led to a watchfulness of the movements of Abolition in the Northern States. In its success, the South could see no result, but ruin to its industry, to its social and political relations — and to the sacred cause of religion. Home would be blotted from the South; and our land would become one vast battlefield, where the torch of the incendiary would blaze at every hearthstone, and bloodshed and crime, would reign in the sunny domain, where pleasant associations, and the dignity of virtue, and every Christian grace had made their abode for a century.

If men and women were not prepared, at the risk of property and life, to defend home, civilization and religion, in the fear of God, and without the fear of man, then the South would have proved unworthy of a place among nations, and derelict to the mighty trust, which God had confided to their keeping.

Look now at history! Forty years ago, the North violated the Constitution, as the Supreme Court of the United States, have recently decided, by excluding the South, with its social institutions, from lands purchased with the common treasure of the country, This was a step to increase the power of the North for political action. It disturbed the balance of power. The South complained, but acquiesced for Peace and the Union.

Fifteen years later, the North flooded Congress with Petitions for interference with slavery in the South. It was then almost universally conceded, that the Constitution did not allow such interference. The South said — "If you have no power to act, why disturb our peace by these constant clamors for action? Why insult us in our common counsels by denouncing the domestic relations of our homes? If we are entitled to have slavery, surely we are entitled to hold it in peace."

These appeals for action, at last generated action. Negotiation gave us Oregon. By express law, the South was excluded from it forever. The country became engaged in war with Mexico. Peace brought accessions of new territory. The arms of North and South had united to win a rich domain — and the money of both contributed to acquire it by conquest and purchase.

The North with almost entire unanimity demanded the whole domain for their own colonization and settlement, and the entire exclusion of the South. By direct and indirect means, it succeeded — and the slaveholder could not take his slave to any part of that vast domain, for acquiring which, he had poured out his blood and treasure.

This was a deep wrong! It was a gross insult! it branded such infamy upon the South, as proclaimed it unfit for association with the people of the North. The South was made use of to acquire, what it was thus declared unworthy to enjoy. This action changed the political balance in every department of the Government. The united North, from that moment, could pass any law, and could elect a President against the will of a united South. Thenceforth the South was at the mercy of the North, and held its dearest rights, at the will of the dominant section.

The South still clung to the hope that the North would. do it justice. It tried by the strategy of party combinations, to divide the dominant section, and thus defeat action fatal to its rights and liberties.

But the North, from the moment the balance of power was disturbed, began to consolidate parties in that section, and abolitionize the whole. That once accomplished, the union of the *will* and the *power* to do, made its warfare upon Southern interests effectual, and the consummation of its ultimate purpose, certain. Time would work out the result — and the ruin of the South would be only a question of time.

The North knew this. The South saw it. Still the South struggled to awaken or keep alive in some of the Northern people, a sense of justice to the rights which the Constitution designed to protect. The States labored for this end and the Church prayed for it.

But the North was conscious of its new-born power, and was proud of the mastery it had at last achieved. Its churches pointed to the sin upon the Southern soul — and its demagogues to the stain of slavery on the flag of the Union. Agitation deep and strong took hold of the masses — books and sermons were written — speeches and lectures uttered, all with one aim — to show that the sin of slavery must be extirpated by the Church, and that the black blot on the American name, imprinted by this Southern crime, must be washed from the flag of a free people forever

In 1856, this Abolition party, (numbering 60,000 in 1844,) had grown to 1,300,000. It only sustained defeat by the accidents of a canvass. But it felt its power, and the South read its doom.

This success was a truce, not a victory. Both sections felt it, and subsequent events proved it. Abolition approached its flood tide, and Northern friends of the South began to give way.

On the memorable night of October 17th, 1859, the oldest commonwealth in the Union, first in settlement, first in organization — Virginia, which had granted a domain to the Union, now forming five great States of the North-west; Virginia, which, in council had done more for the formation and progress of the Union, than any other State; Virginia, which had given her Washington to the military and civil administration of the new-born Republic; this "Ancient Dominion," was the scene and the victim of an Abolition raid, designed to raise her slaves to insurrection, and to devote her homes to flame and desolation and outrage! The project failed; the invasion was suppressed; the leaders were executed!

We now sadly smile to think, how far less criminal was John Brown, than those Northern professing friends, who, three years ago, hypocritically denounced him, and now, equal him in brutality of purpose and surpass him in its successful execution. *His raid* was, but a faint type of *their cruel war.*

Throughout the North, bells tolled, eulogies were pronounced, the drapery of mourning was paraded, in honor of these martyrs in the sacred cause of Abolition. Instead of the dreadful event producing a reaction against the sentiment, which had originated it, it strengthened and advanced.

The friends of Abolition organized anew for the Presidential election. All available opposition to it was overwhelmed; and the tornado of Anti-slavery swept resistlessly over the North, and bore to the Executive chair its idol, (and such an idol!) and to the halts of Congress a delegation, intent upon adverse action to the institutions of the South.

The North was united upon its idolatrous worship of Anti-slavery; and the South was as united against it. The fatal hour had come, when in solid phalanx, the North took hold upon all the power of the Government, against the impotent voice of a protesting South. Both sections were united — but in stern opposition, the one to the other. They became in fact, *two nations* in sentiment, linked together by a feeble political bond.

The Union had ceased in truth; it existed only in form. As well attempt to hold France and England under the same Government, as to hope the North and the South could remain longer in Union, when the one purposed a destructive policy, which the other was yet more strongly bound to resist with all its energy.

The President elect had declared there could be no peace for the South, until the North "could rest in the belief, that it" (slavery) *"is in the course of ultimate extinction."* He had gravely written, that "those who deny freedom to others, deserve it not for themselves, and under a just God, cannot long retain it." He has realized the truth of this sentiment for the North! It has denied freedom to the South, and it has lost it; it has struck a blow at the liberty of the South, and has fatally pierced its own!

Mr. Seward was made the Premier of the new administration; a man, possessed of more power and influence with his party, than any other. He had, in a public speech, a few years ago, declared its fixed policy in these terms:

"Free labor has at last apprehended its rights and its destiny, and is organizing itself to assume the government of the Republic. It will henceforth meet you boldly and resolutely here, it will meet you everywhere, in the Territories and out of them, wherever you may go to extend slavery. It has driven you back in California and in Kansas; it will *invade* you soon in Delaware, Maryland, *Virginia,* Missouri and Texas." (Was not the crack of the rifle of John Brown, the Mere echo of the sentiment of the Senator?) "It will meet you in Arizona, in Central America, and even in Cuba."

"You may indeed get a start under or near the tropics, and *seem safe* for a time, but it will be only a *short time.* Even there you will found States only for free labor to maintain and occupy. The interest of the whole race demands *the ultimate emancipation of all men."* Now mark the menace:

"Whether that consummation shall be allowed to take effect, with needful and wise precautions against sudden change and disaster, or be *hurried on by violence, is all that remains for you to decide!"* "It is for yourselves-, and not for us, to decide how long and through what further modifications and disasters the contest shall be protracted before *freedom shall enjoy her already assured triumph!"*

The policy of the Republican party had been boldly avowed. The exclusion of slavery from the common Territory, and the refusal to admit any more slave States; Abolition in the District of Columbia, and in all forts and arsenals; the outlawry of slavery, by treating it as out of the protection of the Government; the denial of the surrender of fugitive slaves, or so to trammel it, as to involve the liberty, and life of the master; the proclamation of the equality of the two races in the South; agitation for Abolition in Congress, in the States, in the Church.

And finally, the throwing of the moral influence of the whole Union against the social institutions of one half of it; the surrounding of slavery by a cordon of free States, thus shutting it up within its present limits, with the avowed purpose, so to endanger our peace, limit our prosperity, and press the growing population of the two races together, as to work out the "ultimate extinction" of slavery, and the revolution of Southern society!

All this was purposed to be done under a Constitution, which recognized and protected slavery — and treated, as .equals, free and slave States — and by a Government formed and bound to protect, defend and advance each and all the States, in all their interests and institutions.

The South was told it had but one thing to decide: Shall the result be rapid and violent — or slow, torturing, and debasing, though not less certain?

The States of the South have humbly appealed to God, and may boldly appeal to Christendom, to justify them in refusing the alternative presented. To accept either horn of the dilemma, was to accept degradation and ruin. What would remain of dignity or virtue in civilization — of liberty and right in Government — of order and progress in society — should a people consent to so base a surrender of its ALL, to the violence of the marauder — or to the slow poison of a torturing and wasting assassination?

The South could never, thenceforth, have been free, prosperous or happy — and without these, its civilization — its claim to a place, as a people in Christendom, must perish forever!

The Church of the South can make its appeal to its brothers in Christ, throughout the world — for its justification in sustaining these States in the defense of these great temporal interests. If the Church has ever, any where, prayed and labored for its country in great war struggles, let such Church furnish a parallel to the interests staked upon the cause of the South.

If the welfare of the Church is bound. up in that of the State — if her safety under the shield of civil government, depends on its integrity and the defense of its law and its Constitution — if there can be no well ordered and prosperous church, where the State is torn by social disorder, or oppressed by external tyranny — then was the Southern Church bound to pray for, and defend these States, from the threatened violence of Northern tyranny, and the menaced convulsion of Southern society.

Where would be the Church interests of Great Britain, should a mad fanaticism proclaim to its laboring classes the overthrow of its monarchy, its aristocracy — its ecclesiastical polity? Where was France and its Church, when social revolution, in its red torrent, rushed through the streets of Paris, with the cry of no government — and no God? Would the Church, in these cases, be justified in throwing its power into the scale of order and law, and ancient Church polity?

And should the Church of God, in these Southern States, remain passively neutral, when a crusade is proclaimed by Abolition, which will raise four millions of slaves, ignorant and debased, into brutal insurrection against their masters — And drench Southern fields in blood, or stain Southern homes with murder, rapine and rape?

Can the followers of Christ remain at ease in their Zion, when the wildest tornado of revolution menaces society — and the Communion of Saints — of masters and servants — was rent by the wedge of cruel hatred and savage War? Could the Church, the guardian of religion, see its foundations upturned, its loving people roused to fury by the teachings of an insane fanaticism, and stand all the day idle, in the midst of such a crisis? Could it deny its mission of peace?

We appeal to Christians everywhere! Are we not justified in standing by our country in the breach, which Abolition threatened to make in our society and in the Church of God?

We believe no such issue was *ever* presented in *menace* to a *Christian nation,* which was not met by *war.*

But let it be remembered, *we* did *not* resent the menace by war. We sought to avoid war. We prayed, and asked for peace!

The Cotton States decided it was no longer safe to remain in the Union. Eight of them withdrew, by ordinances of Secession. Upon written terms, and for specified purposes, they had *acceded* to that union. They *seceded from* it, when the terms were violated, and the purposes were defeated. They did no act of violence. They neither threatened, nor desired war. They withdrew in peace, and to secure Peace!

The whole question, as presented to them, was, shall we act for our safety upon the menace of violence? or, shall we await the development of the hostile policy of our foes?

As most people have done in human history, who have succeeded in achieving liberty and independence, they acted promptly, and did not await the fall of the blow before taking steps for safety.

In February, 1861, these States adopted a new Constitution, differing but little from the old, and formed a new Confederation.

But they declared no war against the United States. They made provision, it is true, for Public *Defense,* but in their official documents, deprecated the resort to war. They made the navigation of the Mississippi, free to the Northern States.

But they did more — they tendered the Olive branch of Peace.

In their very Constitution, they provided that "the Government hereby instituted, shall take immediate steps for the settlement of all matters between the States forming it and their other late confederates of the United States, in relation to the public property and public debt, at the time of their withdrawal from them — these States hereby declaring it to be their wish and earnest desire, to adjust every thing pertaining to the common property, common liability and common obligations of that union, upon the principles of right, justice, equity and good faith."

Commissioners were appointed, and were sent to Washington, to propose and to negotiate a peaceful adjustment. After repeated delays, upon pretexts feigned for a purpose, all overtures for peaceful separation, were rejected, and the war policy was proclaimed.

Meantime, the United States continued to hold some of the forts in the Seceded States. These places ceded by the States for the security of their liberties, were bristling with guns, loaded and pointed at their cities and homes — as the securities of Despotism, for its continued oppression!

The President of the United States declared, officially, his purpose to hold, permanently, these forts, and to recapture, by force, those taken by the Confederate States, within their borders. Such a policy could not be permitted — unless these States were prepared to surrender their position of independence. Each fort was a key to our commerce — and to our liberty.

In the hands of a power, which denied our independence, these keys would forever debar us from attaining or enjoying it? The holding of a fort within our borders, was war upon us — and could not be acquiesced in. The Confederate Government so declared to the United States. Submission to this policy would have made secession an empty formality.

But the United States, in possession of Fort Sumter, Knight to reinforce and supply it. This effort, and the rejection of the overtures of peace, made. its bombardment a necessity. It surrendered on the 13th of April, 1861.

Two days after its surrender, the President issued his proclamation of war — his call for 75,000 troops — his denouncement of insurgency against 8 large States — and his purpose to suppress secession, by force of arms. This had been a covert policy until Sumter fell: That event compelled its disclosure.

These States sought only to be free and independent. They preferred no claim against the United States. They said, we cannot live under your Government in safety — seek your own welfare in peace — let us seek ours without war — we will settle all questions amicably — since we cannot live together without conflict and contention, let us separate in peace: — "Let there be no strife, I pray thee, between me and thee; for we be brethren. Is not the whole land before thee — separate thyself; I pray thee, from me — if thou wilt take the left hand, then I will go to the right, or, if thou depart to the right hand, then I will go to the left."

Could anything be more reasonable and just? Could the South propose terms more Christian in their character?

But Pharaoh was resolved not to let the people go! Eight sovereign States, were denounced as insurgents, and were told. to return to their homes — or war was declared. The riot act was read to eight. commonwealths; and a bill of indictment was found against 12,000,000 of people!

The will of the free people of 8 free States was to be constrained by a free (?) Government, by force of arms! In the name of liberty — liberty to choose their own Government was denied, at the point of the bayonet!

Virginia and the Southern States remaining in the Union, were summoned to arms, by President Lincoln, to suppress the Southern Rebellion. They were, thus, compelled to make war. They could not choose peace and avoid war. They could only choose on which side to array themselves in the war, forced upon them. Could they hesitate?

They chose, upon the issue of war, to take the side of the oppressed, against the arms of the oppressor.

We appeal to Christendom — to Christians everywhere — could the South submit to the rule of the North, whose menace of wrong was thus backed by violence? Could the Christian Church in the South fail to pray for the defense of rights threatened by a usurping Government, or refuse to unite in resistance to that usurpation sustained by the force of arms?

The war has been waged without mercy — barbarously, cruelly and wickedly. If we were regarded by our enemy, as an independent nation, the conduct of the war is contrary to all the rules of civilized warfare, and a violation of the law of nations.

No war in modern times, among Christian nations, has been marked by such ferocity — such disregard of private rights of persons and property — such assaults upon the liberty and conscience of private citizens — such atrocities towards non-combatants, men, women and children — and such wicked violations of all sanctions of our Holy religion.

In the estimate of international law, our enemy must stand for condemnation in the Pillory of Nations!

We may waive all questions of minor consequence — and the mention of all acts of subordinate officers, which have made a grievous cry ascend to heaven for justice. We may fail to recount the brutal orders of a Pope, a Hunter, and a Butler Humanity through all thine, will remember such men, only to detest and execrate them. Theirs will be an immortality in infamy!

But we choose to rest our charges upon the official action of the Government.

The Federal Government refuses to recognize our independence, and still claims these States as members of the Federal Union. And yet, at every step of this contest, that Government, in its own view, of the relations of the parties to it, tramples under foot the Constitution, its officers are sworn to support, and which it falsely professes a purpose to restore.

It has made war upon these sovereign States, whose delegated authority it claims to exercise — and without which it would never have existed. It has made war upon them, without justice or mercy, as if these people were aliens and savages.

It has blockaded our ports, which the Constitution guaranteed should be open and free. It has declared the universal confiscation of all property held by those it terms, Rebels, in the teeth of the Constitution, and without trial or conviction of the owners for any crime. It has thus, by a general law of Attainder, condemned a whole people, when the Constitution declares, *no Bill of Attainder shall be passed.*

It has sanctioned the act of its President in his unconstitutional annulment of the *habeas corpus.* It has established a military Star Chamber, for the trial of its citizens, without authority of law, against the express mandate of the Constitution, without indictment, without a trial by jury, and for crimes not defined by law, but created by military order!

It has muzzled the press, abridged the freedom of speech, and has prohibited the free exercise of religion, even in the Northern States.

It has emancipated millions of slaves by a dash of the pen of its President, thus by imperial edict devoting to destruction $3,000,000,000 worth of property, without compensation and for no public use!

It has stirred up these slaves to insurrection and war upon their masters, and enlisted them in its armies. It has given freedom to the slave, and put chains upon his master, without warrant of law, and beyond the hope of relief.

It has reduced sovereign States to mere provinces, and superseded their Governments by its own military satraps. It has declared its ferocious policy to subjugate or exterminate, to ruin or destroy. It has invaded, by force, the homes of unarmed citizens and burned or plundered them.

It has driven helpless women and children from their blazing homes, without shelter to shield them, or food to support them, It has destroyed the implements of husbandry, thus seeming to purpose, what is openly avowed by its agents, the starvation of our people.

It has desecrated our houses of Worship; has stifled the voice of prayer by violence and his dragged the ministers of religion from the sacred Church for the utterance of supplication to God for their bleeding country It has committed the worst crime against the human soul, by requiring men to take its oath of allegiance, as a condition for the privilege of purchasing needful supplies for their families, thus compelling to perjury, or condemning to starvation.

It has so conducted this war against us, as (if we were still Members of the Federal Union,) would violate every principle of the Constitution under which it was created. It has defeated every object for which it was formed. It has done gross injustice, though formed "to establish justice." It has stirred up servile insurrection, though formed "to insure domestic tranquility,"

It has made fierce war upon us, though formed "to provide for our defense." It has spread ruin and desolation in its march, though formed "to promote our welfare." It has destroyed liberty of thought, of speech, of action; liberty of the press — liberty of religion — though formed "to secure the blessings of liberty to us and our posterity!"

It has destroyed our lives — confiscated our property — invaded our homes — engendered a war of races in our midst. It has, when defeated by our armed men in the field, meanly turned its weapons against non-combatants — our women and our little ones. It has traitorously intervened between the conscience and God, and made religion a mockery and last, and perhaps worst, it has dared to tempt our people to perjury, by the alternative of starvation to their wives and children!

These wrongs against us — these crimes against God and the human race, are enough to justify these States and the

Church, in combined resistance to such an enemy — our resistance now, is a resistance against the destruction of our All.

But let it be remarked, that these acts are, but the execution of the previous measure. Though done subsequent to the war, they demonstrate the existence of a purpose and intent on the part of our enemy, to avoid which, some of these States sagaciously seceded prior to its commencement.

None can doubt, that the atrocious vengeance of the North, is but the rapid manifestation of covert purposes as certain of consummation without secession, but which that event ripened into the overt act of wrong and outrage. The war has, in the language of Mr. Seward, already quoted, hurried on the consummation of their policy by violence — which by slower, but equally sure means would have followed, had the South continued as submissive vassals to their unbridled and absolute power!

We insist, then, that the menacing attitude of the North, was not empty bravado — but was the manifestation of a real purpose to destroy the South — and the vengeance, which secession has roused, has only demonstrated that fact the more clearly, by more rapidly maturing the covert and deadly intention. Hatred of the South has been felt for years — and only waited a fit occasion, to ripen into the deadly fruits of a war of desolation, plunder and ruin.

These facts demonstrate further, that civil liberty was imperiled by the continuance of the Union. We have escaped great danger. The people, who have, in two years, so carved out every spark of constitutional freedom for themselves, were never safe guardians of *our* liberties, but sooner or later, must have destroyed them. With the loss of civil liberty, religious liberty must have perished: and hence, the Church was deeply involved in the issue, as has been already shown.

The facts which we have thus presented, in review, show that our people have only sought to preserve their liberty, their type of civilization, and their religion; that in doing so, the change of our Government was necessary: that we seceded to effect this change — that we did so with the tender of the Olive branch of peace, and the proposal of negotiation to settle all differences; that we were met with the declaration of a war of subjugation —

A war for the ruin of our property, our society and political institutions; that it has been waged fiercely and wickedly — and that, as a Christian people, we stand in the thresholds of our homes, to repel violence, to defend our God-granted rights — -to save our free institutions — our civilization and our religion.

One further view may be presented.

We feel, that where two types of civilized life, come into irreconcilable and "irrepressible conflict," under the same form and system of Government, it is an indication of Providence, that separation between them, is, according to the purpose of God.

Two such types, require two nationalities for their appropriate development. The difference between the North and the South, representatives of two distinct civilizations, grew from small beginnings, until the conflict was angry and fatal to the interests of both in continued Union.

Fortunately, the Confederate form of our Government made secession an easy and proper remedy The finger of God pointed it out — and all subsequent events have only demonstrated. the total incompatibility of the Union of the two sections.

It is in this way, that the Divine hand has divided continents, and established nations. The consolidation of a continent, under one Governmental system, has continued, only so long, as some providence did not open the way for separation into distinct nationalities. When that has been accomplished, the world has perceived, how such an event is fraught with the blessings of a larger progress — a better assured liberty — and a more varied and comprehensive civilization.

Europe was consolidated under Roman dominion. It was rent into separate nations by the seeming overthrow of the best hopes of man. Centralization has since been often attempted; but the Hand which scattered the world at Babel, has as often frustrated the attempt — and Europe, in its decentralization, finds today, a more varied, broad and comprehensive development of all the elements which constitute highly civilized life, than were it but one great nation, under a Caesar, a Charlemagne, or a Napoleon!

Is it not the finger of God, which has dispersed the Babel builders of *this* wide-reaching Union, and has ordained a better destiny in separation, for the two distinctive types of American civilization?

And why should it have been followed by violence? The South sought it in peace. The North opposes it by war!

Do not the events antecedent to the war, justify secession? Do not succeeding events confirm the wisdom and necessity of that action? Does not the history we have traced, show that we should never look back to that Union, but in gratitude to God, that we were rescued from the evils, that must have followed its continuance, and that now, rather than return to that Egypt of our bondage, we should die in the wilderness of revolution?

And is not the Christian Church justified in its attitude of prayer for the success of Our cause, and in its heroic and patriotic maintenance of our civil and religious liberties?

Christianity has furnished during this war the noblest types of heroic patriotism, which history records. The seal of their blood attests their devotion to the rights and the liberty of their country.

Death has just closed the career of a man, whose name will live, while military genius excites admiration, or Christian virtue has a votary.

Amid the clouds which hung about the dawn of the war, the sun of Jackson arose from obscurity It has gone down at noon, amidst the splendors of achievements, which have had but few parallels in the past.

The beginning of our struggle, found him a modest and unobtrusive professor of Natural Philosophy, in the Virginia

Military Institute; a simple hearted, sincere and devout Christian, the teacher of a Bible class, the superintendent of a Sunday school, for negro slaves. His was a nature strong, resolute and firm, because guided only by the Divine will: a mind in perfect peace, because stayed on God.

Faith in Him was the motive power of every action — a sense of His omnipresence the air he breathed — submission to His providence, the permanent condition of his soul. In politics he had no aspirations. He clung to the late Union, with the hope of justice to his country, until the proclamation of April 15, 1861.

When that event occurred, the sword he had laid aside from aversion to strife, and love of peace, he resumed, from the conscientious conviction, that civil and religious liberty were staked upon the issue of the war firm and decided, but never violent or vengeful, he fought as a Christian should, for right and not for blood.

Of undaunted courage, with the real intuition of military genius, he, by fervent prayer, committed our cause into the hands of God before, and *during* battle, and when it closed in victory, he ascribed all the glory and honor to the Lord of Hosts! This was no affectation. It was sincere and true reverence of soul.

He had no ambition for military glory He wished the war to end: He desired to sheath his dripping sword in the scabbard of peace. He pined for the haunts of his mountain home — for the pleasant affections of family and friends — for the closet of sweet prayer — for the quiet sanctuary of God!

Brought from obscurity by a sense of duty, he struck every blow for his country, as if it were impelled by God's directing hand; and fell a martyr to her liberty, in the arms of a victory, whose glory is immortal.

In the exodus of our people, from the oppression of the old Union, this extraordinary man, meek in submission to his God; holy in Christian virtue; calmly brave, and devoutly prayerful, in the dreadful shock of battle; a Captain of undoubted genius; a victor upon an hundred fields; this Moses of our host, from Pisgah's top, looking to and hoping for the independence of his nation, but doomed, without reaching and enjoying it, to die in "The Wilderness;" resigned his mighty soul to heaven; met its solemn decree, with the trustful words, "It is all right;" and left the glorious heritage of his name to the Christian Church and to his weeping country!

Christianity may well cherish the memory of this holy hero, as the noblest example of pious patriotism; and appeals to his name, as an imperishable proof, that the devout conscience of the South, in the tear and love of God, is constrained to yield up life, a bleeding sacrifice upon the altar of its country independence! For, can any man believe the heroism of Jackson was inspired by any other motive, than the liberty of his country, the honor of God, and the glory of his kingdom?

In concluding this address, it may be proper to suggest to our Christian brethren throughout the world, the aid they can render us.

We ask no material aid. We need their prayers — their Christian sympathy We have presented our justification before God and men. We have received reproach and defamation, from ignorance and malignity Our conscience is void of offence in this war. We stand in our lot, to defend our right.

We have been reviled abroad for slavery. If it were a curse, *we* are the sufferers, though we did not bring it on ourselves. If it were an evil, we might, claim pity, and surely should receive no blame. We deny it is either an evil or a curse, as those terms are intended, when used respecting slaves. But whether so or not, we found it here, and must deal with it, as we found it.

One thing we know. We understand our own business, greatly better than those who are 3,000 miles away We dictate to no Christian people, nor provoke their ears with faults we think we see in either their social or political systems.

Let each be less ready to pluck the mote from the eye of the other and more intent upon the beam in his own. Let each study to fulfill its mission, according to the dictates of an enlightened Christian conscience.

We are striving to do our duty. We are a superior race, with an inferior race to deal with. We are its guardians, and it is our pupil, and all this under God's good providence. As a Christian people, we have a work of evangelization to do. We have Africa at our doors. The light of the gospel shines brightly in the cabin of the slave — but is extinguished in the hovel of the Hottentot.

We repeat, God put the negro here, and placed us here in authority over him — to regulate him — to make him useful, instead of being unthrifty — industrious and not idle — Christian and not savage. This work we mean to do, despite the efforts of our foes in arms, and the revilings of ignorant fanaticism throughout the world.

All we ask is, that Christian charity may judge us fairly, and give us credit for doing our duty, according to Christian conscience, in protecting our social institutions, as a God-given heritage, against the malignant assaults of our enemies. Beneath the frown of the world's prejudice; beneath the cloud of this cruel war, we feel the smile of God's face, and the pleasant shadow of His Almighty wings!

In His arm, we trust — in His might, we have triumphed; His pillar of fire and of cloud is our guide and we bless Him, that we can still cherish the confiding hope that in His own time and way, He will, through this sea, red with the blood of our bravest and our best, mark a pathway for His people to the Canaan of Peace, liberty and independence!

Christian brothers throughout Christendom! pray for us! for we trust we have a good conscience, in all things willing to live honestly. Pray for us that we being delivered from our enemies, and the hands of all that hate us, may serve our God without fear, in holiness and righteousness before Him, all the days of our life.

Finally: Let us pray for each other! that the God of Peace, that brought again from the dead our Lord Jesus, that great Shepherd of the sheep, through the blood of the everlasting covenant may make His Catholic Church perfect in every good work to do His will, working in it, that, which is well pleasing in His sight, through Jesus Christ: To whom be glory, for ever, and ever! Amen.

The Blessed Dead Waiting For Us

A SERMON
PREACHED IN

ST. JAMES' CHURCH
MARIETTA, GEORGIA

ON THE
FESTIVAL OF ALL SAINTS

NOVEMBER 1ST, 1863

BY

REV. SAMUEL BENEDICT

RECTOR OF THE PARISH.

1863

"If I Go And Prepare A Place For You, I Will Come Again And Receive You Unto Myself."

"This Same Jesus Which Is Taken Up From You Into Heaven, Shall So Come In Like Manner As You Have Seen Him Go Into Heaven."

"From Whence Also We Look For The Saviour The Lord Jesus Christ."

"Looking For That Blessed Hope."

"Looking For And Hasting Unto The Coming Of The Day Of God."

"When He Shall Appear We Shall Be Made Like Him."

"Even So, Come Lord Jesus."

A SERMON

Heb. 11:40 "that they without us shall not be made perfect."

Today is All-Saints' day. We today commemorate all those who "having finished their course in faith, do now rest from their labors." That long line of faithful ones, of whom St. Paul, in the chapter of which the text is the conclusion, gives only a few note-worthy Scripture names, has been year by year, rapidly and steadily augmenting.

It now includes many familiar to our minds and dear to our hearts. Towards that great "cloud of witnesses" all living saints are steadily advancing and rapidly passing. A few years and we, too, shall have been numbered with the dead. God grant to all of us, that then we way be reckoned among those, of whom a future generation may take up the strain of Apostolic rapture, "These all, having obtained a good report through faith, *received not the promise*, God having provided some better thing for us, that they, without us, should not be made perfect."

Yes, we can hope for no better condition after death, and, before the resurrection, than all the saints of all the former ages have enjoyed. They, in their triumphant, their blessed state, still wait for us. How near this thought brings all the departed good to us! not gone on to their eternal, their final reward, and, for the present separated from us in hope and sympathy; but, still with us in a state of expectancy, with us, waiting for a still brighter day, for a still more glorious fruition.

Abraham and Moses, and Joseph and David, and all the saints of the world's earlier days have not yet received the promise! Why? "God having provided some better thing for us" *also*, (for that is what the verse plainly means: not that God has provided some better thing for us, than he did for them, but that God for us, *as for them*, has provided some better thing, than in this world is offered to us, and, therefore, they do not receive it in advance of us;) "God having provided some better thing for us" *also*, "that they without us should not be made perfect."[1]

In these words, is, we say, contained the doctrine of the intermediate state of the departed saints; a doctrine which comes naturally to our thoughts, when we dwell upon the memory of those who, once with us in the communion of the Church on earth, are still with us in the communion of Christ's body, although taken from our presence and our sight. One with us still!

How? As the angels are? No, not so. In a closer, in a still nearer sense. Still related to us, by the ties of a mortal nature; still destined with us to the glad bursting of the resurrection morn; still to pass with us the ordeal of the judgment; still with us to hear the approval "well done" from the lips of our Judge; and still, with us, to be admitted for the first time, "to the kingdom prepared" for us and for them "from the foundation of the world."

There is, we maintain, in this doctrine, a peculiarly sweet and animating reflection: the dead in Christ, our own loved ones gone before, still waiting for us, still delaying their entrance into their highest glory, till we with them can enter there.

We consider this doctrine as it is here so plainly stated, in a two-fold aspect;

1. In regard to the condition of the body.

2. In regard to the condition of the soul.

I. As to the body. Outside every city and town and hamlet where human beings live, there grows up rapidly and steadily, the more thickly populated city of the dead. In Christian lands, the dear lifeless forms are there disposed with care, in recognition of the fact, that, in this condition, a great and mighty transformation awaits them.

Soon, very soon, the population in these silent streets, and these lonely tenements, far exceeds that of the busy town, with its bustling crowds, and its homes of gaiety and happiness. Every year the stream flows on from the busy to the silent city; from the homes of the living and the loving, to the cold, dark, unresponsive chambers of the tomb.

Christian faith may teach us, that the state of the soul is vastly more important than the disposal made of the material form, and that he who has Christian faith will think only of the soul of his departed friend; that, in his view, the body will be only the deserted cell, the cast-off fetter, the forgotten aurelia of the released, the exultant spirit. So, in one sense, it does.

But still, under Christian teachings, the resting-places of the bodies of departed friends, are places of special interest to the bereaved. There the heart naturally feels that the loved one *is* lying. Despite the voice divine that tells them "he is not here," the heart still clings to the form, lifeless and moldering, though it be, beneath the stone. There *is* the father, the mother, the husband, the wife, the child, the friend, that once I loved. "Here he lies" is the true, the appropriate epithet on Christian tombs.

And so he does. It is no mere concession to the dullness of the mental vision that we turn to the graves of our dead ones, with the yearning of loving hearts, and so tenderly guard their resting place. It is no mere yielding to the weakness of the flesh, that we enclose the precious dust and so carefully mark the spot where it is deposited. Here he does lie. Not only the earthly form now turning back to dust; but here lies the form that is to rise immortal, to stand with us at the judgment, to enter with us the golden gates.

True Christian faith, sitting at the door of the sepulchre, thinks not only of the form that was carried lifeless and corruptible to its last earthly sleep; but also, of the body that shall wake in immortal energy and issue forth in glorious beauty. And so as the Christian tends carefully and visits lovingly the place where sleep the companions of the past, he feels that it is with the companions of the future, rather, that he is holding silent communion.

It is a mistake, into which even Christians fall, to speak of the immortality of the soul, as if the body, too, were not immortal. The immortality of the soul was a speculation of heathen philosophy, and rested on the supposed indestructibility of the spiritual part of man. The immortality of man, body and soul, is a doctrine of the Gospel, and rests on the revelation of God, and gathers its confirmation from the resurrection of the man Christ Jesus.

Those Christians, who, in their conceptions of heavenly felicity, leave the body out of account, and make the disembodied spirit at once to mount up to the highest glory and enter upon its perfect reward, seem to me, to be rather believers in Plato than in Christ. For it surely is around the tomb, that His disciples are taught to anticipate that perfect day, when mortality shall put on immortality, when weakness shall gird itself with strength, when corruption shall be raised in incorruption, and when all the blessed children of the resurrection shall "inherit the kingdom prepared for" them "from the foundation of the world."

The fact then that the body is to be raised and made a participator in the full, final reward, proves the doctrine of which I speak.

II. But while the flesh thus rests in hope, the spirit is in its proper place. Where that place is exactly, we care not to discuss. It is called Paradise in more than one passage; in one other, it is Abraham's bosom; and, in others, the invisible place, denominated in the Psalms, and in the Acts, hell — i. e. the covered place, because no human eye can penetrate its shades.

In the old heathen mythology, this place of the dead was beneath the surface of the earth. There were bright elysian fields, the counterparts of the pleasantest spots of the upper world. In these the spirits of the good disported themselves as they had been wont to do in the happiest days of their earthly life. And that was all. The body was left forever. It was the soul, and the soul alone, in its disembodied state that occupied their contemplations of the condition of the departed.

Now the Scriptures, all in harmony, teach us this one consistent truth, that after death the body rests in the grave, and the spirit in its separate condition, is in the place of departed spirits, wherever it may be, but not in the state of perfect glory destined to it hereafter.

This place is called hell, as where in the Psalms, David says, "Thou shalt not leave my soul in hell, neither shalt thou suffer thy Holy One to see corruption." Of which confidence of David, St. Peter, in his Pentecostal address, asserts that it was of Christ's soul that David, as a Prophet, sung.

He "spake of the resurrection of Christ, that *His* soul was not left in hell, neither *His* flesh did see corruption." This place, or at least one portion of this place of departed spirits is Paradise; for to the penitent thief our Lord promised "Today shalt thou be with me in Paradise." For its locality we do not contend.

The word Paradise is a sweet word, and carries back our thoughts to Eden's garden of perfect and delightful beauty, where man talked face to face with God, and innocent and immortal, lacked nothing to his present enjoyment or his future expectation. The word strictly means a kind of park or pleasure ground, and is suggestive of peacefulness and repose.

In our conception of such an earthly paradise, there may be included the idea of a noble mansion, to which these lovely grounds belong. In such an earthly paradise, the invited guests who have already *arrived*, may wander at will, amid its cool shades and fragrant breezes, pleased with a thousand charms of sight and sound, happy in their present delightful repose, and in the expectation of the rich entertainment to which they have been called.

In such a state of actual joy and of still more joyous hope, they wait till the time shall have fully come, till all the guests shall have arrived. Then the doors of the mansion are thrown open and all go in together and sit down at the banquet. So in the Paradise of God,[2] the blessed dead, full of present peace and of joyous hope wait for us. In such a happy state, and with such a blessed hope, a few years, or even a few centuries, are in comparison with the eternity before them, but a waiting moment.

They wait in joy, and when the appointed time shall come, when the number of the elect shall be completed, then again, as once for Jesus, our ascending Lord, so now for those, who are made like unto Him, shall the everlasting gates lift up their festal heads, and all the saints together shall go in and sit down at the Marriage Supper of the Lamb.

We hold this to be the one great central fact of all the glorious truths concerning the invisible world, and man's condition therein, at which Scripture gives us transporting glimpses, more or less distinct: i. e. Christ is the *Resurrection and the Life*. The Resurrection and *therefore* the Life.

First, He raised Himself, and so became the Giver of Life. Through death He overcome death. By His raising His human body, and re-uniting it to the human soul, He burst the dominion of the king of terrors. Till His resurrection, He was not Himself delivered from the power of death and the captivity of the grave.

But when on the third day He came forth, the conqueror of death and hell, then the triumphant exultation began to be shouted, "Oh, Death! where is thy sting? Oh, Grave! where is thy victory?" Not till He had overcome death, and wrested from him everything that he had subdued to his power, do the Scriptures exhibit Christ as the Life giver.

"Because I live, ye shall live also." Or, as St. Paul, who so plainly points to the bodily life, "If Christ be not raised, your faith is vain, ye are yet in your sins."

And on this truth depends another. Till the moment of His victory, Christ was in His state of humiliation. For three days His body was held as the trophy of death, thus far the victor even over the Life-giver himself. Thus far, He was Himself the Captive. And can we imagine, that the Paradise, to which His soul went, was the state of triumph and the place where the conqueror of Death was received with all the glory of the Victor over death and hell?

No! not till He led captivity captive, not till death's dominion had been completely shaken off, not till all immortal, body and soul, Jesus had overcome death, and reclaimed from him all His human nature, did the city of our God, resound with the hosannas of triumph, and the challenged gates lift up their heads, and the everlasting doors give way, to let the King of Glory, the conquering Jesus in.

And then, is the disciple above his Master? Shall the servant, at once, after death, enter the full triumph of the redeemed, while his body is in the place of corruption, when so did not the Lord himself? No! Certainly in this respect "it is enough for the disciple to be as his Master, and the servant as his Lord."

And in harmony with this view Scripture teaches that our bodies shall in the tomb await a glorious resurrection; that they are to be made like unto His glorious body; that our flesh shall rest in hope of the time when Christ shall come again, and, in the form of the Son of Man, shall call forth from their graves all His sleeping saints; that then before His bar the gathered nations shall be judged; and that then to His saints, in their restored human nature, body and soul reunited, He shall address the welcome, "Come, ye blessed children of my Father, receive the kingdom."

Then shall come the blissful reception into the palace of the King of Kings. Then shall the righteous enter "life eternal." Then bearing the image of Him who reigns in glory, shall they in His likeness be perfectly glorified with Him.

And we do maintain, that it is a false and marring view of this great and symmetrical truth, to make the soul of the departed saint, immediately after death, enter upon the perfect and final glory.[3]

Such a conception of the state of the departed, reduces the body to a useless appendage to the redeemed and glorified man, and not a part of the man himself; such a conception sinks the resurrection of the body to a useless display of Almighty power, not longed for by the saint, because not needed, in order to his further advancement in glory. Such a conception makes the judgment but the idle re-enacting of a long finished drama, and the sentence of that day but the reiteration of a welcome already extended and already accepted.

No! Not so. Think of our departed friends as we may — as happy as we may fondly believe them to be — at rest from all earthly labors, and that is much — free from sin and temptation, and that is more — secure in their title to their eternal inheritance, and that is the great thing — in Paradise, the celestial ante-type of Eden's perfections of beauty and of peace — in Abraham's bosom, and so in the sweet companionship of all the saints — present with the Lord, because absent from the body, and hence with him in a closer union than to us here is possible — in heaven, perhaps, if by heaven you simply mean some happy place, away from this stricken, groaning world, and nearer to the glory of God's immediate presence, where sin and sorrow never enter.

Think of them, I say, as we fondly may; but oh! let us not forget that a higher state, a more glorious destiny, a fuller fruition yet awaits them, which shall not be by them enjoyed till we, too, if we are so happy, till we, too, are ready, till all the sons of immortality are ready and Christ comes again. Then, side by side, we who have taken sweet counsel together, and gone to the house of God in company, shall be glorified together — together receive our reward — together go in at the heavenly mansion and sit down at the Marriage Supper of the Lamb.

Oh! this waiting for us of the blessed dead! How closely it still knits them to us! Waiting for us! All of the same company still. Waiting for us! Not to welcome us to their perfect state. That is but half the truth. But waiting for us, with us to be advanced and crowned.

Half the truth, did I say! It is but the merest fraction of the truth. Glorious and happy as we may conceive our departed loved ones now to be, and happy as we may be when, in their paradise, we enjoy their present joy, it will still be but the beginning of an endless advance, the first step, although a lofty one, in a succession of upward mountings into light and life; the first enlarging of a free spirit, that is more and more, and forever more and more, to be filled with all the fullness of God.

Our departed friends, just across the dark river, in those bright fields which — "beyond the swelling flood, Stand dressed in living green," wait for us, to enter with us, as conquerors, into the Heavenly City. And then all immortal, body and soul, we in one triumphal throng, with Jesus at our head, shall pass on to the heavenly Zion, receive our crowns, and reign with Him forever and ever.

At the old Grecian games, the victors in the amphitheatre were removed from the arena to that part of the stadium, where the judges sat, and where the prizes had been displayed. Not at once were the crowns put upon their brow. The contests in the amphitheatre were still going on. One by one the victors passed out of the place of conflict and entered the place of honor and repose. Was anything then wanting to their satisfaction? Their breasts swelled with exultation.

They occupied the place of honor — the admired recipients of a nation's envy and applause. Yet for a while they waited. Then when the games were ended,[4] the judge pronounced the names of the victors in all the games. Then the paeans burst forth; then the crowns descended; then the palms were grasped, and the conquerors went forth to banquet and song amid the ringing plaudits of the rejoicing city.

So in our Christian course, which the Apostle likens to these contests of ancient Greece. A long line of the conquerors through faith have passed out of the arena of earthly strife to the presence of their Judge — to the post of security — to the place of honor, of happiness and of repose.

Still they have not yet received the promise. The games of life are still progressing. Other victors are to be added to this faithful throng. Other crowns are to be won.

Then when all this earthly probation is closed, the Judge shall arise, the victors shall be proclaimed, the crowns awarded, the harps struck, the song awakened and the triumphal procession of the redeemed shall take up its march to the uplifted gates; and the marriage of Christ and his spotless, perfect Church, shall cause the golden streets of the New Jerusalem to resound with the welcome acclaim.

The Church of Christ, then, is to be considered in a three-fold aspect. Here on earth, it is the Church Militant, where the struggle is still going on, where the victories are to be gained, if gained at all, and the prize of everlasting life secured, if secured at all. Then beyond the resurrection of the dead and the eternal awards of the Judgment, is the Church Triumphant, where the victorious saints enjoy their triumph together, the proclaimed, the received inheritors of the kingdom and the crown.

Between each one's death and resurrection, there is the Church in another state, properly called the Church Expectant, where, the contest finished, the prize secured, the successful, happy champions of faith, in present honor and delight, delay their entrance into the still higher glory, till we whom they love, and for whom they wait, shall have finished our course with joy, and are ready with them, in body and soul, to "have *our* perfect consummation and bliss," For "they, without us, should not be made perfect." Oh! what an incentive here, to strenuous, unintermitted labor in the Christian course.

"Wherefore, seeing we also are compassed about with so great a cloud of witnesses, let us lay aside every weight, and the sin that doth so easily beset us, and let us run with patience the race that is set before us." Christian champion, have you among this cloud of witnesses, a departed parent or child, husband or wife, brother, sister or friend, in whose communion on earth you delighted? He waits for you there. Great as his present joy may be, he waits for you to enter upon a higher state of glory and felicity. Shall he wait in vain?

In this Church Expectant are many, who have recently, very recently completed their course on earth, There are many now there, who but lately drew near to *this* altar, and participated in *this* feast of love. Within the five years that I have ministered to you, in this part of the Church Militant, six of the forty-six communicants whom I found here, have been laid by me in the grave.[5]

Their spirits, we trust, are in that blissful, waiting throng, waiting for us, who are here today, mutely but eloquently calling to their beloved ones, to join them in their coming day of triumph.

In this view of the relation between the Church Militant on earth, the Church Expectant in Paradise, and the Church Triumphant beyond, the history of each Christian Parish, becomes deeply interesting, and its Register extremely suggestive. During the five years just closed, there have, in this parish, been admitted to the Christian Church, by baptism, seventy-eight children, and twenty-eight adults. In the view, upon which, this morning, we have been dwelling, these are one hundred and six members of Christ, children of God, inheritors of the kingdom of heaven. It would be a blessed thought, that all of them shall ever thus remain; that their names shall never be blotted out of that book of life, which will at the last great day be opened.

Within these years seventy-six of God's baptized children have here renewed their baptismal promises and avowed themselves the soldiers and servants of Christ, and have set out in the Christian course, to win the prize of their high calling. Here are seventy-six enlisted competitors for the crown. How inexpressibly delightful it would be to the pastor's heart, to believe that each admitted competitor, would so run as to obtain.

Twenty-one times have I joined in Holy Matrimony those over whom I have uttered the prayer of benediction, "May you so dwell together in this life, that in the world to come, ye may have life everlasting." Would that in every case, we could feel, that Christ and His Church were so present in this earthly union, that, with assurance, we could anticipate for every one a more glorious espousal, and a never-ending reunion.

Forty-three times have the words been said over the open grave, "Blessed are the dead who die in the Lord." Many of these, we are sure, are now sleeping in Jesus, their flesh resting in hope, their spirits joyously in Paradise awaiting the day when corruption shall put on incorruption, and mortality shall be swallowed up of life. Oh! that no sad foreboding of a resurrection unto shame and everlasting contempt, mingled with our anticipations of that glorious day.

Over and over again, as we are today, soon to do, have we gathered around this table of our Lord. One after another has disappeared from our number, to join the greater communion beyond the veil. Others have come in to fill their places, till now where forty-six stood, five years ago, now one hundred and ten are registered as the communicants of this Parish.

Month by month the sacrament of this communion has been renewed. Your pastor's heart is animated with the confidence that many here are going on from strength to strength — till they appear before God in Zion; that they are growing more and more meet for the blessed supper above, where none but the tried and the purified shall be admitted.

While on the other hand, his heart is saddened with the reflection, that many seem to care little for their privileges, and try little for their glorious crown; and over some such, even among his communicants, the sigh will arise, that the records of the Church Militant, will not, perhaps be ratified by the records of the Book of Life. The sad thought will intrude, "that many" even here, are to be found, who, at the last, "shall seek to enter in, and shall not be able."

Oh! these records of the Church of Christ! How they speak of privileges and of responsibilities, of hopes and promises, of God's mercies and of man's accountabilities, of present grace improved or neglected, and of future glory or despair! Let us ever, my brethren, remember that other book of God's account, and strive so to keep our place in His family that from the Church Militant on earth, we may pass to the blessed company of the faithful dead, who, in the Church Expectant, wait, in sure and certain hope, for their perfect consummation and bliss in the Church Triumphant, in the immediate presence of Christ, our risen and glorified Lord.

"The Spirit and the Bride say, come — and let him that is athirst come." Do not these sweet words of invitation from the Bride of Christ, this gentle persuasion of the Holy Spirit, come to you today, with a strange new power and tenderness — blended as they are, with the voices of the fondly remembered, the loved, the sainted dead? Can you not hear them say, "Come, for all things are now ready." Yet there is room." Room at this table of our Lord, room in our expectant ranks — room at that feast above, to which, we wait, with you to enter.

And now to Jesus, the Author and Finisher of our Faith, our risen and glorified Lord, be ascribed, with the Father and Holy Ghost, as by the angels in Heaven and the saints in Paradise, so by the Church on earth, all the honor and the praise, forever and forever. Amen.

Almighty God, with whom do live the spirits of those who depart hence in the lord, and with whom the souls of the faithful, after they are delivered from the burden of the flesh are in joy and felicity: we give thee hearty thanks for the good examples of all those thy servants, who, having finished their course in faith, do now rest from their labors. And we beseech thee, that we, with all those who have departed in the true faith of thy holy name, may have our perfect consummation and bliss, both in body and soul, in thy eternal and everlasting glory, through Jesus Christ our lord. Amen.

Notes:

[1] The advantages in this life conferred upon us do far exceed those granted to saints in the earlier ages. But there seems to be no such comparison intimated in these words, or hinted at in this chapter. Our faith needs *some better thing* in the future, to sustain us under earthly labors and sufferings, just as theirs did, v. v. 10, 13, 16, 27, 35.

The systematic contrast between the Jewish and the Christian dispensations, seems to have passed out of St. Paul's mind at the middle of the tenth chapter. From that point, all the faithful, are, in his view, members of the one family of Abraham's spiritual seed, and heirs with him of the same promise, and bound to live, and labor, and suffer, and conquer through faith. And to this victory of faith it is necessary that *some better thing* should be held out to us, of which "faith is the evidence," some future reward "hoped for," of which faith is the present "substance."

To adhere, in this verse, to the idea previously set forth of *some better thing* granted to us in this life than to the Jews was vouchsafed, complicates the interpretation, and confuses the sense.

The Presbyterian divine, Dr. McKnight, while needlessly laboring to incorporate both ideas in his paraphrase of this verse, yet uses the following words, "*God having foreseen* that by the Gospel He would bestow *some better means of faith on us* in order to our becoming Abraham's spiritual seed, resolved *that the ancients without us, should not be made perfect*, by receiving the promised heavenly country.

For He determined that the whole spiritual seed of Abraham, raised from the dead, shall be introduced into that country in a body at one and the same time; namely, after the general judgment." And in his annotations, he says more fully: "*Made perfect*, here signifies made complete, by receiving the whole of the blessings promised to believers. These blessings are the resurrection of the body, the everlasting possession of the heavenly country, and the full enjoyment of God as their exceeding great reward."

The Apostle's doctrine, that believers are all to be rewarded together and at the same time, is agreeable to Christ's declaration, who told His disciples that they were not to come to the place He was going away to prepare for them, till he returned from heaven to carry them to it. *St. Jo. 14:3.* Further, that the righteous are not to be rewarded till the end of the world, is evident from Christ's words. *St. Matth. 13:40, 43.*

In like manner St. Peter hath told us, that the righteous are to be *made glad* with their reward, at *the revelation of Christ. 1 Pet. 4:13.* When they are to receive *a crown of glory that fadeth not away. 1 Pet. v, 4.* St. John also tells us, that *when He shall appear, we shall be made like Him, for we shall see Him as He is. 1 Jo. 3:2."*

The following are a few of the many passages bearing on this truth. Let them be consulted in order: *Dan.12:2, 3. St. Jo. v, 29. St. Lu. 14:14, 20:36. Rom. 8:23. 1 Cor. 15:54. 2 Cor. 4:14. 1 Thess. 4:14-17. Heb. 9:28. 1 Pet. 1:3-7. St. Matth. 13:43. St. Matth. 25:21, 34, 46. Col. 3:4. Ps. 17:15. 1 Jo. 3: 2. 2 Tim. 4:8.*

[2] Does not this view satisfactorily explain such passages in Scripture as are quoted against the doctrine of the intermediate state? Such passages are *Acts 7:59. Phil.1: 23. 2 Cor. 5:6, 8, 12:4.* On this passage, Dr. McKnight says: "Clement, of Alexandria, Justin Martyr, Irenæus, Tertullian, and most of the ancients, except Origen, and among the moderns Bull, Whitby, Bengel, &c., were of opinion that the Apostle had two different raptures."

The language of Bp. Bull is, "First he had represented to him the most perfect joys of the third or highest heaven, of which we hope to be partakers after the resurrection; and then, lest so long an expectation should discourage us, he saw also the intermediate joys of Paradise; and for our comfort tells us, that even these also are inexpressible." *Sermon III, on the middle state, &c.* Olshausen, while dissenting from the idea that St. Paul speaks of two visions, yet says, "The distinction between an upper and a lower paradise entirely corresponds with the Biblical doctrine."

[3] "Now I do affirm the constant and consentient doctrine of the primitive church to be this: that the souls of all the faithful, immediately after death, enter into a place and state of bliss, far exceeding all the felicities of this world, though short of that most consummate perfect beatitude of the kingdom of heaven, with which they are to be crowned and rewarded in the resurrection." *Bp Bull, Sermon III.*

"It was the Popish Convention, at Florence, that first boldly defined against the sense of the Primitive Christians. That those souls which, having contracted the blemish of sin, are, either in their bodies or out of them, purged from it, do presently go into heaven, and there clearly behold God Himself, one God in three persons, as

He is. And this decree they made, partly to establish their superstition of *praying to the saints* deceased; *but chiefly to introduce their purgatory.*" Ibid.

Dr. Whitby says: "And the Trent Council, sess. 25, hath laid this as the foundation of the invocation of saints departed, that they do now reign with Christ, and enjoy eternal felicity in heaven." Annotations on *2 Tim. 4:8.*

[4] So testify Theodoret and Theophylact. Dr. McKnight, however, on what authority I do not find, says that all the victors of the day were together, at the close of each day, proclaimed and crowned. The difference is unimportant. When all the contests of this earthly life are over, or what is the same thing, when the day of probation comes to an end, then shall the crowns of immortality be awarded.

[5] In the order of their decease these are Jeremiah B. Elmer, a Vestryman of the Parish, J. Mongin Smith, Junior Warden, Mrs. Eliza McDonald, Mrs. Barbara Pulliam, Mrs. Mary W. Berry, Benjamin Green, Junior Warden.

Of the forty-six communicants on the Register five years since, fifteen have removed, leaving only twenty-five of that number at this time on our communion list. Forty-four have been added by removal, sixty-seven anew, make the sum total of communicants in these five years, one hundred and fifty-seven.

Of these additions two have died, and twenty-four removed, leaving our present number one hundred and ten, as given below. In this are reckoned a very few who on this (All Saints) day received their first communion. None are included in this number however, who, resident it may be for a longer or shorter time, have yet parish relations elsewhere in the Confederacy.

Festival Of The Ascension

A SERMON

DELIVERED BEFORE THE

ANNUAL COUNCIL

OF THE

DIOCESE OF NORTH CAROLINA

UPON THE

FESTIVAL OF THE ASCENSION

MAY 14, 1863.

BY

REV. ALFRED A. WATSON
ASSISTANT MINISTER of ST. JAMES' PARISH
WILMINGTON

1863

SERMON

St. Matt. 13:52. — "Every scribe, which is instructed unto the Kingdom of Heaven, is like unto a man that is an householder, which bringeth forth out of his treasure things new and old."

Not only new, but old things also; not bending his diligence only to amuse "itching ears" and Athenian searchers after "some new thing," but producing old truths, and thus laying a firm foundation; building up with those massive principles which know no change.

Yet not only old things, but new also; adapting himself to the times — so as to make the old fundamental truths practical guides to present conduct, and in present circumstances — erecting upon the fixed and unchangeable foundations, a superstructure to suit the season — teaching not only the great principles of the Truth, but also the lessons of the Hour.

Such was our Saviour's estimate of a wise Scribe. The Scribes were the appointed Teachers of the Church. They represented the Church, in that department of her work.

We may generalize the text and apply it to the Church and her Teachers now.

When, as on this day, our Saviour ascended up on high, it is recorded by S. Paul (2nd evening lesson: Eph. IV) that he "gave gifts unto men." When the King of Glory entered the eternal gates and took possession of His throne, He distributed largess to his subjects.

And what gift was worthy of such a King and of such an occasion? Not gold, dug from the dirty mine; nor jewels; bright daughters though they be of base earth; but, beyond all gold or rubies, the means of heavenly wisdom for His Church — the agencies of sanctification and pardon and Eternal Salvation.

It is written, "He gave some, Apostles; and some, Prophets; and some, evangelists; and some, pastors and teachers; for the perfecting of the saints, for the work of the ministry, for the edifying of the body of Christ." "That we henceforth be no more children, tossed to and fro, and carried about with every wind of doctrine, by the sleight of men, and cunning craftiness, whereby they lie in wait to deceive."

Thus when Christ would bestow upon His people a gift worthy of Himself, He gave them Teachers. And, that their instruction might be thorough and reliable, He made their teaching two fold; giving them, first, a permanent code of instruction, in the Holy Scriptures; wherein to represent and hold, as it were, in stereotype, the great fixed, unchanging, principles of His Truth and Law — a teacher impersonal, inanimate, of necessity as ignorant of all of us now present upon earth, however accurately meeting our cases by analogy, as were the Stone tables of the earlier Law, but infallible, and always and everywhere essentially the same.

Secondly, His Church — fallible, as made up of men — liable to change and to some degree of error, but endued with the advantage of being living — able to take cognizance of present circumstances, however peculiar, and to adapt her instructions to the necessities of individual, or local, or temporary cases — to bring forth things new as well as old — able, therefore, to teach, the lessons of the Hour — enabled to do so, by teaching through a living ministry who, dwelling in the hour themselves, can see what are its lessons.

And the Church is bound to teach "the Lessons of the Hour." Else is she no faithful guide to her children; else are her watchmen, like those rebuked by Isaiah, "dumb dogs that cannot bark." But not with frivolous haste: perpetually hunting novelties, and degrading the dignity of the pulpit, and seeking to catch the attention of a giddy world to its solemn lessons, by weaving into their fabric all the petty excitements of the day.

Nor yet with laggard indifference, or stiff disregard of the actual, daily, moral and spiritual necessities of her hearers — with a dry and dull propriety, handling only universally recognized truths, and old facts — walking the ramparts of

Zion in formal round — making no sallies upon the actual, present assailants.

Adopting neither of these modes, but teaching with the dignity and yet the earnestness becoming the Bride of Christ — refusing, on the one hand, to turn aside to "vain janglings," or to make her pulpits the show places of all the straw floating by upon the human current; but on the other hand, teaching the Lessons of the Hour; dwelling in living sympathy with her children; helping them grapple with their local trials; in their sunshine, warning them against the seductions of the Tempter; and when dark clouds gather over them, and their path becomes dim and perilous, guiding them through the gloom, and comforting and strengthening them for the moment of distress and danger.

And how shall the Church now guide her children aright, if she looks not around her at the actual horizon; if she perceives not the circle of lurid flame that engirdles her; if she sees not the heavens black and still gathering blackness; if she feels not the earth as it rocks to the tread of armies and the roll of artillery; if she sees not the burning homes and trampled harvests of her children; or her widows and helpless infants and aged women, driven forth at one moment with a view to swell the supposed ravages of famine, and at another compelled by the invaders to remain as a breastwork for themselves; if she hears not the groans of the wounded and dying or the moans of the widow and fatherless, as, not one by one, but in great sheaves, the dread mower reaps down on the red field of battle, husband and father and brother and son?

How shall God's Church teach faithfully the lessons of the hour, if she fails to see that War is in the land — or, seeing it, thinks it beneath her dignity to take notice of it in her pulpits? Far be it from her to sound the dread tocsin; to excite war, or stimulate bloodthirstiness. We may congratulate ourselves that in the South, at least, this war has not been brought on by harangues from the pulpit; nor when it burst, was the emblem of secular power permitted to shroud the sacred desk or flaunt from the spires of God's house.

The Church of the South has not attempted to declare war, or lash on the hesitating politician to his bloody work; nor have her great religious conclaves, of various names, been degraded into arenas for denunciation, or the venting of bitterness towards those she hopes to conquer. It is a condition of things which she cannot help.

I do not mean to intimate that on such questions the Church must surrender her conscience, or do implicitly the bidding of the State. I do not hesitate to say that were this war both unjust and offensive upon our part, we could as Christians have nothing whatever to do with it. No earthly authority would have the right to force us into it. The Church would be bound so far as she could do so, to thunder her denunciations; and though the consequences were imprisonment or a felon's death, there would be no choice for us, as Christians, between such a fate, and the enormous crime of carrying fire and sword into the territory of an innocent neighbor.

But happily we are placed in no such alternative. The Church of the South can with a clear conscience, take her stand by the side of her battling children. She can send her soldier to the field, as to a part of God's work for him, in this present strait; she can teach him his duties there — the duties of subordination and discipline — of temperance and regularity; she can teach him to restrain his temper from outbursts of animal ferocity — to be chivalrous as well as brave — while he wars with the armed man, to respect the aged, the woman and the child — to endure hardness, as a good soldier of Jesus Christ.

And she can teach him true courage and rational confidence; she can point his faith to an Almighty Protector, who is with him as truly in all the terrible storm of the battle-field, as in the quiet of his home.

She can remind him that even to escape death in battle is not to escape it long, but that, in fact, he is "immortal till his work is done" — that he is immortal even in death — that for the Christian, death upon an honorable battle-field is but one great pathway to eternal glory. And though she draw not the sword herself, nor descend to the dust of the field of strife, yet can she take her stand with God upon the Mountain, and by prayer uphold her warrior's hands.

And she has lessons of the hour for the citizen also; lessons of caution, lest led by avarice, he forget his duty to his country and his kind, and fatten himself upon his neighbor's wasting flesh, to his own life-long, his eternal infamy — lessons of hospitality, which, due at all times, from the Christian, is now specially due from those whom a kind Providence has thus far permitted to remain under their own vines and fig trees, towards brethren who have lost their all to the enemy and so in the common cause.

How sad their lot! Exiles from the homes of their fathers, they have wandered forth, too often to be inhospitably repelled by their own brethren. Cut off from the temples of their childhood and from the worship of their reason and of their affections — by distant waters, they "weep when they remember Zion."

But the Hour has its lessons not only for individuals and individual interests, but for communities also — lessons not only to circumscribed localities, but for the Church throughout the world, and to the world itself — lessons which are peculiarly and emphatically, the great lessons of the hour, taught by the Providence of God, and with a force unattainable without that special Providence, which makes them the Lessons of the Hour.

It is a momentous hour for the Church; — an hour of rampant fanaticism — of forgetfulness of first principles and of the most familiar and fundamental truths — of bitterness of feeling obliterating principle and overruling conscience — an hour of division — an hour of depressed finances — of zeal cooled down — of forgotten work — of the smoking embers of many a neglected or trampled religious enterprise.

God is teaching us some things with peculiar emphasis; — vindicating His Church and His truth by a broad and bloody experience — warning that Church of some unexpected dangers, and establishing for her some new and most important responsibilities. And these lessons He expects her to teach her children — like the well-instructed scribe, bringing forth from her treasury, things new and old.

Among the lessons of the hour, and especially appropriate to this occasion, is the testimony, which God in His providence is giving to the adaptation of the Church, as we understand and define it, to the work of God and the wants of men.

Let me not be misunderstood. I bear cheerful testimony to the personal piety and excellence of many who differ from us as to the nature of the Church. They may be much better men than I am. But neither my membership of any religious body, nor my father's before me, nor my neighbor's, can determine its claims as God's appointed instrument for His own work or for the greatest good to men.

In our human fallibility, we and all ours, may for generations have been connected with an incomplete, erroneous, or even injurious system. The true question is not one of persons, or one in which our feelings should be allowed to influence us. It is a question of systems. So let us regard it.

The national contest in which we are involved, is in great part a religious war; and that, both as to its origin, and as respects the persons who are our principal enemies.

We need not deny, that other and great political causes have been at work. The vast extent of our territory, and the conflict of interests, commercial, manufacturing and agricultural, thereby resulting, had doubtless done much to unsettle us. But fanaticism — religious fanaticism — was the lever.

Abolitionism was the LEVER used by those who drove us into the conflict. And abolitionism found — certainly at the first — no fulcrum in the Episcopal Church, either North or South.

True, her congregations and her Clergy at the North have yielded to the pressure, and have sided with our enemies, to a degree mortifying to us. They have suffered themselves to be upheaved with the rest. But they constituted no appreciable part of the upheaving influence. Abolitionists there were within her ranks; we know them well. But we could almost have counted them upon our fingers. That noxious plant found in her no genial soil.

Year after year she repelled the question from her Conventions, both Diocesan and General; and that by immense, overwhelming majorities. And so far as the Northern Dioceses have arrayed themselves against us, it has not been primarily through the power or influence of fanaticism, but because of the disposition of the Church to uphold the powers that be — the civil government under which she dwells.

This was characteristic of her course in the revolutionary war, and while constituting, perhaps, a guaranty for her stability and conservatism, is for that very reason, no evidence — but to the contrary — of any liability to the influence of fanaticism.

I do not say how far this war may or may not abolitionize her Northern Dioceses, or may or may not have done so already. What I say is this: — that her part in the war was not, in the first instance, due to any sympathy felt by her for the fanatics who built their circles of fire around us, and drove us into the dissolution of our union with them.

The Northern Episcopal Dioceses had nothing to do with bringing about this contest. They accepted it as a fact — joined more zealously than we could have wished with our enemies; but did so, we maintain, actuated by a notion — a false one we think it — but still a notion of loyalty, and not by fanaticism.

And even since that whirlwind at the North has arisen in its fury, and gathered into its tempestuous movement all things and nearly all men, how has the action of the Episcopal Conventions there, both Diocesan and General, contrasted with that of some other religious bodies![1]

Where else at the North will you find the comparative moderation which has marked her assemblies? And where, in all her assemblies, will you find the counterpart of such a meeting as was held in Democratic New York, in April, and reported in our papers — tumultuously affirming the incompatibility of slavery with Christianity; and where professed ministers of Jesus Christ proposed to treat those who among themselves were of opponent politics, by hanging them, or by stamping them under their heels?

I venture to think that, when this war is over and the truth is discoverable, it will be ascertained, that among our strongest friends and allies have been many of the Churchmen of the North; and further, that the main body of Churchmen will be found to have been either averse to this war altogether, or in favor of a moderate mode of conducting it. That they support the government under which they live, and condemn our secession, may be true. But they have not been possessed, as have many others, with the demon of ferocity, and the desire of our extermination or subjugation.

Many of them, I am persuaded, have never been willing to support the war at all. Even while condemning, perhaps, our secession, they have not wished to put the question to the bloody issues of the sword.

In all this I may, of course, be measurably mistaken. But that will not invalidate my assertion that the Episcopal Church, throughout this country, had been comparatively free from the fanaticism which has brought the war and all these sorrows upon us, and, that had she been the prevailing Church of the country, there would have been comparatively no soil wherein for that pernicious plant of abolitionism to grow — there would have been no need of secession — no cause of war, at least on that account. Whatever evils other and political differences might have precipitated upon us in time, this war has been brought upon us by fanaticism which knew no footing in the Church to which we belong.

But there are other religious bodies at the North, who, like ourselves, have comparatively kept out, or kept down this moral miasm, though, excepting the Church of Rome, not, we think, so fully as among ourselves. All honor to them. And if we can detect the common principle, which has been for us all so great a prophylactic, we will assuredly have learned one of the most important lessons of the hour.

I am persuaded that, aside from the divine character which we claim for the Church, the great secret — philosophically speaking — has been in the traditional character of her belief and teachings. She accepts no novelties in religion. She admits novel applications of old truths; things thus new and old she has among her treasures. But the truth, or the principle, is always an old one; and so far as circumstances remain the same, the application is the old one also.

What was the truth, whether of principle or of application, to the first Christians, she believes to be the truth now. What was the meaning of the Gospel, when St. Paul wrote the Epistle to Philemon, or when St. Paul or St. Peter in the flesh, commanded servants to be obedient to their masters, she believes to be its meaning now.

If slavery were wrong now, and to be condemned, she believes it would have been wrong then, and would have been condemned then. She accepts no new Gospel, according to Garrison, or Phillips, or Beecher, or anybody else.

She remembers that immediately after enforcing upon Timothy to teach obedience to servants, St. Paul adds: "If any man teach otherwise and consent not unto wholesome words, even the words of our Lord Jesus Christ, he is proud — or, as in the margin, he is a fool — knowing nothing, but doting about questions and strifes of words, whereof cometh envy, strife, railings, evil surmisings, perverse disputings of men of corrupt minds, and destitute of the truth."

She takes the old Gospel, with its old traditional interpretation. — And so long as she is faithful to this rule, no fanaticism can creep in. And you will find that the exemption of other religious bodies, at the North, from the taint of abolitionism, has been in direct proportion to the prevalence among them of this same traditional principle;[2] while just in proportion to its abandonment has the door been opened for new notions, new translations, new interpretations, heresies, schisms, fanaticisms..

And I believe that one great lesson which God is teaching us at this dark hour, is the value of a traditional religious system. It is the only safe system. It is the only system which gives us any security for the religious belief of our neighbors or of our descendants — the only system which can secure us against agrarianism, abolitionism, or any other heresy, which, like them, may uproot the social compact, or our religious faith.

But, because traditions have been forged or abused, and because our Saviour condemned those "traditions of the elders," which contravened the law of God, and because Rome has brought in many unfounded doctrines, under the name of tradition, multitudes of superficial thinkers have gone on to condemn all traditions — forgetful of St. Paul's express injunction to the Thessalonians — (2. Thess. 2:15) to hold the traditions they had been taught, and (3:6,) "to withdraw themselves from every brother, walking not after the tradition received of the Apostles."

Traditions were doctrines or practices handed down. Of these some were inspired and good; others were human and bad. The bad were to be rejected; the good were to be preserved. But the Gospel system was to be traditional. And the great principle of the traditional system, such as our Church maintains, is that of holding nothing as revealed truth, or as the sound interpretation of revealed truth, which we have not received from the Apostles, and which was not received by the first Christians from the Apostles.

We reject all new Revelations or developments of Revelation; and upon points of practice, in common to us with the first Christians, all new interpretations of Revelation. And so we exclude in the mass, both Romanism and Neology — all the modern developments of Romanism on the one hand, and all the still more modern inventions of Puritanism and Neology on the other.

As the first Christians were not Abolitionists, so neither can we be, so long as our system remains traditional.

And I maintain, that the importance of a traditional system of Faith and Interpretation is one of the great Lessons of the Hour, which God is teaching us.

But I have said more than this. I have said that I think God is also teaching us the value of our own Zion, as the maintainer and champion of a sound traditional faith — teaching the whole Country and the world her value — her peculiar adaptation to the work of God and the wants of man.

It is true, that other religious bodies, at the North, have shared with us, our exemption from the fanaticism of the abolitionist, who, nevertheless, reject our doctrine of tradition. But what security have we that they will continue thus exempt?

Their freedom thus far has been owing to the fact, that their faith and practice have been in reality traditional, even while they themselves have condemned the principle of tradition in theory. But the theory will in time eat out the principle, and their safeguard will be gone.

This seems to be rapidly coming to pass at the North. Here, at the South, our circumstances have well nigh compelled us all to be of accord thus far upon the great disturbing question of the day. But how can we feel assured, that without this traditional principle, it will so continue? — that Southern sects will not arise?

It is not many years, since an abolishing clause with respect to slavery existed in the Discipline of one of the largest and most respectable religious bodies of the South. It has, I believe, been expunged. But what security have we against its reappearance, if the traditional interpretation of the word of God be rejected — as rejected it is by all who reject Episcopacy?

I would not be understood, in what I am saying, to speak with bitterness; or in a mere spirit of controversy; or with any vain estimate of our own personal piety or personal superiority in any respect. I would have it a question of systems, not of persons. Nor would I forget, how in this great national struggle, we are all, of every religious name, standing shoulder to shoulder in a common cause. — I desire to consider this question one of common interest — one, in which we are all, in reality, interested upon the same side.

In the interest of Presbyterians, and Methodists, and Baptists, and others, as well as of Episcopalians. I desire to discuss the comparative benefits and practical working of the systems we have tried; and to inquire, with perfect impartiality, so far as that is possible, whether of all these is the true Church for our country — which of them is best adapted to the preservation of its peace, and the exclusion of fanaticism. I put the claims of our Church, of course, upon far higher grounds. But I am content, at present, to urge her claim in that, while Protestant, she is a traditional Church — that she is the Church for the Country.

Nor do I forget the Abolitionism of our brethren of the Church in England.

It has been one of the riddles of the day; but I think it may be read by the light of several considerations, as: 1st., An ignorance of the system of slavery as it exists among us — an ignorance sustained by the enormously false representations of some writers of our own: 2nd., a strong leaven of puritanism still extant there; 3rd., erroneous ideas of Christian unity, which forget that the very force of the Apostle's illustration is due to the fact, that the slave, while still remaining a slave, is one in Christ with his master.

Other solutions may be offered, but the one important fact for us is, that in this country where we live, and where our interests are to be secured, if at all — that here the Episcopal Church, North as well as South, has by virtue of her traditionary faith, kept herself free from that gigantic fanaticism from whose effects we are now suffering. Henry Clay is reported to have said that she was one of the three great conservative agencies of the Country.

We think that History has justified the wisdom of the remark; and we further believe, that God is, by the history of the last few years, and by the fiery light of this war, teaching this whole nation, that she is His true Church — the Church for this Country. It is one of the great Lessons of the Hour.

Whenever we are in danger of forgetting great principles, they become thereby — Lessons of the Hour. That which is specially endangered must be specially defended. And, therefore, this seems to me a time for specially asserting the Church's Independence.

Both at the North and at the South this principle has been endangered. At the North by actual assault. Things have occurred there within two years, which, if predicted three years ago, would have been scouted as the dreams of an alarmist, or the notions of a Neapolitan despot. Steeple and desk and pulpit and altar have been compelled to wear the secular livery; while organs attuned for the praise of God, have been made to peal forth the war notes of a wicked invasion.

In portions of the South, which have fallen under the Federal power, the temples of the Most High have been forcibly closed, or as forcibly opened at the order of some petty military tyrant.

Prayers have been dictated to the priesthood; and on their refusal to bow the neck to such outrageous tyranny, armed men have been intruded into the Sacred Presence, and the priest of God has been dragged by foul hands from the very altar — all surpliced, as he was, to some military guardhouse. Numbers of the Clergy have been imprisoned or exiled. The Missionary Bishop of the Southwest was placed in confinement and that confessedly without provocation on his part.

Thank God that no such scenes[3] have characterized the South. Yet in the South also, has the independence of the Church been specially endangered: not by assault, or opposition, but by her own forgetfulness, and because she has no quarrel with the State: endangered because — and so much the more because — we believe the State in which we live, to be right in her present action — because we go heart and hand with her in the war she is maintaining for the defense of our firesides and all we hold dear. The Church of the South, I say, is in danger of voluntarily abandoning her own independence and allowing her own action to be too hastily determined by that of the State.

But she should not forget her own royalty — that she is a nation and a kingdom of herself — THE nation of the Earth — the Kingdom of the King of kings — the government of the Lord of the whole Earth. Earthly monarchs are among her subjects. Invincible, except by her own fault — liable to no foreign conquest — to no possibility of final decay — the universe her dominion — all time her history.

But the weapons of her power are not carnal, but spiritual. And it is only in her own department that she rightfully governs at all. Except by moral influence, she interferes not with the secular government; nor in secular affairs, disturbs the earthly nations within whose borders she dwells.

Rome forgot these principles, when with ban and interdict she broke in upon the quarrels of princes, or, with the sword, attempted to open the way for her doctrines into the hearts of unbelievers; or to brand them in with the faggot and the stake.

Puritanism forgot this when she set up the Kingdom of God, as she called it, in the English commonwealth. And the Church forgets it whenever she attempts to grasp the secular sceptre, or by bodily penalties to enforce her doctrines. She cannot now, as in the days of the Jewish Theocracy, "bind Kings with chains, and nobles with fetters of iron." Such honor have not now the saints. In secular matters she obeys, and teaches her children to obey, the civil Ruler. She upholds his arm. In her own domain she is a Queen, whom none may despise or resist, without despising or resisting God. For she has been crowned by God Himself as the Bride — the Lamb's wife — "the fullness of Him that filleth all in all."

"He that will not hear the Church, let him be unto thee as a heathen man and a publican," is the decree of Christ, the King. As she cannot rightfully interfere with the secular ruler in his department, so neither may he interfere with her. He has no right, without her consent, to divide her Dioceses, or interfere with her councils, or control her worship, except so far as she first abandons her own province and intrudes into his. If he does, he must answer for it to the Great King, upon that day, when provost marshals and generals and presidents and kings will stand in helpless weakness before His bar.

And so in our present strait, it has been for the Church herself and not for the State, or for human beings outside the Church, to decide whether, here at the South, she should secede from her sister Dioceses at the North. I do not question the propriety of the general decision to which the Church has come. On the contrary, all my feelings and my judgment go with it. We could not have remained in present legislative union with the Northern portion of the Church after what has occurred. And the preface to our Book of Common Prayer, declaring our ipso facto separation from the Church of England, by virtue of our severance from the English Government, left open, as it seems to me, a formal door for our departure now.

No decree from the Confederate Congress at Richmond, or the Federal at Washington, could by itself have effected the separation. Only by the Church's own action or provision could it be accomplished. But it may be a fair question, whether the provision in the preface of the Prayer Book, to which I have referred, is itself strictly consistent with the true doctrine of the Church's independence and unity.

The hour requires the warning: lest in the heat of this war, we forget the high doctrine of the independent Sovereignty of the Church.

And so also, it is a time especially demanding the reassertion of the Church's Unity and Brotherhood. It may seem to some, as, precisely, not the time. But I think it is. If that Unity and Brotherhood be, as we hold, one of the fundamental doctrines of Revelation, than which none has been more earnestly taught, by both our Lord and His Apostles, then no storm of human passion has the right to suspend it, or cloud its shining light.

That doctrine, as set forth in the New Testament, is, that all Christians are baptized into One Body — made members of one great Family of God — that the Church in all nations, whether Jew or Greek, Barbarian, Scythian, bond, or free, is itself at last one great nation, having no national or continental boundaries — the one kingdom of the one God, the God of the whole earth — beyond the authority, therefore, of any earthly ruler or earthly government to divide her — with provinces territorially, limited, yet as a whole, indivisible.

In that she is divinely one, far more indivisible than any free masonic or other human organization can be — one by the will of Christ — one by the decree of God — one, therefore, in the face of all human decrees and all human struggles to the contrary — one, not only over all the present world, but one, through all time also — not only one in fact, but bound to acknowledge her own Unity.

A doctrine so cardinal, that it is set as one of the Articles of the Apostles' Creed — The Holy Catholic Church.

When the Caesars lived, and the Apostles wrote, Rome and her enemies had but one Christian brotherhood or Church. In those days, when Princes made war upon their own caprice, without consulting their subjects, and with little or no reference to their feelings or wishes, it was easily true that two nations might be at war, while yet the portions of the Church in both might be at peace, preserving undisturbed their unity and brotherly love. But now and with us, it is the people themselves — the members of the Church themselves — which make war, and, therefore, make war upon each other.

Thus national alienation now produces individual and ecclesiastical alienation, and so, the Unity of the Church, at such times, seems unavoidably broken. And yet, our experience in this is not entirely new.

The Psalmist was constrained sadly to write of his enemies: "It is not an open enemy, that hath done me this dishonor; for then I could have borne it: neither was it mine adversary, that did magnify himself against me; for then peradventure I would have hid myself from him; but it was even thou, my companion, my guide, and mine own familiar friend. We took sweet counsel together, and walked in the house of God as friends."

Such contentions are deep wounds, severing the sacred flesh of Christ's mystical body. And yet, the parts are still one; and, however deep the wound, may hope for reunion. I speak not of civil re-union. That I regard as forever impossible.

The feeling of abhorrence and detestation, with which the South regards this invasion, is so deep, and is daily so deepened by the ferocity with which the war is waged upon the Federal side, and by the atrocities which mark its progress, that it will take long generations to obliterate it. But I speak of the re-union of the Church.

Nor even of that, in the way in which it has heretofore existed; but only, so as it may exist between us and the mother Church in England. Such a re-union of the now bleeding portions of the Church, we may look for. Proud flesh may rise — much may be sloughed away — but if the true life be there, the re-union of its parts, so far as to make them parts of one great body again, will ultimately take place.

Wars like the present, raise momentous problems respecting the Church's Unity. It will be difficult, if not impossible, ever to feel as we felt before, towards those who have so bitterly, so wantonly, so cruelly, assailed us. Yet should the Church at such a time be specially careful, how she forgets the great doctrine of her own Unity. Nor must her children forget that she is Christ's kingdom, and, therefore, far above all human interference.

Human governments, as individuals, are subject to Christ; and were all the kings on earth and were all their parliaments — were all forms of earthly government — were all mankind with one voice and consent — were even the Church herself in Council to repeal God's law of the Church's Unity, their action would be void; only of effect, as it would be treason against their Almighty King, and would subject the guilty upon the last day, to the eternal penalties of treason.

We cannot repeal that law. But the difficulty we feel, in our present circumstances, in realizing this principle of the Church's Unity, as still prevailing, makes it one of the great Lessons of the Hour for us.

The next Lesson of the Hour, to which I will refer, is that which teaches us that, more than heretofore, we are thrown upon our own resources, in the maintenance of all religious enterprises; and the need of greater exertions than ever heretofore, in order to keep in full action the machinery of beneficence and education in our midst. Henceforth we must organize our own missions, and maintain them.

We must erect our own Theological Seminaries, and support them. We must establish colleges and schools for ourselves. We must prepare school books. Our whole system of education, and training, must be within ourselves. It will be impossible, at least for some time to come, consistently with self-respect — consistently with our maintenance of healthful truth — consistently with our responsibilities to our children, and those under our charge — consistently with our duty to our country, to resort to schools or colleges, Northward of our own line.

So far as mere pecuniary outlay is concerned, this will, perhaps, cost us no great struggle. But something else will be needed — personal care, personal exertion; the consistent refusal to resort to any institutions but our own, no matter how great their seeming advantages; the patriotic, and sometimes self-sacrificing determination, to sustain exclusively, the educational institutions of the South, as well as use exclusively Southern educational books.

Among these objects, as commending itself more especially to the attention of a body like that I address, is prominent, the necessity for Theological Seminaries of our own, whether Diocesan or General. To a remarkable extent, hitherto, the North has supplied the ministry of the South. This cannot well continue. The means of training must be provided here. And, what is of equal importance, the supply of living material should be found at home.

Let this hour of separation and of cutting off from old resources, teach our young men the lesson, that the Lord has need of more of them to do His work. Let us hope, that the perils of the battle-field and its narrow escapes, the many conspicuous mercies of a soldier's life, will not be without effect upon the minds of our young men. And let parents be more willing than they have been, to devote their sons to the service of the Lord.

What strange inconsistency for a professed follower of Christ, to be ashamed or unwilling to have his son become Christ's minister! While seeking for him all earthly honor, to despise or reject the honor of being the ambassador of the King of Kings! The harvest-field will be large, but where are the laborers?

Pray the Lord of the harvest, to send his laborers in; but while praying thus, be not so inconsistent as to withhold your own sons from the noble work. And that the young men of our country may be more encouraged to undertake it, strive to surround it with all suitable secular advantages. Degrade it not, in the eyes of your children, by withholding its proper honor, or its proper support. Nor doubt for one moment, that all you do in this direction, will redound to your own advantage both here and hereafter.

It is a time, brethren, for special exertion, and special zeal, and special contributions of the means which God has allowed you. And unless you render all these, you will not have learned the Lessons of the Hour. With many of our best contributing parishes cut off, and with what remains of the Church's income depreciated immensely in value, the work of the Church must stagger, and her standard-bearers come nigh to fainting, if there kindle not within those who remain, a warmer zeal, a more earnest action.

It is the hour of darkness, and want, and suffering, to very many. Let it be, also, the hour of self-denial, and liberality, and flaming enthusiasm, for Christ and His Church.

She is the Church for the future. We believe it. God is teaching it. His hand is writing it in letters of fire and blood, since otherwise we have refused to learn it. The little one will become a thousand. Give her honor then as the Bride of Christ, the mother of human souls; maintain her independence; keep firm her unity; sustain her institutions.

These are God's lessons of the hour for us.

And when did ever any hour teach, with such sad emphasis, the lesson of religious consolation, and the power of holy Hope?

When our blessed Lord as on this day ascended; and His bereaved followers gazed after Him with aching hearts, and no doubt with weeping eyes, God sent His angel to comfort them, with the assurance that as He had gone, so should He one day come again. And so, as one by one, our loved ones, the young, the noble, and the brave, are lost to sight — as they are swept from us in this fearful war — it is God's lesson of faith to us, with respect to many of them, that when Christ comes again, "them that sleep in Jesus, will God bring with Him.

As in a just cause, the Christian may find his Master's work upon the field of battle; so in an honorable death there, he may find the gate to Paradise. Beyond this life there bursts a brighter one upon the vision of the dying Christian soldier. In that brighter world, he will meet his blessed Master, Who as on this day took up His journey thither; that going on before, He might prepare a place for him, and welcome to his Father's house of many mansions, each faithful soul, as it might be released from the confinement of the flesh.

And now, in our hour of mourning for a great Captain, whom God had invested with qualities which had won him a nation's love and reverence, and whom in the hour of victory, he has taken from us, perhaps because we trusted too much in him and too little in God — what a comfort, to know that he died in faith! How it lightens the grief which weighs our hearts, and makes us feel that we would rather have lost a battle-field than to have lost him; how it lightens that grief, to regard him as but gone on to glory.

And when the day comes at last, for us to join that bright assembly round the Throne, how trivial will seem all earthly trials. Loss of property — hardships — defeats even — subjugation itself — their horrors will all fade out, on that day when in the blaze of Heaven, all earthly interests will pale away. Let us do our duty here and now, as citizens, as soldiers, as churchmen.

Let us strive to learn the Lessons of the Hour, and put them into practice. So may we hope to make part of that glorious triumphal procession, one day to follow the footsteps of our ascended Lord. Let us set our affections on things above, that, "when Christ our Life shall appear, we may also appear with Him in glory."

Notes:

[1] There can be no better exponent of the Northern Episcopal Church, than its General Convention, held at New York in October, 1862. In Art. VI. of the January No. of the Christian Remembrancer — an English Quarterly of high rank, published at London — there is a review of the proceedings of the Convention, from which I extract the following statements:

The opening services were marked by a sermon by Bp. McCoskry, of Michigan, containing an earnest appeal against meddling with secular politics.

In the House of Clerical and Lay Delegates: —

After "shelving" various resolutions condemnatory of the South, the whole subject was committed to a Committee of 9, who introduced a report, expressing a "deep sense of the wrong inflicted by the rebellion;" but recommending abstinence from terms of condemnation or reproach.

This document, says the Remembrancer, was about as decided a rebuke to the spirit of the Lincoln Government, as was Mr. Seymour's subsequent election.

When Judge Hoffman, of New York, introduced resolutions more strongly condemnatory, they were voted down by 14 Dioceses to 7 among the Clergy, and by 14 to 2 among the Laity. On the other hand, when Dr. Mason, of Maryland, moved to lay the whole subject upon the table, he was defeated by only 11 to 9 Dioceses among the Clergy, and 10 to 7 among the Laity — the Clergy of N. Y., Western N. Y., and N. J., and the Laity of N. J., sustaining him.

The Clergy of California, Kentucky, Maryland, Minnesota, New Jersey, Vermont, and Western New York; and the Laity of Illinois, Kentucky, Maryland, New Jersey, and Vermont, sustained a resolution by Rev. Mr. McAlister, of California, against all political pronunciamentos.

In the House of Bishops: —

An address to Mr. Lincoln, moved by Bp. Potter, of Pennsylvania, was voted down.

The pastoral letter was first prepared by Bp. Hopkins, of Vermont, as Chairman of the Committee. It avoided denunciations of the South, and was at first adopted by the whole Committee. Afterwards, Bishop McIllvaine, of Ohio, introduced one of his own, which, after considerable maneuvering, was adopted instead of the first. At its reading to the Church, however, it was observed, that the seat of Bp. Hopkins, the presiding Bishop, was vacant.

The Remembrancer thus sums up its notice of the Convention: "Bating the "Episcopal laches, the Convention very unmistakably, refused to lend itself to "the war-at-all-price party. Abolitionism was ignored, even to a fault. If we take into account the large and weighty minority of the lower house, who voted against any resolutions (condemnatory) we are led to the conclusion, that with all its vacillation of conduct, the representative Church of the Northern and border States, is, so far as the Presbyters and Laity go, on the side of peace, though the misfortunes of the time, and their own want of firm standing ground, have driven them to clothe their feelings in the language of the Northern Democratic "platform. Is it past hoping, that in the march of public opinion, the Church, "recovering more of self-respect and self-confidence than it now shows itself mistress of, will be an influential agency towards that inevitable and blessed result, "the recognition of the Southern Confederacy."

[2] Thus it will be found that the Roman Catholics, the Episcopalians, and the Old School Presbyterians, have been more free from the Abolition

taint; while from the New School Presbyterians down, it has prevailed more and more widely and fatally.

[3] The number of the Christian Remembrancer which I have quoted in my first note, remarks upon "that marked aversion to the (Episcopal) Church, which has "made the Lincoln Government seize on all the Episcopal Churches in Washington "for hospitals, while there were other buildings as commodious standing empty "by."

A SERMON DELIVERED

On the Day of Prayer

Recommended by

the President of the C. S. of A.

the 27th of March, 1863,

AT THE

GERMAN HEBREW SYNAGOGUE

"BAYTH AHABAH"

BY THE

Rabbi M. J. MICHELBACHER.

RICHMOND:

1863

SERMON

Nehemiah 3:33, to 5:13, inclusive

BRETHREN OF THE HOUSE OF ISRAEL: It is due to you, to whom I always speak of your faults, without fear, favor or affection, to say, I have carefully investigated your conduct from the commencement of this war to the present time, and I am happy in coming to the unbiased conclusion, that you have fulfilled your duties as good citizens and as men, who love their country.

It has been charged by both the ignorant and the evil-disposed against the people of our faith, that the Israelite does not fight in the battles of his country! All history attests the untruthfulness of this ungracious charge, generated in the cowardly hearts and born between the hypocritical lips of ungenerous and prejudiced foes. The Israelite has never failed to defend the soil of his birth, or the land of his adoption — the Emperors of France and Russia will bear evidence to the verity of this assertion.

In respect to those Israelites who are now in the army of THE CONFEDERATE STATES, I will merely say, that their patriotism and valor have never been doubted by such men as have the magnanimous souls of Lee, Johnston, Jackson and others of like manhood. The recorded votes and acts of the Israelites of this Confederacy, amply prove their devotion to the support of its Government. They well understand their duties as citizens and soldiers, and the young men do not require the persuasion of conscription to convert them into soldiers, to defend, as they verily believe, the only free government in North America.

Many of our young men have been crippled for life, or slain upon the field of battle, in the service of THE CONFEDERATE STATES, and there are several thousands yet coursing the campaigns of war against those enemies of our Confederacy, who are as detestable to them, as were the Philistines to David and his countrymen.

The humanity and providence of the Israelite for the distressed families of the soldiers of our army, have allayed the pangs of poverty and brought comfort to households, wherein before were only seen hopelessness and misery. In this you have performed your duties as Israelites and as citizens — and, for this, may the God of our fathers shower upon you all the blessings which He confers upon His favorite children!

There is another cry heard, and it was even repeated in the Halls of Congress, that the Israelite is oppressing the people — that he is engaged in the great sin of speculating and extorting in the bread and meat of the land. To discover the character of this accusation, I have made due inquiry — the information I have acquired upon this head, from sources that extend from the Potomac to the Rio Grande, plainly present the fact, that the Israelites are not speculators nor extortioners.

As traders and as merchants, they buy merchandise and sell the same immediately; the merchandise is never put aside, or hoarded to enhance its value, by withdrawing it from the market.

Flour, meal, wheat, corn, bacon, beef, coal and wood are hardly ever found in the mercantile magazines or storehouses of the Israelite — he buys some of these articles for his own consumption, but he buys none of them to sell again — he does not extort — it is obvious to the most obtuse mind that the high prices of the Israelite would drive all his customers into the stores of his Christian neighbors; but is such the effect of the price of the Israelite's goods?

The peculiar characteristic of the Jewish merchant is seen in his undelayed, rapid and instant sales; his temperament does not allow him, by hoarding his goods, to risk time with his money, which, with him, is as restless as the waves of the sea that bears the ships that convey the manufactured goods of his customers.

I thank God, that my investigation has proved to me that the cry against the Jew is a false one — this cry, though cunningly devised after the most approved model of villainy, will not subserve the base and unjust purpose of hindering the virtuous indignation of a suffering people, from tracing the true path of the extortioner, and awarding to him who deals in the miseries, life and blood of our fellow-citizens, that punishment, which the traitor to the happiness and liberties of his country deserves to have measured unto him.

That you may never waver in the strict and cheerful performance of your duties as citizens, listen attentively to the words of God, and may you profit and improve by their instruction! Amen.

"And I looked, and rose up, and said unto the nobles, and to the rulers, and to the rest of the people, Be not afraid of them: think on the Lord, the great and terrible, and fight for your brethren, your sons, and your daughters, your wives and your houses." (Nehemiah 4:8.)

BRETHREN AND FELLOW CITIZENS:

The duties of the citizen are so intimately associated with the services he owes to God; his creator and master, that the patriotism which is comprised in the former, must necessarily depend in its expression upon our hearty and faithful obedience to the commands of Him, who hath taught us the ways of Righteousness in the paramount institutes of Moses and the prophets — who, hath furthermore, impressed upon His people, for the conservation of their happiness and prosperity, a constant recollection of the Divine Code with an humble compliance with all its requisitions.

Patriotism has in all ages been the chief theme of the historian and the poet, and we need not turn to the partial pages of profane history, nor go beyond the general chronicles of our own people, in the times of their obedience to the voice of God, for noble examples of self-sacrifice and that pious sentiment, with which they were inspired by the Almighty through the Captains of old, who set their squadrons in the field under the light of the Divinity.

The undaunted Nehemiah, in calling upon the Jews, to defend the unstopped breaches of the walls of Jerusalem against Sanballat and Tobiah, and the Arabians and

Ammonites and the Ashdodites, said unto the nobles and to the rulers, and to the rest of the people, "Be not afraid of them: think on the Lord, the great and terrible, and fight for your brethren, your sons, and your daughters, your wives and your houses."

These are diamond words, brilliant with the love of country, and pointing with heavenly rays of truth to the Great and terrible Lord of the universe as the friend and protector of him, who defends, against a public enemy, his home and his family.

The inspiriting words, "Be not afraid of them," gave vigor to every arm and courage to every heart. The admonition, "think on the Lord, the great and terrible," recalled the ancient faith of Israel, when nature obeyed the voice of Moses, and the sea divided itself to save, the retreating multitude and peacefully stood on either side, to give free passage to the chosen people, and came down again with lashing and furious waves upon Pharaoh and his hosts as they adventured in, to defile its bed with the feet of the wicked and the enemies of God.

They recollected the ancient faith of the wandering Israel in the desert, when the people were parched by thirst, and "the Moses of the Lord" smote the rock, which sent forth living streams at his command. It was then they remembered the Lord with increased faith, as retrospection brought, in sublime array, the gracious deeds He had executed aforetime, for the salvation of their fathers, and their souls were animated with heroic daring and invincible determination at the eloquent and heart-stirring appeal of Nehemiah to their manhood, as he stood before them, and, pointing to Heaven in the character of the servant of God, the loyal citizen and patriot exclaimed: "fight for your brethren, your sons, and your daughters, your wives, and your houses!"

It was on this momentous and perilous occasion, he solemnly reminded them of the *first duty of the citizen in connection with the first duty of man* as the obedient servant of the most High God. The people were not only taught the divine duty of defending their country in battle, with the death-dealing weapons of war, but they were, through

Nehemiah, also commanded to set a watch upon the walls of the city, during the day and night, with the implements of *building and fortifying in the one hand, and the instrument of defense in the other.* "And the builders, had every one his sword fastened around his loins, while they were building. And he that blew the trumpet stood along side of me."

While the Judean patriots were thus progressing in strengthening the defenses, the insidious Sanballat with Geshen sent four times to Nehemiah to meet him, but unavailing were the invitations; and the fifth time, he sent by his servant an open letter to terrify and to cause him to take counsel with his enemy; yet was Nehemiah stern, resolved and unyielding, and to the contents of the letter, made fearlessly an instant declaration of their falsehood in the words: "There had been done nothing like these reports of which thou speakest; but thou inventest them out of thine own heart." (Neh. vi. 8.)

And, thus he continued his course in building and repairing, with the assistance of his countrymen, till through his wise administration, clear foresight and courageous conduct, his enemies went from before him, and departed in fear and trembling. In this wise, he and his compatriots faithfully performed the first and transcendent duty of the citizen; and the Lord was with them.

From this brief, but beautiful and instructive scriptural history, may our fellow-citizens and the Government of THE CONFEDERATE STATES OF AMERICA take lessons of profit, and heed the reserved conduct of Nehemiah towards those, who were hostile to him, when they sent messengers and an open letter to deceive and betray! Let it not be, that we take counsel with our enemies, or any portion of them, in the critical period of their warfare against us; and, above all, let us keep our watchmen upon the walls during any term of cessation of arms, as well as in active hostilities!

Our business and our duty are to deal in the rugged matters and measures of the latter, till the offenders, who desecrate our soil and pollute our atmosphere, depart from our country in fear and trembling — this is all we require as an independent people, and it is what we will accomplish; if so be, we retain the blessing of the Great Creator by our humility and righteousness before Him, with the spear in the one hand, and the implement of industry in the other — *so help us God!!*

Our enemies may have their intestine feuds — civil war may rage among them — and they may fiercely quarrel among themselves, they may lament the loss of their own liberty, sacrificed to fanaticism, cupidity and ambition in the attempt to enslave us, and may point to us as the cause of the maledictions of offended Heaven against them, and they may even seek our aid in the hour of their calamity, which will surely overtake and crush a wicked people; yet, let us not be deceived and entrapped by the specious words, nor the open letters of a people and government of cunning and treachery!

They may even throw out as a bait, the hint of serious divisions in the North and Northwest, to lull our manly fears and to allure us into a policy, dangerous, if not destructive to the liberties and independence of THE CONFEDERATE STATES. If there be incidental advantages accruing to us, from pretended differences and divisions in the condition of their political or military affairs, it will be well for us to be lookers-on, with sword in hand, ready at all times, for every emergency — we can afford to look on with keen watchfulness and unabated activity and vigor; but we shall not, we must not touch the accursed thing arising from the pollution of Northern necessities, nor permit it to be brought into our camp — and, if we must reply, let it be in the words of Nehemiah: "There had been done nothing like these reports of which thou speakest; but thou inventest them out of thine own heart."

We have fought, and are now fighting, by reason of a virtuous resolution to live apart from those, who for many years marred our peace and increased our anxiety for the preservation of our institutions and our safety, and, who down to the moment of our separation, derided our solemn protests against their repeated violations of our sovereign rights, and have converted a Federal government into a central one, for the purpose of founding a despotism, that we may the more speedily receive the lash of a tyrant.

Solemnly, have we appealed to God to examine our hearts for the honesty of our intentions; hence, it is no light thing with the sole Creator of the Universe and Supreme Director of our destiny, that we halt for one moment in pursuing that course we have chosen before Him, and for which, at sundry times, our people and our President have implored His guidance and blessing — *and may His guidance and blessing lead us unto the desired attainment of liberty, independence, happiness and prosperity!*

Surely, it is no light thing, if we now exhibit before God our friend, the want of any trait that belongs to the perfect character of the defender of one's country. The mission of the patriotic citizen, is a great one — with a broad patent in legible characters, all may know him to be a servant of the Lord, and a soldier of the people, whether he belongs to the council or the camp.

May we not reverently conceive, that the Almighty, in listening to our prayers, has in the High Courts of Heaven graciously ratified our choice? the wonderful victories of our arms in answer to our petitions, impress us in our faith therein with this belief — and, if this be so, let him beware, who is slow to perform the first duty of the citizen!

Shall we then trifle with the Great God of Israel, and offend His terrible Majesty, by entertaining alien messengers, whatever the Import of their character, or receiving open letters, written in deceit and falsehood by a treacherous foe? shall we be so weak and credulous, as to trust for our salvation in the false reports and varied rumors adapted to peculiar occasions, and invented for the covert purposes of our circumvention and ruin!

Ah, my God, let us not put from us our confidence in Thee, nor forget the wonderful manifestations of Thy power in our behalf within the last twelve months! Thou only art our Saviour and Redeemer, and Thou hast graciously assisted us in building the high wall of separation; and, even now, Thou dost call upon the people of the South in the words

Thou gavest to Nehemiah: "Fight for your brethren, your sons, and your daughters, your wives and your houses!"

Who will dare turn a deaf ear to this Heavenly command, to perform the most eminent work pertaining to the duties of the citizen, while every soul should be clad in the panoply of war, to take just vengeance in the name of the Lord, upon His enemies and Ours, for the manifold wrongs they commit against His laws, His justice, and His mercy, in the pretended name of truth, by cruel imprisonments, and unprecedented deeds of rapine, arson and murder! These things cry unto Heaven for retribution, and "vengeance is mine," saith the Lord.

Arise then, all ye people of the South, doubly armed with your trust in God, and the remembrance of your sufferings, and the wrongs done unto you, "your brethren, your sons and your daughters, your wives and your houses," and let the shout of your confidence in God go forth to the discomfiture of the enemy, while the thunder of your guns, the flash of your swords, and the gleam of your bayonets, shall give the seal of the blood of the invaders, as a witness unto the Lord of hosts, that we, who have trusted in Him, have signalized the vengeance which is His, and performed the first duty of the citizen, in obedience to His mandates through Nehemiah, in calling upon the name of the most High in the spirit of piety, and, "fought for our brethren, our sons, and our daughters, our wives and our houses."

But is the physical defense of one's country against invasion, the only duty required of the citizen in the period of war? In what terms shall we condemn them, that have taken advantage of the necessities of the times, to reduce the poor to a condition so deep in poverty, that on the coming of every morrow, the gloom of troublous anticipations thickens with the approach of the fearful period when in the words of Jeremiah, it shall be said in bitterness:

"Happier are those slain by the sword, than those slain by hunger; for those poured forth their blood, being pierced through — these perished without the fruits of the field."

We already hear a great cry of the people and of their wives against their brethren, who have speculated in the blood of the living, and whose song of joy, in the amassment of wealth, is heard above the fury and horrors of war, the groans of the dying, the screams of the wounded in the battle fields, upon which our gallant soldiers are offering their lives in defense of our brethren, our sons, and our daughters, our wives, and our houses!

What answer shall we make to the noble defenders of the country, when they, garlanded with the victories of a hundred fields, return and behold the wan features of their brethren, their sons and their daughters, and their wives — and their houses, no longer the abodes of plenty and cheerfulness! well may they, in surprise at the ingratitude and atrocity of their countrymen, exclaim: "Happier are those slain by the sword, than those slain by hunger; for those poured forth their blood, being pierced through — these perished without the fruits of the field!"

Will it come to that pass, that they too shall be compelled "to mortgage their lands, vineyards and houses that they may buy corn," and against which the Jews complained in the presence of Nehemiah, as a great evil, inflicted upon them by their brethren? The generous heart and noble spirit of Nehemiah became inflamed with a just anger, when the great cry of the people and of their wives against their brethren, the Jews, came up before him; and, he thus describes his feelings and conduct upon that occasion:

"And it displeased me greatly when I heard their complaint in these words. Then I consulted with my heart, and I upbraided the nobles, and the rulers, and said unto them: Ye exact usury, every one of his brother. And I brought together a great assembly against them."

And in the concluding part of his address, we are affected with admiration at the justice he meted to every man, who had wronged his neighbor and sinned against God. His remarkable words are well adapted to the present times and events — *O may they be borne by some gracious breeze of Heaven to every village, town and city of our Confederacy!* — let it then be known to all the people of the land, that Nehemiah, the servant of God, said in the settlement of this question before him and the great assembly, which he set against them,

"Give back to them, I pray you, even this day, their fields, their vineyards, their olive yards, and their houses, also, the hundreth part of the money, and of the corn, the wine, and the oil, that ye have lent them. Then said they, We will give back and we will require nothing of them; so will we do as thou sayest.

Then I called the priests and made them swear, that they should do according to this promise. Also I shook my lap, and said, so may God shake out every man from his house, and of his toil gotten wealth, that performeth not this promise, and so let him remain shaken out, and empty. And all the congregation said, Amen, and praised the Lord. And the people did according to this promise."

These events occurred when Sanballat and others, enemies of the Jews, conspired to come and to fight against Jerusalem, and to hinder the building of the wall; yet did not Nehemiah neglect the civil affairs of his country in the midst of a war, that threatened the enslavement of his people with the destruction of the capital city of Judea; but with the steady character of a great chief, that trusts in the Lord, he introduced reformations, which at once remedied the defects, exhibited in the disposition of the people and restored to them that moral feeling, whose basis is religion.

They became regenerated under his potent and pious sway, and the citizen and soldier adorned with their virtues both, the camp and the path of civil life. The people repented and made restitution; and, the dark cloud that hung with evil portent over Judea's plains, passed away before the sun of righteousness.

Usury and practices of a kindred nature fled from the searching eye of Nehemiah. The man, who had inspired his people with the heroism, to defend unto death their brethren, their sons, and their daughters, their wives and their houses, could not patiently observe the oppression of the poor, nor the extorted wealth of the rich; and with a strong hand, supported by the people, rescued them and his country from the most corrupting vice, that can deform the moral constitution of a nation.

He saw the beginning of that *divided sympathy* among the people, which is the forerunner of national degradation with the loss of liberty; and, in the midst of the Great Assembly, he denounced the usurer and the despoiler of the poor, and sealed his righteous denunciation with a curse: "Also my lap did I shake out and said, So God shake out every man from his house, and from his toil-gotten wealth that performeth not this promise, and so let him remain shaken out and empty. And all the Assembly said, Amen, and praised the Lord. And the people did according to this promise."

The extortions practiced throughout the length and breadth of THE CONFEDERATE STATES, and which appear to have superseded honest trade, to ride upon the back of speculation for the purpose of hunting *"the dear life"* wherever an article of food, fuel and raiment may be found, has already given rise to a fearful cry of the people, who are patriotically assisting to build the wall of separation between the South and the treacherous North.

They justly consider that these heartless demons, whom we call speculators and extortioners, are giving aid and comfort to the enemy; and, there are not a few who believe, these men would in no wise assist in subduing the conflagration of a city, because, even in such a calamity, they would seek food for speculation in the ruin of its inhabitants, and, at some brief future day, extort from their wants, the wreck of property saved from the flames!

Will the speculator and extortioner heed the cry of the people and their wives for bread and other provisions, necessary to the sustenance of life? Will they listen attentively to instruction and humbly receive rebukes before the Great Assembly, and swear to give back ill-gotten gains, as did the Jews under the inspired counsel of Nehemiah?

Will they retrace their steps from the road of wickedness towards that path to which Nehemiah directed his countrymen, and in which only can they ever hope to regain the lost character of the virtuous citizen and patriot — the only path that can direct them aright, because it is the path of righteousness!

Come up to the bar of Justice and of God, ye vile citizens of a country, ye have caused to bleed at every pore — ye, who are ever ready to plunge the traitor's dagger with stealthy hand into the bosom of your mother in the moment of her most critical danger! *Desist from the sins* charged against you this day — desist from the sin of oppression over the people and the sin of disobedience against the terrible God of Israel, and — *repent, and give back, or, "ye shall be shaken out, every man from his house, and from his toil-gotten wealth and be empty."*

It is not true that you have been compelled to oppress the people, by reason of the peculiar difficulties of your own situation, in respect to your families. It is, because you have the power, or are permitted by the silence of the municipal and civil law and the public authorities, to retain, or, remit under usurious contracts; and, you, yourselves, have generated the circumstances to bring forth your own extortion — the monstrous and evil thing that draws its nourishment from the heart's blood of men, women and children!

And, it is also, because you have strengthened your power, by sweeping the circuit of many districts of our country, and, have thereby come into possession of those things, that God intended for the common benefit. You have seized and engrossed the meat and flour of the poor — and, while these starve, you complacently look forward to the crisis of famine, with your warehouses filled with the life-giving food, which, by right of nature and nature's God, belongs alike to all, under the wise restriction of just compensation! You purchase the rich offerings of the generous Earth — and await famine and high prices! *If this be so, O God, "let them be shaken out, every man from his house and from his toil-gotten wealth and be empty!"*

I thank God, that this curse comes not within the circle, or reach of my congregation, and, that its members have kept their skirts clean, and have not committed this great crime against man and Heaven. Continue thus, O my brethren, to fulfill your duties, and turn not away in their performance, to stain your hands with that sinful gain that cometh from extortion.

It is the duty of the Great Assembly of the people to set their face against this iniquity, and it becomes us on this occasion to pray, that we may not be tempted to commit a sin so heinous before the God of Israel.

It is the duty of the people to satisfy the Lord that their hearts are against this sin, that the skirts of the nation may be cleansed from the curse that He will measure unto the unrepentant individually — that punishment justly due to the enemy of God and man — that punishment justly due to those who refuse to perform one of the first duties of the citizen by reformation and restitution, with a solemn promise before God, the author of all good, to do this evil thing no more!

Let the skirts of the people be cleansed by prayer and humiliation, that the Almighty may continue to protect and bless the Confederate States of America, and that He may presently and with great haste drive far away from our land the Northern armies that now disturb its tranquility. Let our land, O Lord, be dedicated to Thee and Thy service only; and may the holy name of the God of Israel be forever among us! Amen.

PRAYER

Again, do we approach Thee, O God of Israel — not as a single meeting of a part, but as the whole congregation of all the people of the land, that trust in Thy protection forever, and who do now come before Thee, to seek it in the midst of dangers, yet *more* appalling than those of the past, that Thou didst put aside without harm unto us!

We are Thy people, O God! who, whether in times of want or pestilence, distress or danger, cannot be kept back from coming unto Thee.

Thou only art our father and friend, and we come before Thee in the dutifulness of children, and with abiding faith in Thy love and a constant fear of doing aught to offend Thee.

O God of our fathers! God of Abraham, Isaac and Jacob! hear our prayers, and listen graciously to our supplications, this day, for our salvation as a people, struggling before Thee for our liberties and independence, now threatened with renewed dangers and calamities, from the combining and concentrating powers of our enemies.

Thou hast, O God, in Thy mercy unto us, foiled from good time to good time their efforts, to circumvent and to subdue and to subjugate Thy people, that trust in Thy mercy and omnipotence! Now, O God, we who trust in Thee, beseech Thee to look into our present condition. Then dost see, O Supreme Giver of Good, the red and savage hand of massacre held with the menace of foreboding evil, over the innocent and nursing infants of our people!

Thou doest see, O Supreme Giver of Good, that we are threatened with the destruction of our men, women and children by cruel enemies, that laugh and clap their hands at the calamities, they desire to bring upon us, whereby they may outrage and scoff at Thy Super-Excellent Majesty, and say within their hearts that vengeance is theirs and not Thine! O God of Israel! hearest Thou this, and art Thou still or silent?

No! Thou, God of our fathers, that art a jealous God, Thou art not silent, nor unmindful of our terrible straights, and, neither wilt Thou permit this wicked intent — neither wilt Thou let come to pass this atrocious thing of blood and crime against Thy people, that this day, in the presence of all the nations of the Earth, proclaim Thee as the only true God, and Saviour!

The man-servants and the maid-servants Thou hast given unto us, that we may be merciful to them in righteousness and bear rule over them, the enemy are attempting to seduce, that they too may turn against us, whom Thou hast appointed over them as instructors in Thy wise dispensation!

Because of Thy strength in aid of us, our enemies have failed against us, in all the modes and means of warfare known and adopted among the men Thou hast civilized — *because of Thy strength* they have failed; and, behold, O God, they incite our man-servants and maid-servants to insurrection, and they place weapons of death and the fire of desolation in their hands, that we may become an easy prey unto them; they beguile them from the path of duty, that they may waylay their masters, to assassinate and to slay the men, women and children of the people, that trust only in Thee. In this wicked thought, let them be frustrated, and cause them to fall into the pit of destruction, which in the abomination of their evil intents, they digged for us, our brothers and sisters, our wives and our children.

Our land and our waters are troubled with the presence of the foes of Thy people. Drive them away, O Lord! Let it be, that their boasted ships of terror may come to naught before the breath of our Lord God, as He sendeth it forth upon the waters of the Great Deep.

Bless, O God, the tillage of our fields, that they may bring forth abundantly for the wants of the people! Give unto each one the bread of life, and let the fat of the land be seen in plenty in the home of every family of the Confederate States of America.

O God! We acknowledge our manifold sins, but look to Thee for forgiveness with deep contrition and repentance.

We implore Thee to turn the hearts of the people of THE CONFEDERATE STATES OF AMERICA generously and kindly every one to the other, that, in the midst of common tribulation, they may cheer and sustain each other till they shall have safely passed through the troublous flood of war, to the happiness of a peaceful land, regenerated by Thy favored presence forever and ever!

O God! we invoke Thy holy name for protection, because we know, that, without the aid of our kind Father in Heaven, we of ourselves can do nothing.

We believe, O God, that piety cannot subsist apart from patriotism — we love our country, because Thou hast given it unto us as a blessing and a heritage for our children; and, now, O God, we call upon Thee, to bring salvation to THE CONFEDERATE STATES OF AMERICA, and to crown independence with lasting honor and prosperity.

O God! Give cheerfulness to the hearts of our people; and, as a sign of our confidence in Thee and Thy especial protection over us, let the play of the children be seen in the streets of our cities, towns and villages and all places of our country. Let no fear come near our maidens, and be Thou unto our young men a tower of strength, that they may stand with undaunted hearts to shield and sustain the matrons and patriarchs of the people!

Drive, O God, the fear of black famine far away from our borders, and open the Omnipotent hand of Thy Heavenly bounty upon all these — the people of this Thy land, which we dedicate anew to Thee this day. And, O God, keep in remembrance this day forever!

Be Thou, O God, with our armies, and inspire the leaders thereof with a pious fear of Thee. Endow them with the faculty of anticipating the designs of the enemy and the wisdom, to thwart every movement of hostility!

Inspire our soldiers with that patriotic courage, which comes from the thought of duty to Thee and to their country. Give unto them, sleepless vigilance, vigorous and active bodies and hands, to wield in victory the weapons of battle. Give unto them, when in pursuit of the flying foe, the swiftness of the eagle, and in the fight, let them be as fierce lions among the prey!

Send, O God, Thy protecting messengers to our ships of war upon the waters of the rivers and of the great deep! Shield our infant navy from all the dangers of storm and battle; and, in all its engagements with the enemy, let the power of the wonderful arm of the God of Israel be its succor, defense and victory! Let the boast of the enemy's naval superiority in numbers over us, be unto Thee, O Lord, their weakness and destruction. And give unto us, Thy people that trust in Thee, O God of Israel, the crown of triumph!

O God! Give counsel and wisdom to Thy servant, JEFFERSON DAVIS, PRESIDENT OF THE CONFEDERATE STATES of America, and grant speedy success to his endeavors to free our country from the presence of its foes.

Be Thou with him and the legislature of the CONFEDERATE GOVERNMENT OF AMERICA, and give unto them Thy care and blessing.

Send us peace, O Lord God, we humbly implore Thee! and let the buds, that spring forth in this present spring of the year, burst out in smiling blossoms over a land of tranquility and prosperity! Amen! Hallooyah!

True Eminence Founded on Holiness

A DISCOURSE

OCCASIONED BY THE DEATH OF

LIEUT. GEN. T. J. JACKSON

PREACHED IN THE

First Presbyterian Church of Lynchburg

MAY 24th, 1863

BY

REV. JAMES B. RAMSEY

1863

True Eminence Founded on Holiness

"I will set him on high, because he hath known my name." PSALMS 91:14.

"How are the mighty fallen in the midst of the battle! O, Jonathan! thou wast slain in thy high places." Such was the lament of David and Israel over the brave and generous Jonathan, slain in the high places of the field, in defense of his country and people, against their hereditary foes: and such is now a nation's lament over a greater than Jonathan the son of Saul.

With a stricken heart, and bitter tears, this whole people bow in grief, and as one man, are ready to utter the touching words of David over his friend: "We are distressed for thee: very pleasant hast thou been unto us: thy love to us was wonderful, passing the love of women. How are the mighty fallen, and the weapons of war perished!"

Our beloved JACKSON was slain emphatically in his high places; in the high places of his God's and his country's service, in the very zenith of his fame and usefulness. Few men in our world have ever attained to greater eminence: none to purer. The nation accorded to him its entire confidence; it rung with his praise, and its whole heart thrilled with true affection for him.

Our enemies at once feared and honored him. His praise is heard in distant lands. Envy had to gnash her teeth in silence, for in the universal enthusiasm, she dared not speak. The Church of Christ praised God continually for such a burning and a shining light, and multitudes of souls, especially in our army, high officers and privates, will rejoice eternally in that light.

This eminence was not the result of brilliant and towering genius, or of a chance combination of favorable circumstances. His whole history shows a combination of circumstances against it, such as is not often overcome. Success was in his case extorted, compelled from unwilling and adverse events, and in spite of difficulties that at first sight might have been regarded as insuperable.

A brief sketch of his life will show this, and will best prepare the way for the important truth wrapped up in all that life, and blazing forth in all his character, that it was God who made him great, by making him holy.

Lieut. Gen. THOMAS J. JACKSON was born in Clarksburg, Harrison county, Virginia, in January, 1824.[2] His ancestors were from England. Some military taste and talent appears to have been inherent in the family. His own father was a successful lawyer, and at one time, a man of considerable property, but by suretyship for others lost it all, and died leaving three children only, one of whom, a daughter, is now living.

THOMAS, at his father's death, was only three years old. About six years after, his mother died in the triumphs of Christian faith and hope. Her memory was always very precious. Do we not see here the first of that chain of influences that made him what he was? Who can ever tell the power of that mother's example and prayers?

Thus, bereft of his father and his mother, the Lord took him up. He found homes among his relatives; especially his uncles. His early education was irregular, and necessarily imperfect, until he entered the West Point Military Academy. There he manifested the same traits of quiet indomitable perseverance and singleness of purpose that afterwards so distinguished him, and that then went very far to make up for his very imperfect preparation.

From the Academy he at once entered the service of his country in the Mexican war. By his promptitude, bravery and coolness, he there highly distinguished himself. It was during this campaign, or while quartered in the halls of the Montezumas — as we are assured he literally was — that he first seems to have become impressed with a sense of the

---

[2] For most of the interesting facts in this sketch I am indebted to a connection of his, a valued friend, who for years was in daily and familiar intercourse with him.

importance of personal religion, partly, at least, through intercourse with the pious Colonel of his battalion.

With the same prompt energy, and thoroughness, and zeal, that he always manifested in whatever he regarded as present duty, he resolved to examine the whole subject of religion in its personal claims, and its system of truth.

Being satisfied that the Bible was from God, the great question was, where and by whom, was its truth most fully and purely held?

Determined to take nothing for granted, or at second hand, he at once availed himself of what seemed to him the rare opportunity there afforded of examining the Roman Catholic religion, by waiting on the Archbishop of Mexico, with whom he had frequent interviews, extending through some months, I think, during which he was taken in order over the main parts of their whole system, and propounded his own difficulties.

These last could not be resolved to his satisfaction, and the result was a firm conviction that this, at least, was not the Bible system. With the same impartial zeal and love of truth, and disregard to mere human authority, did he pursue this search for some years before his mind became satisfied.

Gen. JACKSON was therefore the farthest possible remove from being a bigot. His views of each denomination were obtained from itself, not from its opponents. Hence he could see excellencies in each.

Even of Popery he had a much more favorable impression than most Protestants, and it would be well for the Church of Christ, and would greatly tend to promote fraternal feeling and kill bigotry, if we would all, in our search for truth, gather our views of others, not from their opponents alone, but from the best and wisest of themselves, as JACKSON did.

After his return from Mexico, and being quartered for a time in South Carolina, Florida, and New York, his health became so shattered as to nearly unfit him for any active duty. It was at this time, and while endeavoring to regain his health, that he was elected to the Professorship of Applied Mathematics in the Virginia Military Institute. In his very entrance on that work with very feeble health, and eyes that totally forbade his using them at all by night, he exhibited that same quiet energy of will and mental discipline that afterward contributed so greatly to his success in the field.

Running rapidly over many pages of mathematical reasonings before night, he would, as we learn from members of the family who knew his habits well, after dark, without book or help, holding the complicated materials before his mind, examine, analyze and thoroughly master the demonstrations.

There he first entered into full connection with the church. From that time, the harmony and force of his character became still more apparent. With him, to know his duty and to do it, were the same thing. Humble and *retiring* almost to a fault, he would never shrink from any duty, whatever sacrifice of feeling it might cost him. A striking instance of this I had from his own lips, when speaking of the trial it cost him to speak before an audience.

Being on a visit to his sister, where were residing a number of professed infidels, and where there was but little religious influence, the thought occurred to him that, being a military man, they might be willing to listen to something from him, more favorably than from others, though it might be much inferior. And he at once resolved to prepare and deliver a few lectures on the evidences of Christianity, which. he did; though the delivery, he said, was one of the greatest trials he ever had.

Where, among a thousand, is there another of like temperament who would not, at once, have excused himself from such an obligation? He formed a class of young men for instruction in the evidences of Christianity; and for years he superintended with great zeal and efficiency a Sabbath school for the instruction of the colored people of Lexington, the beneficial example of which has been widely felt. Liberal to the full extent of his means, God prospered him according to his promise, that "the liberal soul shall be made fat."

When he entered the army at the beginning of the war, he did it in obedience to the call of his God, as well as of his country. Hence, no love of ease, of friends, of home, or domestic joys, could induce one moments relaxation of energy in the single line of his duty. He never, during the two years of his service, left the camp — never saw his home and for thirteen months at a time was separated from his beloved wife.

Of his military life and exploits, this is not the place or the time to speak; the country and the world knows them and they will yet appear, doubtless, in fitting narrative. But his deep interest in the spiritual welfare of his army, deserves here special notice. Who does not know that this was an object for which he labored most assiduously and during the last year, especially with great success? Busy as he was with personal attention to every thing connected with the efficiency of his army, both at rest and in motion, he always found time to attend to this.

He devised and suggested a great comprehensive plan for the organization of the chaplaincy system, which is now being carried into effect with prospects of great success. To his pastor, Dr. White, he wrote a long letter on this subject, which would itself be a most noble portrait of his religious character All his letters showed how full his heart was of this matter, and all seemed to be written from the very precincts of the throne.

In a letter received from him, only about a month before his death, he thus speaks:

"Whilst as Christians we must all have trials, yet we have the precious assurance that they work out for us a far more exceeding and eternal weight of glory. If you had the physical strength, I would be greatly gratified to see you in the army. It appears to me that I have never seen such a field for Christian effort. I am greatly gratified at having Mr. B. T. Lacy with the army. His labors, I trust, will be greatly blessed. So far, great encouragement has attended them. I am much obliged to you for your prayers, and beg that I may still have an interest in them. It is to God that we must look for peace, and for its enjoyment when it is bestowed."

But the following extract from a letter to his pastor, the substance of which the latter read at his funeral, has special interest as showing his moral greatness.

"The death of your noble son[3] and my much esteemed friend, Hugh, must have been a severe blow to you, yet we have the sweet assurance that, whilst we mourn his loss to the country, to the church, and to ourselves, all has been gain to him. 'Eye hath not seen, nor heard, neither have entered into the heart of man the things which God hath prepared for those that love him.' That inconceivable glory to which we are looking forward is already his.

I greatly desire in the army such officers as he was. When in the Valley there was much religious interest among my troops, and I trust that it has not died out. It appears to me that we should look for a great work of grace among our troops, officers and privates, for our army has been made the subject of prayer by all denominations of Christians in the Confederacy.

I am very grateful for your prayers and the prayers of other Christian friends. Continue to pray for me. I wish I could be with you in the church and lecture room, whenever our people meet to worship God.

Let us work and pray that our people may be that nation whose God is the Lord. It is delightful to see the Congressional Committee report so strongly against Sabbath mails. I trust that you will write to every member of Congress with whom you have any influence, and do all you can to procure the adoption of the report. And please request those with whom you correspond (when expedient) to do the same. I believe that God will bless us with success if Christians but do their duty. For near fifteen years Sabbath mails have been through God's blessing avoided by me, and I am thankful to say that in no instance has there been occasion for regret, but on the contrary God has made it a source of pure enjoyment to me."

---

[3] Capt. Hugh A. White, who fell in the second battle of Manassas.

On this subject of Sabbath mails he felt very deeply, as he did on everything affecting the favor or the frown of God upon our country. Just before his last battle, he wrote a long letter on this subject, perhaps the very last he ever penned, to his connection, Col. Preston, who was a commissioner to the General Assembly, requesting him to secure some appropriate action from that body in favor of their abolishment.

His heart seemed thus to be so full of deep interest for the spiritual good of the army, and the advancement of the church's interest, and her enterprises, as if it were the one and the only thing to which his energies were devoted; and yet the country and the world and especially the army know that the minutest military duty or interest was never by him neglected or postponed.

The sad circumstances of his wounding, his sickness and death, are well known and need not here be repeated. A perfect knowledge of all the facts will, we are very sure, remove all suspicion of imprudence or rashness from the movement which led to his wounding, and will show it to have been an event which no human skill or foresight could probably have prevented in the case of one whose fixed principle it was, we believe, to see with his own eyes whatever was necessary to the disposition of his troops in battle, and whose success was doubtless greatly owing to this fact.

You have heard how looking at his stump and wounded hand, he said, "I would not be without these wounds now, even if I could. God has sent them upon me for some good purpose. I regard them as one of the greatest blessings of my life." With what true Christian submission and heroism he received the announcement that he had but a few more hours to live, answering, "Very good, very good, I will be an infinite gainer, to be translated."

When his little child, which had been baptized in the camp only a few weeks before, was brought in — he exclaimed, with all the fullness of a father's heart — *"my darling child!"* and having attempted to amuse it with his crippled hand for a few moments, he commended it to God. His wife asked him, are you perfectly willing that God should do with you just as he pleases? With characteristic simplicity and decision both of language and tone, he replied, "I prefer it, I prefer it."

Such a death was a fitting close to such a life. It was emphatically a translation from the high places of his earthly fame, to the infinitely higher places of heavenly glory. To the church, and the country in this hour of our peril, his loss seems irreparable.

But the God that raised him up, can raise up others in his place, — his resources are not exhausted, — and what is more, can make that life now ended a greater blessing, a mightier power for good than ever before. This will be so if he only makes it a means of impressing on the heart of this whole people the truth, of which it was such a brilliant illustration, — that holiness is power, and it alone secures true eminence.

Our text which is but a statement of this truth, is a concentration of Gen. JACKSON'S whole history. It is his life and his character, his fame and its secret source, all in a single sentence. It declares the secret of his great eminence. God set him on high, because he honored God.

This whole Psalm beautifully and strikingly applies to him. It describes the Divine protection and honor of the man that dwelleth in the secret place of the Most High, that says of the Lord, He is my refuge and my fortress: my God, in him will I trust. It is of him that God here says, "I will set him on high, because he hath known my name."

To *know the name of God* is to recognize his true character, and to love, serve and trust him accordingly. It is but another expression for true godliness or holiness. The text is, therefore, but the declaration of God's purpose to honor those who honor him: "I will set him on high — I will make him safe and great because he hath regarded not his own name and glory, but mine.

Or in the language of the immediate context, — "Because he hath set his love upon me therefore will I deliver him. He shall call upon me, and I will answer him; I will be with him in trouble, I will deliver him and honor him." The same purpose he elsewhere thus expresses. "Them that honor me I will honor, and they that despise me shall be lightly esteemed." "If any man serve me," says Christ, "him will my Father honor."

To this as a general truth some will be disposed to demur, and to say that religion does not always secure eminence; that cases like this are exceptions to the general rule, — that so far from the fear of God elevating men in view of the world it has the opposite, object, inasmuch as men do not love but hate holiness, and religion prevents men from using the means necessary to secure earthly honors; indeed, that it is inconsistent with entering upon the eager strife and contention made necessary by the rivalry they awaken.

Much of this is doubtless true. In the arena where worldly honors are the prize, the man of God may not and will not descend. For him they have no charms. He knows their emptiness. To him they are the veriest baubles. And no man ever held them in more utter contempt than JACKSON did.

These are not the high places to which the man of God aspires, and in which God has here promised to put him. To be elevated to them alone is no *real* eminence. When properly understood there is no exception to the principle of the text that the fear of God alone can raise any man to the highest eminence of which he is capable.

1. To make this clear consider first what true greatness real eminence, is. It is not mere worldly honor, or high place, or great power. To attain these, indeed, needs no religion, they are, when taken apart from moral excellence, the rewards with which the devil has always lured his willing victims to the giddy heights of their own ruin.

As he tempted our Saviour, so he tempts men still; pointing to the kingdoms of the world and the glory of them, he says, "All these will I give thee, if thou wilt fall down and worship me." The devil has his high places, which however similar they may sometimes be in appearance, are as different from the real eminence to which holiness exalts, as darkness is from light, as the height of the gallows is from that of the throne.

The great ones of this world have by their fame and their glory only been pilloried on high to the pitying or contemptuous gaze of all succeeding generations of the wise and good. So it has been with almost all who have filled the thrones of earth, with all indeed except where moral worth has been eminent.

So with a Byron in the loftiest flights of poetic genius; with a Laplace in the sublime researches of the astronomer; with an Alexander and a Napoleon in the highest and widest sweep of military achievements. Men may and they will wonder at their genius, their vast acquirements, their power and deeds of daring, but where is the wise and good man, the enlightened lover of his race, who does not lament over the shameful prostitution of all this talent, learning and power to the purposes of a low and selfish ambition; and regard them as brilliant wrecks strewed all along the shores of time as beacons to future generations?

If mere intellectual superiority or artistic skill, or indomitable energy and vast power could raise its possessor on high, then has the devil attained an eminence that none of the sons of men may hope to reach.

True eminence is inseparable from holiness. In this consists especially the glory of God: without it all his other attributes would be objects of horror and dread just in proportion to their infinite greatness. Although it is true that men hate holiness naturally, when its claims are urged upon their hearts filled with fleshly and worldly lusts, or when it shines so near and so brightly upon them as to disclose their own moral deformity, yet it is also true that God has so created us that we are irresistibly impressed with the feeling of its infinite excellence, and compelled to conscious veneration for it.

Did not the proud and envious Pharisees even when they sought to slay Jesus, feel and shrink in shame from the dazzling brightness of his unspotted holiness? You may gather round your name all the glory that genius, learning, skill, or military prowess can impart, yet if this one grand element of moral excellence be not there pervading and controlling and modifying all the rest, that name will only go down to posterity to carry your shame and disgrace on account of God's perverted gifts.

2. But more than this. True religion has a necessary tendency to produce those qualities that alone can fit men for the highest stations and the noblest deeds. We do not mean to assert here merely that the possession of those dispositions of heart and principles of action that constitute true religion fit a man better to fill any position in life whatever. This none will dare deny.

Truly to fear God must produce an elevation of character, a purity of motive, a superiority to temptation, a sense of accountability, a submission to lawful authority, that cannot but make men better, whether as servants or masters, citizens, soldiers, generals or rulers. But in addition to this it tends to develop to the highest degree those other mental qualities necessary to fill most completely the highest offices and to meet the most responsible trusts.

What greater obstacle is there to the full development of *intellectual power*, vigorous thought, close reasoning, and clear and bold and lofty conception than the workings of pride and passion and appetite, or the distractions or care, or fear, or the influence of conflicting motives, or the want of one great noble end of life? And what influence ever entered a human heart that could so effectually remove all these, and relieve the intellect from every clog, and banish every disturbing element as the fear and love of God?

Again, nothing so warps the *judgment* as passion, impatience, fear and selfishness — and whatever else weakens the intellectual or moral force, and as nothing so completely corrects these as true holiness, nothing contributes so largely and effectually to soundness of judgment.

There are natural incapacities that of course no religion can remove, but there are no capacities so feeble that true religion will not thus enlarge and invigorate and make them to accomplish far beyond what any culture could do without it. And there are no capacities so great, no genius so brilliant that true holiness — the excellence of God himself, would not have made far greater, and covered with a brighter brilliance and power.

Many a man of far inferior talent has thus been set on high above the child of genius, both in intellectual power, in sound judgment and in the influence exerted. But in nothing is the elevating power of religion greater and more manifest than in the *singleness of aim* it secures and the concentration of all it energies on one grand end. This is the deepest secret of all high success in any pursuit.

Sin disorganizes and divides; holiness unites. This is especially true of the human soul. When the soul truly knows God as its God and trusts him, when it has no will but his, and no end but to obey him, it acquires a force and vigor, a concentration of energy otherwise impossible. There is then no waste of power; every little rill of thought and feeling, and desire and hope flows into the great current of the leading purpose, and from that purpose every selfish end is excluded.

There are no by-ends to divide and divert the attention and energies. Not a particle of power is lost. Fear and anxieties about the future cannot disturb it, for all that it trusts in God's hands; the possible results to itself cannot come into the account, for that too belongs to God to arrange; there are no conflicting motives and purposes as self-indulgence or ambition, for these are all set aside by the one absorbing and comprehensive end of life and rule of duty.

Nothing but holiness can perfectly unite the soul, and develop its full energy. In every other case where it seems united by the overmastering force of some ruling passion, as in the case of Napoleon, by an ambition that sacrificed at its shrine every dictate of conscience and feeling of affection, there is this great element of both of weakness and shame —

The moral nature is crushed, and that which ought to rule, and which ruling by the fear of God, would contribute an energy and force beyond any other single element, is not only lost, but much of the soul's true power has been used up in resisting and crushing it, and even then the disturbing voice of an overborne and abused conscience will still at times be heard causing more or less wavering and indecision.

Thus, true religion, by the pure stimulus it applies to intellectual power by its removal of all those mists of self-love, passion and prejudice which becloud the judgment, and by that power which it alone possesses of producing entire singleness of aim and concentration of energy, must tend to secure to its possessor the highest eminence of which his nature capable. In the very constitution of our being God has thus secured the fulfillment of the assurance — "I will set him on high, because he hath known my name."

3. Still, again. To deny that holiness secures the highest eminence is to deny that a holy God governs the world. "The Lord reigneth," and therefore all who do sincerely and wholly serve him, who make his will their only law and his glory their great end, must fall in with the line of his designs and providences, and secure his favor and blessing." For promotion cometh neither from the east nor from the west, nor from the south. But God is the judge; he putteth down one and setteth up another."

The reason why so many of his people are visited with disappointment and grievous failure in their plans; why instead of attaining eminence in character, reputation, and influence, they are kept in obscurity and visited with shame and confusion, is that their knowledge of God, and concentration to his service is so imperfect, so marred by selfishness and worldliness that instead of their lives being radiant with the beauty and power of holiness, their inconsistencies secure the contempt even of the world, and they prevent themselves from attaining the very elements of character necessary to high success; and success, even if possible, would only be their ruin, their final elevation to glory requiring the present severe and continued discipline of worldly dishonor.

Since, then, holiness is an essential element in all true greatness, all other eminence being only in the end an eminence to shame; since it is necessary to give to the intellect its full vigor, to the judgment its clearest light, and to the whole character the full force of undivided energy; since it is necessary to secure the Divine favor and the special blessing of Providence, it is evident that the true and the highest eminence cannot be attained without it, and must ever be secured by it.

The history of our world affords many illustrious examples of eminence secured by holiness. Joseph in Egypt, Hezekiah on the throne of Judah, Daniel in Babylon, Paul in the early Church; and — in latter times an Edward VI. on the throne of England, an Andrew Mellville in Scotland, a Gustavus Adolphus in Sweden; a Sir Matthew Hale among lawyers, a Thomas Budgett among merchants, a Gardener and Havelock among soldiers — are a few of the most familiar names, together with a whole multitude of others whose names are perpetuated in their writings.

But, although others have stood higher in position, and in attainments, none stand forth as more truly illustrious, or will go down to posterity with greater honor and a more powerful and blessed influence than the name of our own beloved JACKSON, as one whom God hath set on high, because he honored God with all his heart and life.

His character, as far as known must secure this. There was something in it so unique and yet so simple, — it was at once so severe and yet so gentle, so daring and yet so shrinking, that I will not even attempt a full delineation of it. A few traits only will be here presented, such as show him to have been an embodiment of the truths we have been discussing.

And in speaking of his character we speak with confidence; for we speak what we do know. An acquaintance of years, that had ripened into a warm friendship, — and habits of special intimacy with those who were in daily intercourse with him, and to whom his character was always an object of admiration and study, enable me to speak with assurance.

That in him holiness was power, seems to be almost universally granted. Is there a man in this Confederacy that has any doubt as to the secret of JACKSON'S greatness? It was not that in grasp of native intellect, in brilliancy and breadth of conception, in vigor of reasoning he excelled others so much; — many others surpassed him in each of these, both in the lecture room and the camp, who must ever hold a far inferior place in the world's history.

God indeed had gifted him with a mind of no ordinary force and clearness, and great native energy of will; but it was not this alone or mainly that made him great; it was that in him above all other men I ever knew, the only object of life was just to do the will of God, and the constant posture of his soul one of unhesitating confidence in God.

To obey God in all things, and at all costs, and to trust him implicitly seemed for many years to have been the fixed habit of his soul; not so much to have required an effort, as to be the steady and spontaneous working of his whole being. It almost seemed as one who watched him as if he could not help it; his whole happiness consisted in it. He seems to have been deeply impressed in early life with the power of habit; and from the very beginning of his Christian course he sought to form fixed holy habits, extending to the minutest matters of life, from which nothing could ever make him swerve, and which were the secret of his close walk with God.

"I never," said he to a very dear friend, to whom he was accustomed to unbosom himself most fully, though even to such he never spoke of himself except when constrained by a sense of duty, — "I never take a glass of water, but the moment it touches my lips, my heart rises in thanksgiving to God and prayer for his blessing." "But, Major, do you not sometimes forget?" "No," said he "I think not. It is so much of a habit now, that I would almost as easily forget to drink."

He added, "I never drop a letter in the office, but it is the signal for prayer to God to bless the errand on which it goes. I never break the seal of a letter but I make it the signal for asking God's blessing on the yet unknown author and its unknown tidings.

Whenever I sit down in my lecture room, and the class are assembling, until all is quiet, — that is my time for prayer:

and when one class is retiring and another entering, then too is my time for prayer. In such things I have formed the habit and I cannot forget it. It gives me inexpressible enjoyment." Thus he lived.

Such was his communion with God, his life of faith and prayer. And here was the secret spring of his strength, the source of his real greatness. He was always with God, and he became like God as very few do.

Reference to another of his habits will show how, in the very least things he made the will of God his sole law, and how sedulously he avoided all doubtful grounds. Of the wickedness of Sabbath mails, he was long firmly convinced. Carrying out his principles to their full length, he would never permit a letter of his to travel in the mails on the Sabbath if it could be prevented.

He would carefully count the number of days required for it to reach its destination, and if that time run into the Sabbath, unless it required a whole week or more — no urgency of business could prevent him from laying it over till the next week. When he entered on his professorship, he refrained, as a matter of conscience, from reading even a single line by night, owing to the weakness of his eyes, — and letters received on Saturday night, though from his dearest friends, remained unopened until early on Monday morning.

And so supreme and controlling was his sense of duty, that this never, according to his own explicit testimony, caused him any distraction of mind, but rather a secret pleasure and gratitude to God that he was thus enabled to obey him in all things.

Yet his was by no means a scrupulous conscience which is always dreading evil when there is none, and distressing itself with imaginary fears; no man was ever more free from this; but one rendered peculiarly delicate and sensitive by the unusual vigor of spiritual life, making it shrink instinctively from the slightest touch of sin.

And that testimony of his already quoted in regard to this matter, deserves to be held in everlasting remembrance, — that for nearly fifteen years, during which he had avoided all use of Sabbath mails, in no instance had there been occasion for regret, but on the contrary, that God had made it a source of pure enjoyment. Let the church and the world both gaze upon the rare and noble example, till they feel its power.

Thus walking with God in prayer and holy obedience, he reposed upon God's promises and Providence with a calm and unflinching reliance beyond any man I ever knew. I shall never forget the manner and tone of surprise and child-like confidence with which he once spoke to me on this subject. It was just after the election in November, 1860, when the country was beginning to heave with the agony and throes of dissolution

We had just risen from morning prayers in his own house, where at the time I was a guest. Filled with gloom, I was lamenting in strong language the condition and prospects of our beloved country. "Why," said he, "should Christians be at all disturbed about the dissolution of the Union? It can only come by God's permission, and will only be permitted, if for his people's good, for does he not say that all things shall work together for good to them that love God?" I cannot see why *we* should be distressed about such things whatever be their consequences."

Nothing seemed ever to shake that faith in God. It was in him a truly sublime and all controlling principle. In the beautiful language of this Psalm, he dwelt in the secret place of the Most High, he made the Most High his habituation, and was thus placed on high from the fear of evil.

Together with that extreme fear of offending God in even the least thing, which was the only fear he ever knew, — this lofty faith was the source of that quiet daring, that lofty heroism, that imperturbable coolness and self possession, even in those sudden and dangerous emergencies which wound up all his energies to their utmost tension, that made him the model soldier, the true Christian hero.

In this connection it may be observed, that he seemed never to hold an opinion that did not at once have its full, practical weight upon his conduct. Nothing formerly struck me more than this in his character. There seemed to be no discrepancy between his head and his heart, his belief and his practice. To believe a truth and act upon it were with him one thing.

And all these together went to constitute that quality which has long been regarded by his most intimate friends, as the main secret of his power and success, — his perfect singleness of purpose.

He had no by-ends to divide his mind or his heart. This self-abnegation was, I believe, as nearly complete as that of any mortal that ever lived. It was mentioned by Dr. White, his pastor, at his funeral, that when that unfortunate difficulty occurred in the Valley which led him to send on his resignation to Richmond, — and all his staff and other officers gathering round him, urged him to go to Richmond himself and set himself right with the government. —

He positively refused, saying, "I have but two things to do, to serve my God and my country. If my country has not confidence in me here, let them put some one in my place in whom they have confidence." These two things in his case really resolved themselves into one, to *obey God*, so that really, he had but one thing to do; hence his judgment was clear, his plans comprehensive, his action prompt, his energy indomitable, and his success unvarying God set him on high, because he knew God's name, he recognized his sovereign claims — God's will was his all.

But I must stop this imperfect sketch. Others will no doubt, ere long, do full justice to his noble character and fully portray his bright example. I cannot, however, forbear to add that Gen. JACKSON was eminently a happy man, cheerful and free from anxious care: that he was just as kind, as gentle and as tender, as he was stern and inexorable in his requirements when duty and the interests of his country demanded, and as he was lion-like in battle.

This picture there and in the camp, where God especially elevated him to the living gaze of a whole people, others who saw him and bore with him the fatigues and perils of two bloody years, can alone portray.

Such was in some respects the man whom God set on high amongst us, as very few have ever been among any people before, and whose loss a bleeding country weeps so bitterly. Will you bear with me a little longer while I add a few reflections. Such an occasion occurs but once in any generation.

1. God gave him to us, let us praise him for the gift. Few nations have ever been blessed in their infancy or even in their maturity, with such a man, perhaps none with such a perfect Christian Hero. We challenge all history to produce his superior, nay, his equal even, in this respect. God wonderfully prepared him for his work, put him in the place for which he had been fitting him, and for two years of bloody conflict crowned him with unvarying success. He never once knew defeat.

Kernstown is covered with his glory, as much as Manassas or Richmond or Chancellorsville. By him God wrought for us repeated and glorious deliverances. For our yet peaceful homes and unravaged fields in this dear old Commonwealth we are under God greatly indebted to his toils and skill and rapid energy and valor, and for these to his religion.

God heard his prayers, guided his decisions, and crowned him with glorious success, and to God he gave always all the glory. Let us not cease to praise God for him, and to be encouraged in our great struggle. Can we believe that God would have given us such a man, and answered in every step his prayers for two eventful years, and blessed him as our defender, if he had not designs of mercy for us, and was not preparing for us a glorious deliverance, and us for it?

2. But again. God has taken him, and why? He finished his work just when we thought he was about to enter upon a still more glorious series of triumphs. We are all bereaved. The nation indulges a personal grief. Never perhaps did such a throe of agony pierce a nation's heart, at the fall of a single

man since the Dutch Republic stood horror-stricken at the assassination of William, Prince of Orange. The inquiry is natural, why this terrible blow? Why raise up just the instrument we needed, and then remove him when we seemed to need him as much if not more than ever?

Who has not already heard in it the voice of God saying to us, "Cease ye from man, whose breath is in his nostrils; for wherein is he to be accounted of?" "Put not your trust in Princes, nor in the Son of man, in whom there is no help. His breath goeth forth, he returneth to the earth, in that very day his thoughts perish. Happy is he that hath the God of Jacob for his help, whose hope is in the Lord his God. "

If this nation had an idol it was JACKSON. If there was any mere instrument to whom they were in danger of giving glory beyond what is man's due, it was he. Wherever JACKSON was known to be, there all was regarded as safe; men hardly ever felt the need of prayer for that as for other portions threatened by our foe — it was already secure.

His past safety too was taken as almost a pledge of his future. God has thus taught us that we must depend directly upon him. Nothing filled JACKSON with greater solicitude than the thought that men were praising *him*. It made him tremble in anticipation of heavier judgments through God's displeasure. God will not give his glory to another. Dependence upon God secured JACKSON'S success, and it will as certainly secure our success. If we will not honor God, he will not honor us.

Nothing we can conceive of could teach us this great lesson, as JACKSON'S death is calculated to do it. If it does this, it will be a blessing full equal to his life; if it fails to do it, it would seem that nothing else can, we can look only to be a cast off people. Let it then be a voice to the church calling her to rally round the throne of grace as never before, and to the whole nation to humble itself under the mighty hand of a holy God.

3. Observe again that while God has taken him away, he has set on high his example, and enshrined it in the hearts of

this people, and is holding it up in its beauty and power, as if to draw us on in those bright footsteps.

The very time and circumstances of his death were all such as to awaken peculiar and melancholy interest, and so force attention to his example, as if God intended not a single element should be wanting to perfect the influence of that example. It is a great thing to be made clearly to see the right way, and to love and admire it. Here it is so exhibited as to stir our deepest emotions.

His death has perfected that example, and spread it out in all its fullness as it could not have been had he lived. Just at a time when sorrow and peril had rendered the nation's heart peculiarly plastic, and when its character is being permanently molded, God has thus thrown out upon it this glorious example of the power of holiness with a force that every heart is bound to feel.

God so ordered his life as to show in the very heavens that his success and eminence was due to his religion — that without this element we never could have had a JACKSON, without it he would have been just like Samson without his locks; he then made him the object of our enthusiastic love, and now by his death he sets him on high enshrined in a glory as unchanging as it is attractive, the very impersonation of holiness in its bearing upon our present success and our future prosperity. A tenderer and more stirring call was never made upon any people to turn to, to trust in, and to serve the Lord.

4. Finally, the spirit of JACKSON, in our rulers, our military leaders, and our people can alone save us and perpetuate us as a nation. In him God has shown us the only way to triumph and perpetuity.

Blessed be his name that he has not left us without some at least who partake of his spirit, and that the noble chief of our armies, our beloved and honored and magnanimous Lee is strong in the fear of God. May he raise up many such!

Who does not fully believe that if our rulers and generals and legislators and a majority of the people had been actuated by the godly spirit of our JACKSON this war would have ended before this? In the light of his example and triumphs, how clearly appears the curse of ungodliness to a nation! How dark the reproach and how damning the influence of sin!

Who now will turn away from JACKSON'S God and the religion of the cross? What patriotic heart will refuse to bow in humble prayer and obedience to the God of nations? If any such there be let him remember that so far as be can, he is intercepting the blessing of heaven, drawing down its wrath upon our suffering land, and blasting his own highest hopes.

To our young men what a noble example! Where is the youthful soul so insensible to all that is lovely and glorious, that he will not aspire to copy it? Where is now that worst of cowards, who is ashamed to pray, and be an earnest and singular Christian?

To our military men his example comes with peculiar force: it shows that the greatest military success, as well as all those high and manly qualities that enter into the very idea of a true soldier, are not only consistent with, but in their highest degree, dependent upon the fear of God; and it also rebukes that ambition and mere love of glory which is the great curse of military life.

To every man, woman and child in our land it appeals, and especially to every Christian, pouring shame on the cold half-hearted follower of Jesus, and calling all to a life of earnest and entire consecration to God, and close communion with him.

Let the watchword then of our whole country in her present bloody struggle, and of the Church of Christ in the great work now devolved on her, to form the moral character of the nation, and of every individual in his warfare with temptation and sin, be that with which on the morning after his fall another gallant officer led his triumphant corps to the charge —

"Forward, and remember JACKSON;" only adding, "In the name of JACKSON'S God." Fear not, falter not, flinch not, trust in God and victory is ours; victory over our country's foes, over all of the foes of the Church of Christ, over sin and hell and death. God will set us on high, if we revere his name.

THE

OATH OF ALLEGIANCE

TO THE

UNITED STATES

DISCUSSED IN ITS
MORAL AND POLITICAL BEARINGS

BY

REV. B. M. PALMER, D. D.

Southern Methodist Episcopal Church

LATE OF NEW ORLEANS

1863

The Duties and Obligations of those Citizens of the Confederate States falling within the lines of the enemy discussed, in their Moral and Political Bearings, with particular reference to the atrocities practiced by Gen. Butler in New Orleans, in a letter addressed to the Hon. John Perkins, of Louisiana, upon the introduction of the following resolutions in THE CONFEDERATE CONGRESS, commending those persons who refused to take the oath. By Rev. B. M. PALMER, D. D., late of New Orleans.

JOINT RESOLUTIONS in commendation of the conduct of those citizens of Louisiana and other States who, falling within the lines of the enemy, have refused to take the oath of allegiance to the United States.

Resolved, That Congress views with pride the course pursued by the true men and women of the Confederacy, who, falling within the lines of the enemy, have resisted all appeals to their pecuniary interest and refused, in spite of pains and penalties, to foreswear their own government by taking an oath of allegiance to support that of the United States, and regards with peculiar satisfaction the conduct of those citizens of Louisiana, who, by refusing the oath and openly registering themselves enemies of the United States in the immediate presence and in defiance of General Butler's military authorities, have borne most noble testimony by their martyr-like courage to the patriotic spirit and Christian faith of our people.

Resolved, That while such conduct has secured them the present respect and sympathy of all good people, it will be esteemed, in the future, a most honorable claim upon the gratitude of their country, and the highest evidence of their devotion to truth and principle.

The Oath of Allegiance to the United States.

COLUMBIA, S. C., Feb'y 10, 1863.

HON. JOHN PERKINS:

My Dear Sir — The joint resolutions submitted by you on the 13th of January, for the consideration of Congress, "in commendation of certain citizens of Louisiana and of other States within the lines of the enemy in refusing to take the oath of allegiance to the United States," have recently passed under my eye. The impulse cannot be resisted of addressing to you some reflections which have long been maturing in my own mind, and which you are at liberty to use in any way you may think conducive to the public good.

Permit me, in the outset, to express my approval, not only of the matter, but also of the form of your resolutions. It appears to me eminently proper that Congress should signalize the fidelity of our fellow-citizens who have withstood all appeals to self interest and to fear, in their country's darkest trial. But I especially commend the moderation which pretermits in the resolution any mention of those who have been caught in the snares of the enemy, and duped into concessions which have filled the land with sorrow.

So long as these unfortunate parties are debarred the privilege of a hearing — the government, from paternal lenity, if not from a sense of rigid justice, may well feel itself restrained from open and direct censure. From the language of your paper, the world is not to know that a solitary individual is excepted from the encomium pronounced by Congress.

Those familiar with all the facts cannot fail, indeed, to perceive a discrimination in favor of some, which, by implication, contain a censure of others. This, however, is unavoidable, and those who may writhe beneath the torture of this implied censure, will yet be compelled to admire the generosity which forebore to stigmatize them in the legislative records of the country.

Nevertheless, from some quarter, and precisely at this juncture, a protest should be uttered against the weakness of those who have succumbed beneath the tyranny of Gen. Butler, and sworn allegiance to the government of the United States.

It may not be too late to rouse those who are involved in this dire calamity to retrieve their lost position, and to wipe off the dishonor which must else cleave to them forever. Or, failing in this, it is still a duty to attempt the arrest of principles which, I fear, are secretly sapping in Louisiana, the foundations of public morality, and destroying the basis on which rest at last the permanence and security of all government.

I undertake, therefore, in this letter, to present the reverse of your medal, and assume the painful responsibility of giving utterance to strictures, from which, as a legislator, you have wisely refrained.

Should apology be needed for this obtrusion of private criticism, let it be found in the relation I have long sustained as a religious teacher to the people of Louisiana, and my common participation as a citizen in any approach which may tarnish the fame of that gallant State.

We should clearly distinguish betwixt two classes of our fellow-citizens, who have submitted to the oath exacted by Gen. Butler. The first class, inconsiderable both as to numbers and influence, embraces those who were never true to our cause.

Some of them, from misconception of the relation between the States and the general government, secretly denied the right of secession, and simply drifted with the popular current which they felt it idle to oppose. Of course, upon the first appearance of the enemy, they ranged themselves, without solicitation, upon the side of the Union, to which they were borne by their political affinities.

Others destitute of all principle, alike political and moral, having no eye but to present gain, and only intent upon opening the obstructed channels of trade, chose to make interest with those who had blocked their ports. Both these are simply traitors to the South — they went out from us because they were not of us — and it is to be hoped, upon the recovery of our territory, they will find it convenient to leave with their new allies and purge our society of their presence.

The other classes embraces those who, in their secret hearts, are still loyal to the Confederacy, and have taken the oath under constraint, regarding it as one of the necessities of war. The universal compassion felt for their distress has almost extinguished censure of the act; whilst the conviction entertained of their substantial loyalty retains them within the embrace of our affections.

The general integrity of many in this class affords a guarantee that conscience has been snared through the sophistry of the understanding; and that by subtlety of argument they have been persuaded into the belief that the oath could be taken *salva fide*. In adjudicating this question, I cannot but think some considerations were overlooked, which should have formed an element in the decision to be rendered, and, which, if entertained must have wholly changed its complexion.

Before canvassing, however, the grounds upon which this oath-taking has been justified, that we may make due allowance for human infirmity, let us look at the peculiar pressure under which these parties were put. In the first place, the demand made upon them was a novelty; and we all know how men flounder in uncertainty without acknowledged precedents for their guidance.

I have in vain searched the records of modern history for its parallel. The famous contest between Philip of Spain and the State of Holland presents some features of resemblance to the conflict now waging between the North and ourselves.

The Spanish power then, as the North does now, branded the attempt of a brave people to frame their own constitution and laws as flagrant rebellion; and conducted a long and bitter war to reduce, as they alleged, a revolted province to allegiance. But in no instance did the cruel Alva — fitting tool though he was of a treacherous and bigoted despot, force a reluctant oath upon the cities which he conquered.

They were held, indeed, by military garrisons until such time as the State of which they formed a constituent part should in like manner be reduced. No attempt was made to cancel their ties of allegiance but through the constituted authorities to whom that allegiance had been sworn.

It has been reserved to our time and to our foes to invent the shameful and cowardly device of dealing with single communities, and even with individual persons, as if they were independent of higher authority.

A magnanimous enemy might have held New Orleans by right of capture; but would have refrained from the imposition of oaths until the State of Louisiana had been reduced to submission, and as an organic whole, had carried over all the parts of which it is composed. But the refined despotism of the Lincoln government adopts the policy of grinding individuals between conflicting jurisdictions as between the upper and nether millstones.

Conscious of its impotence to subjugate, it has been satisfied with disgracing those whom it cannot conquer, and with demoralizing those, over whom it cannot rule. The satanic boast of Gen. Butler has been in part achieved of holding up what he is pleased to term a perjured people to the derision of mankind.

I shall recur to this thought in another connection, and present it as a reason why the oath should have been sternly refused. It is mentioned here only to show how our people were surprised in the historic novelty of their position; and how they were subjected to a rigor of treatment unknown to the worst despotisms of the past.

In the next place the craft by which this nefarious design was accomplished, does full credit to the subtlety and malice in which it was conceived.

Butler's tyranny opened with a prohibition against more than three persons speaking together upon the streets, under the penalty of being dispersed as a mob; the effect of which was to insulate individuals, and to prevent that interchange of views necessary to concert of action.

A system of espionage, most comprehensive in its sweep, was moreover immediately instituted; so that you could not look your fellow in the face, lest the flash of the eye should betray to a paid informer, the secret resentment of the soul.

Even slaves of the household were suborned under promises of personal freedom, to invent charges against the master, which subjected him to examination and search, accompanied with brutal and insulting threats.

With the poison of suspicion thus universally diffused, the infirmity of many yielded to external pressure, as single-handed and alone, they were either bullied or cajoled into a form of submission denied by the heart as often as it was sworn by the lips. But the catalogue of wrongs is only begun.

Placing his mailed hand next upon the separate guilds into which society is classified, and resorting at once to the arts of special pleading and to the display of irresponsible power, he extorted minor concessions from each of these — yielded in the vain hope that this would be the end of their humiliation — but which, though small, were sufficient to break the tone of a spirited people.

"C' est le premier pas qui coute;" when the veil of delusion was rent by the imposition of further tests, they found themselves upon an inclined plane, which had no resting place but in abject submission. Nothing was left but consistency in error and the melancholy confession at the last, *"pas a pas on va bien loin."*

Thus craftily were our unhappy fellow-citizens decoyed into the oath from which, at the beginning, they recoiled with the indignant exclamation of Hazael, "What! Is thy servant a dog, that he should do this great thing?"

The darkest feature, however, in this oppression, is found in the undefined terrors which hung like a portentous cloud over this devoted people; terrors, too, of such a nature as gloomily to impress the imagination and freeze the soul with horror.

The infamous order, No. 28, was not, as usually interpreted, the outburst of a brutal and savage nature in a moment of resentment; but part of a premeditated system to strike universal terror into the heart of the community. The blow was threatened just where the affections were most sensitive; and the violation of the sweetest sanctities of home was set forth as the penalty of resistance to the tyrant's will.

Though directed in form against the women of Louisiana, its evident design was to reach through them their intractable guardians of the other sex. The husband and the father were called to look upon their imprisoned households, and then to survey the hounds of the despot by whom they were held at bay.

A licentious soldiery drawn from the scum of Northern society, the agrarian element always to be found in the mixed population of a large city, and the drunken helots just emancipated from bondage and tricked out in the toggery of their new associates — these were held in the leash to be let loose to sack and plunder at their will, and to gratify the worst passions of the human heart.

Doubtless these fears were, to a large extent imaginary; for they were never realized by those who openly defied the tyrant's power, who seemed rather to amuse himself with playing upon the fears of and with imposing tests of their moral courage, and with mocking those who faltered and trembled under his frown. But though imaginary, they were nevertheless effective.

Our people appeared to feel as though the earth was heaving beneath their tread, and that, in a single moment, they might go down together through the parted crust. These nameless, formless horrors, presented by a morbid fancy, with the desire to preserve their property from confiscation, combined to crush the spirit of a people as noble as any beneath the sun.

My heart, sir, alternately burns with anger and bleeds in sympathy as I contemplate these accumulated wrongs, which are recited with no design to apologize for the oath, but to show that the censure leveled against it proceeds from no insensibility to the distress by which it was coerced. The same tenderness which weeps over the sorrows of our friends, pleads with them to retrieve the still heavier disaster of a dishonorable name.

It is not to be presumed that all were conducted to this fatal step by precisely the same line of argument. Accordingly, we find it justified upon two grounds which are not only distinct from, but even exclusive of each, as the attention happened to be fixed upon one or the other horn of a common dilemma.

The difficulty was how to take the oath without surrendering, on the one hand, a conscious loyalty to the Confederacy, and retaining, on the other hand, something like integrity of conscience. The path was too narrow to allow the slightest deflection without plunging into one or the other of these two quicksands.

Some determined to preserve their interest in the country which they loved, even at the expense of truth; others, to maintain veracity at the hazard of clouding with suspicion their civil fidelity. Let us examine both expedients in detail.

It is alleged, then, by the first of these two classes, that being without liberty of choices, in the hands of an unscrupulous and barbarous enemy, it was lawful to swear an oath with the lips to which the heart gave no response; that no faith was to be placed in an oath exacted upon compulsion, and accordingly it might be taken with a mental reservation to break it so soon as opportunity should be afforded of doing it with safety.

The case is considered parallel with an oath of secrecy exacted by footpad with his stiletto at our throat which it is alleged might be given with the firm but secret purpose of bringing the outlaw to justice as soon as we should be once more within the protection of society and law. I believe I have stated the argument in its utmost strength.

The oath, say they, was taken, but under circumstances which gave the imposer no confidence in the fidelity of the party sworn, and absolved the latter from all obligation to abide by his pledge. It were far better to let this oath pass without defense than to justify it by a doctrine so desolating in its consequences.

Then apparent, or even the real apostasy of many thousands from our ranks, cannot inflict so severe or lasting a shock upon the Confederacy as the promulgation of principles like these. We are all willing, in a superabundant charity, to forgive the weakness of those who have fallen under the cruel oppressions which I have already described; but we cannot permit that weakness to be extolled into a virtue, nor to be extenuated upon grounds subversive alike of morality and religion.

What is an oath, but an appeal to the omniscient God as a witness to the truth whereof we affirm? In this consists the essence of the sin of perjury; that "the juror has the thought of God and religion upon his mind at the time, so that if he offends, it is in defiance of the sanctions of religion, and implies a disbelief or contempt of God's knowledge, power and justice."

Since human society cannot exist without mutual confidence, and this in turn depends upon truth, the oath has been ordained by God for the attainment of both these ends. To guard as far as possible against the temptations to falsehood, the religious sentiment in man is brought into exercise, and the conscience is surrounded by all those motives which can be drawn from a consideration of God and of His retributive justice.

The juror (the term being taken in its etymological, not its technical signification) is cited immediately before the Divine tribunal, that in view of Him who reads the secrets of all hearts, and is pledged to punish fraud as an offence against His authority, he may have the strongest inducement to utter the truth. This of course, is founded upon the idea that human government itself is not only an ordinance of God, but that it is a dim reflection of the Divine.

We could not, indeed, be subjects of human law, if we were not antecedently under the jurisdiction of the Supreme Ruler of the world. Hence human government is not only divinely ordained, but its existence and preservation depend upon those religious convictions which are recognized in the divine law.

With all the temporal sanctions by which it strives to enforce obedience, its control over human conduct is not effectual until it invokes the aid of omniscience, and thus places a police in every human breast. Its strongest protection is found in the oath which takes hold of the religious nature in man. It can rise no higher than this.

It summons us into the presence of the infinite God, and sways His awful sceptre over the soul as it compels our testimony in sight of those tremendous judgments which fence around the prerogatives of that august being. Hence moralists have not hesitated to describe the oath as a twofold covenant made both with society and with God; and in this latter aspect it rises into the solemnity of an act of religious worship.

Thus it is that "men swear by the greater, and an oath for confirmation is to them an end of all strife." The pledge of veracity is deposited with the Judge of all the earth, and upon its forfeiture are suspended the fearful retributions of eternity. If this does not bind the conscience, nothing can bind, and society is without a guarantee for that truthfulness upon which human intercourse must at last hinge.

To trifle, therefore, with the sanctity of the oath, is to strike a fatal blow both at religion and at law. It destroys religion by weakening the sense of God's presence in the soul, and by debauching the very faculty to which all her sanctions are addressed: "he that cometh unto God must believe that He is, and that He is the rewarder of them that diligently seek Him."

It also undermines the foundation on which civil government is built which cannot lose its hold upon the conscience without destroying the very source of its authority. No increase of civil penalties can compensate for the loss of this moral control; for, besides the fact that every addition to the criminal legislation of a country only increases the friction and wears out the machinery of government, there are many offences which cannot be reached by it; and in any case it is but a collateral security which it affords.

I freely confess my alarm at the ventilation of a doctrine which thus summarily dispenses with the obligation of the oath. If it be not arrested, the most complete demoralization of our people must ensue, which will render all government impossible save that of brute physical force. The prevalence, indeed, of this corrupt sentiment is the remote cause of all the troubles in which we are now involved.

Covenants and treaties solemnly instituted by our forefathers were no longer interpreted in their simple and obvious meaning. Ingenuity itself was put to the torture to devise expositions which should eviscerate them of the principles which they were ordained to conserve until at length our modern alchemists found in the doctrine of "a higher law," the mighty solvent which destroyed the power of oaths and covenants at once.

Men swore with due solemnity to uphold the constitution and the laws, but with a mental reservation to uproot these very institutions which that constitution had been framed to defend; until the universal perfidy of the North suddenly burst every ligature by which the States were held together in the Federal Union.

Are our people willing to walk in the footsteps of our foes? And is it a suitable preparation for a new historic career to inoculate this young nation with the virus of that perfidy which has already destroyed before our eyes one of the most colossal governments upon earth? Nor is it difficult to trace the practical operation of this secret poison as it diffuses itself through the body politic.

If the juror may swear no longer *"in animum imponentis,"* but according to a secret intention of his own, then he alone can judge when or how far he is bound. The magistrate may, by this sweeping dispensation, absolve himself from the guilt of malfeasance in office; the juryman upon the panel and the witness upon the stand may combine to defeat all the ends of justice through an oath which opens and shuts conveniently at the bidding of caprice, until, in the total overthrow of morality, society itself shall crumble through universal distrust.

The application may be made to the very parties whose plea we are now considering. They swear allegiance to the government at Washington, raising the hand to heaven in attestation of their sincerity; yet, at the same moment, they require us to believe their affirmation of loyalty to the government at Richmond.

Which of these opposing declarations is to be received? Plainly, this cannot be determined without weighing both in the balance of probabilities; but as far as their naked word is concerned, how can it challenge confidence when, even under the awful sanction of an oath, it confesses to willful falsehood? Can it ever be lawful for men to place themselves in that condition of disability where their simple word can never be accepted as the gauge of truth?

This might be enforced by adverting to the peril incurred by subscription of the Lincoln oath. Being registered citizens of the United States, suppose it had been required of them to bear arms against their brethren of the South, who are now battling for the restoration of that birthright which, in an evil hour, they have bartered away?

And what hinders it but the conviction in the tyrant's mind that they cannot be trusted with the very duties which their oath of fealty implies? A conviction, by the way, which involves him in the still greater disgrace of compelling an oath in which he does not confide, but which also shows the guilt of subscribing to it, since this alone saves from the most fearful crime of lifting the hand against the mother that bore them.

I come now to the second and entirely distinct line of defense raised by some who have been entangled in the snare; among whom are many far too conscientious to assume a position known to be false, or to subscribe an oath with anything approaching a mental reservation.

I cannot refrain, in passing, from the remark that, upon all questions of honor and principle, the first thought of an honest and pure mind is the safest; for in this the instinct of manliness and truth usually finds expression. The second thoughts which prudence is prone to suggest, are generally the inlets of temptation and turn out to be subterfuges for the evasion of duty.

It is alleged, then, by this second class, that the control and protection of the Confederacy being, through the fortunes of war, wholly suspended, upon the principle of submitting to the powers that be, they took the oath to the only authority to which *de facto* existed, and which made this the only condition upon which its protection could be enjoyed.

They took it moreover in good faith, intending to keep it so long as the Federal rule should continue, but in the hope that this rule would, in due season, terminate and restore them to the civil connections from which their hearts were never estranged. This position is impregnable so far as a *de facto* submission to military force is concerned.

Neither the laws of war nor those of reason oblige men to continue a factious and unavailing opposition against overwhelming and crushing force, and no blame could attach to them for simply yielding to the rule of warfare, which connects with a surrender the cessation of active hostility.

But it is an immense leap from this to the making of a solemn covenant, transforming into a government of law what was before only a government of force; for the oath of allegiance transferred with the citizenship all its moral obligations, and invested the authority of Butler with the sanctions of a recognized and legal government.

Had these parties approached the Federal commander with language substantially this: "as a defenseless people, wholly within your power, we submit, without resistance, to military force, and without conceding this submission to be obedience," no censure could attach to them; and they would then be embraced within the terms of the eulogy conveyed in the resolutions you have presented before Congress.

If it be said that allegiance was the only condition upon which protection would be afforded to property and life, my answer is that the hazard should have been incurred along with the thousands who chose to be registered as alien enemies to the United States rather than forfeit their loyalty to the South.

Actual submission to military supremacy was all that could be demanded of them by the rules of civilized warfare; and it was their privilege to stand upon the assertion of this right before the nations of the earth. Notwithstanding the ghostly terrors by which they were surrounded, the government at Washington dared not, under the eyes of mankind, to exact more.

A few victims might, perhaps, be selected from the mass, upon whom to vent disappointment and spleen, and a brief persistence in tyranny might have tested the endurance of the community; but a little firmness would have carried them over the trial, and won for the sufferers an immortality of glory; in proof of which I adduce the fact, that wherever else in the Confederacy the enemy has been stoutly defied, with all his bluster, he has been compelled to yield a reluctant acquiescence in the moral code established by civilized nations for the regulation of war.

But suppose the reverse of this, and the long dispensation of suffering to ensue, are we to avow the doctrine that the most cherished convictions of the soul must be surrendered upon plea of coercive necessity.

I will put the argument in a form most likely to be appreciated by the Christian men who taken refuge under this plea. Should the days of religious persecutions again appear, would it be right, in order to save property and life, to abjure Christianity and to offer sacrifices upon the altar of Jupiter, as was done in the second century? The frailty of human nature might yield now, as it did then, under the fiery ordeal; and knowing that we are men, we might weep tears of compassion, nay, almost of forgiveness, over an apostasy thus extorted. But what judgment would we pronounce upon a cool argument framed to justify this defection?

If we could be brought to pardon the one, we could not tolerate the other. Yet, after all, why is not the argument of coercive necessity as conclusive in this case, as in that we are now considering? I freely admit the disparity between the two; in that one relates to the duties which we owe to man; but I see not why the obligation may not be as imperative to abide by our principles in the one sphere as well as in the other — why duty to our country may not be as paramount in the earthly kingdom as duty to our God is in the spiritual and heavenly.

I have been educated, sir, in a school which regards the obligations we owe to country as only next to those which we owe to God. Our country! what does not the term embrace?

It means our homes and the cheerful firesides, and the prattling babes that gather round the paternal knee; it means sweet neighborhood and friendship, and the tender charities which solace life from the cradle to the tomb; it means the memories of our youth as they grow fresh again in the twilight of age.

It means ancestry and the proud recollection of honored sires, who bequeathed their blessing with the names we inherit; it means our altars and sanctuaries where we have worshipped God and held communion with his saints on earth; it means the graves where our loved ones are lying, consecrated by the tears of a bitter parting when they were laid out of sight forever.

It means all that the human heart can remember and love; all the associations which spread their secret network over human life; all the scattered leaves on which are written the sorrows and the joys through which man travels onward to his rest above.

Our country and our God! The two blend evermore in the Christian patriot's thought, and shall it be said there are no martyrdoms for the one, when the gibbet and the flame are welcomed for the other?

True heroism may be displayed in endurance not less than in action; and our fellow-citizens in Louisiana enjoyed a most distinguished opportunity of rendering a service to the Confederacy quite as valuable as that of the army in the field.

Can any good reason be assigned why they should not run the hazard of confiscation, of imprisonment and of death, equally with those who encountered the risk of capture, of wounds, and of death upon the field of slaughter?

If those may be justified in their apostasy because of the perils by which they were surrounded, why may not these be justified on precisely the same grounds for declining the gauge of battle in the presence of the foe? In short, the plea now under discussion seems to resolve patriotism into an affair of simple contract.

The inability of the Confederacy for the time being to protect them, is viewed as dissolving the bond between them and it; and, like traders in the market, they bargain with another party, purchasing protection with loyalty. Upon this principle patriotism is a word without meaning, and allegiance becomes the sport of accident and chance. I have not the heart to pursue the discussion under this aspect.

I cannot believe that our friends have deliberately brought themselves to rest in this bleak and desolate conclusion. By the instinct which recoils from it let them detect the sophistry of the whole plea from which it is deduced by the rigor of a remorseless logic.

I close this long letter by suggesting two considerations which alone should have deterred these jurors from subscribing the oath in question.

In the first place its imposition was in contravention of a right which ought never to have been conceded. I have already stated that the acknowledged laws of warfare required the subjugation of the whole, before tests of loyalty should be exacted of the constituent parts. Why was not the attempt to establish a contrary precedent, full of mischief to the world at large, promptly met with a manly protest and with an appeal to the verdict of mankind?

Duty, not to their country alone but to the race of man, forbade the concession of such a claim. In the second place, the distinctive ground on which this war is waged by the North is, that the South has embarked in a wicked rebellion, upon crushing which the very life of the nation depends. It totally ignores the authority of sovereign States intervening between the citizen and the central power, and simply for this reason an oath of allegiance is exacted of individuals.

A monstrous despotism has grown up which swallows up all the States alive, and treats their jurisdiction as no more than that of a municipal corporation. Are the jurors in Louisiana willing to lend the sanction of their names to a doctrine which has already converted the freest government on earth into the most corrupt and reckless despotism upon which the sun ever shone?

And are they prepared to brand with the infamy of rebellion that sacred cause for which their own brothers and their own sons are periling life and limb upon many a field of battle? Yet the oath they have sworn sanctions this foul calumny pronounced against the heroes and the martyrs of their own blood.

Could my voice, sir, be heard in Louisiana, I would say to those who once listened to me with affection and respect, cancel this dreadful oath. Before it is too late, retrieve your position by a bold and manly retraction. Before this war rushes on to its close, say to the Federal authorities we have recovered our manhood and withdraw our allegiance unjustly and cruelly extorted at our hands.

If the dangers of such an act be great, remember that in the greatness of these will consist the amplitude of the reparation you make to an injured cause. There is no alternative but that of a dishonored name cleaving to you and to your children as long as history shall last.

It is now almost a century since the first American revolution; and men to this day point the finger and say, "there goes a man through whose veins the blood of a Tory flows." Choose the dungeon and the scaffold a thousand times, rather than transmit the taint of this leprosy to your offspring.

But if you have not the nerve for this, if the oath cannot be retrieved, let it go before the country without a word of defense. Do not, in the attempt at justification, withdraw the underpinnings of a social order, and involve both government and religion in a common ruin. Let the act stand forth a confession of human infirmity; and perhaps, like the recording angel whom Sterne describes, your country may write its censure, and then drop the tear of compassion which will blot it out forever.

I remain, dear sir,

Most respectfully and truly yours,

B. M. PALMER

1864

Vain Is The Help Of Man

PREACHED IN

CHRIST CHURCH, SAVANNAH

ON THURSDAY, SEPTEMBER 15, 1864

BEING THE DAY OF

Solemn Humiliation, Fasting and Prayer

APPOINTED BY

THE GOVERNOR OF THE STATE OF GEORGIA

BY

THE RT. REV. STEPHEN ELLIOTT, D. D.
RECTOR OF CHRIST CHURCH

"God is our refuge and strength, a very present help in trouble." — PSALM 45:1.

1864

A SERMON

PSALM 60:11, 12.

Give us help from trouble; for vain is the help of man.

Through God we shall do valiantly; for He it is that shall tread down our enemies.

Once again have we been summoned my beloved people, to bow ourselves in humiliation before God, and with fasting and prayer to invoke his intervention in our behalf. War and its attendant horrors have come very near our own homes, and we meet today to beseech our Heavenly Father that its bloody tide may be stayed, and its proud waters may not be permitted to roll over us.

For months past has it been steadily advancing toward us; we have heard its hoarse and cruel murmuring as it came nearer and nearer; the spoils of its destructive progress have been brought to our feet in the exiled women and children who have fled to us for refuge, and in the dead bodies of our noble young men which have come back to us for Christian burial. But it has not yet reached us, and we unite today, with the citizens of our sovereign State, to pray that God would utter his decree, "Thus far shalt thou go and no further."

Trouble is near enough to us to make us earnest; already have the flutterings of distress disturbed many hearts; already is the enquiry frequent and anxious, "What shall be the end of these things?" Man is looking to his fellow-man with gloomy face and troubled spirit. Woman is summoning up her fortitude to give her strength in the day of adversity. Our counselors are at fault, and our armies have been steadily driven back. We cry unto man and no help comes; we labor and fight and there is no fruit of our labor, and no permanent success to our arms.

We have nothing left but to follow the example of the Psalmist and crying unto God to "give us help from trouble," to acknowledge that "vain is the help of man."

But this is to us no new phase in our affairs. What have we been engaged in from the beginning but just this very confession that "our help must come from God," and that "it is He that shall tread down our enemies." Had I ever looked to the arm of flesh, I should never have hoped for any termination of this conflict but a fatal one. The odds against us were too great, unless we believed that God was on our side, and that his influences would equalize the conflict.

Almost every six months since this struggle commenced, have we bowed ourselves, as a people, before the Lord of Hosts, and prayed for his mercy and protection from the fury of our mighty foes. And never have we cried in vain! He has always answered our supplications, and has thus far supported us under all our trials, and sustained our cause against the overwhelming masses of our enemy.

Our case is no different now, save that the peril and the desolation have become more personal to ourselves, and that we feel its presence more sensibly. We clothed ourselves in mourning then for the Confederacy; we now keep our day of humiliation for the State. We fasted and prayed to the Lord of Hosts upon those occasions for the general cause. We now are in bitterness for our own fair heritage, and for the sufferings of our personal friends, and for the slaughter of those who are near and dear to us.

Louisiana and Mississippi, and Arkansas and Tennessee, and above all, high souled Virginia, have all passed through the desolation which seems approaching us; have all wept over their ruined homes and their despoiled estates; have carried their loved ones to the grave with firm hearts and unshaken spirits, sustained by the assurance that they have died in the noblest cause in which blood can be shed, or life poured out.

They are still unconquered; the wave has passed over them, but has not overwhelmed them; they have shaken its waters from them, as the Lion shakes the rain drops from its mane, and yet breathe defiance and maintain hope. No new thing has happened unto us. We are only passing through the fiery trial which has tried most of our sister States, and while it is right that we should humble ourselves before God, and implore his help in our day of necessity, it is also right that we should imitate the proud example of those desolated States, and prove that we are worthy to be classed among the sovereignties which can suffer and die, but cannot pass under the yoke of servitude.

Why should we, of all the States of the Confederacy have hoped to be exempt from suffering? Are we better than they? Have we a higher tone of morality and religion than that proud mother of States for example, who has for three years been the battle ground of the revolution? Her cities have been captured, and placed under the iron heel of the vilest fanatics of the age; her rural population has been driven from their beautiful homes, and are now wanderers over the Confederacy; her Churches, sacred relics of the past, around which are clustered the graves of generations, have been burned with fire; her archives, memorials of the long line of her heroes and statesmen, a loss irreparable, have been rifled and destroyed.

Has she quailed before these things? Have her hands been made to hang down and her knees to become feeble? Has she even complained? Why should we expect to escape our share of the punishment which comes from God, especially when that punishment seems to be the chastening of a Father and not the judgment of a consuming fire? Nay more, should we desire it? Are we self-righteous enough to imagine that we do not deserve our share of the chastisement which is abroad?

God forbid! for it would prove that we were in a condition which might demand a fiercer cautery. Better for us to share our portion of the passing evil, than to be spared, in the future, for some sorer punishment. Were we to come out of this conflict, alone of all the States, rich, unharmed, undevastated, we should come out without a local history, without any thing for tradition to hang glory upon, without those scars of honor which designate the veteran hero.

We might be pointed at as a State which had reaped nothing but gain from the conflict, and had accumulated wealth at the expense of the sufferings of others. We might be left with a sordid spirit, caring more for money than for honor, more for gain than for reputation. Better, far better for us, as a State, that we should bear our portion of the general suffering, should be able to point to battle fields hotly contested upon our own soil, should have tales to tell in the future which would prove us to have been an heroic race, and not distinguished alone for our powers of acquisition, and our habits of trade.

A national character is a most important element in the future of a State, and in no way is it so certainly gained as by passing a people through a fierce struggle, in which they have been brought face to face with suffering and peril. All those States which in the old revolution bore the brunt of the British fury, have to this day maintained their reputation, and have stood conspicuous upon the pages of our public history, Massachusetts, New York, Virginia, South Carolina!

Their battle fields have made them historical, and they have kindled within them, ever since, a national feeling which has helped to make them conspicuous. It operates upon States, as a line of heroic and renowned ancestry operates upon individuals. Just as the French proverb, "Noblesse oblige," marks the effect upon the individual whom nobility distinguishes, so does the history of a State operate upon its people. Their past requires a present which shall be correspondent with its fame, and harmonious with its character.

The eye of the world is upon them; they know it and feel it, and they rise up, under the consciousness, to a level very much above that which, under ordinary circumstances, they should have attained. Even under this point of view, the invasion of our State is not so great a calamity as many feel it to be; individuals may suffer deeply, but the State may be elevated immeasurably; our fields may be sown with blood and desolation, but the harvest may be one of national character which shall bless us for long generations.

But putting aside this view of the subject, may we not have expected just such a visitation? Have not our own statesmen and orators been predicting, for the last eighteen months, just such results as the consequences of the iron grasp with which many of our citizens have clung to their property and their ease? Has not the voice of the truest of our patriots,[4] been ringing through the State exhorting our people to feed our armies, to clothe our soldiers, to furnish to the Government the necessary material of war? Have not his words of power and of sarcasm been hurled in vain against these very men who are now likely to lose the whole because they would not yield a part to the just demands of their country?

Have not our Generals in command cried for men and cried without any answer, until the strong arm of power has been obliged to drag them from their skulking places and force them to their duty? What can our State expect but subjugation, if her citizens will not consent to supply our armies with food and with men?

We think upon an occasion like this, when a foe is upon us, whom we now clearly understand to have determined to extirpate our race as a pestilent one, and to fill up the seats of our ancestors with hirelings from every land under the sun, that every sword would leap from its scabbard, every arm would acquire fresh power, and in one solid phalanx we would arise and annihilate the invader.

If we do not we deserve our fate and it will come upon us justly. We should fast and pray, but not for our danger; our humiliation should be for our covetousness, for our low-mindedness, for our indifference, for our apathy. If the Lord answers us aright, his answer would be that which he made to Moses, when the people of Israel were crying unto him from among the mountains of the Red Sea, and were saying,

"Is not this the word that we did tell thee in Egypt, saying, let us alone that we may serve the Egyptians? For it had been better for us to serve the Egyptians, than that we should die in the wilderness?" "Wherefore criest thou unto me? Speak unto the children of Israel, that they go forward!"

Yes, this is what we are called to fast and pray for, that we have not the liberality to pour out food for the necessities of our Government, nor the manliness to unite as one man and

---

[4] Howell Cobb.

hurl our foe across the borders. It requires nothing but the resolution; the act would follow it as certainly as united Greece rolled back the myriads of the Persians. No army has ever yet been able to withstand a people rising in its power. Even Napoleon, in the height of his dominion, quailed before regenerate Germany, when Körner awoke his people to resistance by the magic of his song, and the Father-land was free!

There is no inconsistency, my hearers, between saying that, "the help of man is vain," and "that it is God who is to tread our enemies under foot," and yet calling upon our people to awake and buckle on the armor of heroic citizenship! God works by means; we must not expect in these days, to receive help from Him through miracle.

He will help us in time of trouble, but through ordinary means. He will help us by giving us strength in the day of adversity; by opening our hearts to sustain our Government; by quelling dissensions among ourselves; by infusing courage into all those who are weak-minded and timid; by confounding the devices of our enemies. These are the ways in which he now manifests himself, and it is for these ends that we are called to fast and to pray this day.

If any one expects that the results of this humiliation will exhibit themselves in some extraordinary shape, he will be sorely disappointed. If any results flow from it, and they will be dependent upon the sincerity and faithfulness with which it is observed, they will come in the shape of renewed faith, of enlarged hope, of fresh confidence, of reviving courage.

They will be seen in the readiness with which our people will rally around the Government — in the healing of dissensions among our authorities — in the decrease of selfishness — in the determination of every one to do his part, whatever it may be, in flinging back, into the face of our enemies, his insults and his cruelty.

These are the legitimate consequences of humiliation and prayer, because these are the means which are natural and which God is accustomed to use in these days when miracles are no more required. Our text combines the two very beautifully. "Through God we shall do valiantly," is its expression. It is we who are to do valiantly, but yet it is through God. And so shall we find it. He means us to work out our own deliverance, but to work it out in subjection to his will and in subservience to his purposes. He will be the sovereign ruler of his people, even while he may be guiding them to their heart's desire.

In this conflict, more perhaps than in any the world has seen, must it be God who shall tread under foot our enemies. It is a conflict involving the future of a race, whose existence or extinction depends upon its result. The white race of the South, even though subjugated might continue to exist, to live on for a time in shame and degradation, and at last to commingle, as the Anglo-Saxons did, with their Norman conquerors.

But the black race perishes with its freedom. They will die out before the encroaching white labor of Europe, which will be poured in upon them, as the Indians have died out before the progress of civilization, or they will be banished to other lands to perish there, forgotten and unlamented.

The Puritan code of mercy has always been the harsh one, "If you cannot do for yourself you must die." If God therefore has any meaning in his past dealings with this race, in permitting it to be brought here, to be preserved, to increase, to be civilized, it is not his purpose that they should be given the liberty which their pretended friends are seeking for them.

To protect them, he must protect us, and therefore is it, as I have said again and again, that I have full confidence in the successful termination of this conflict. What we may suffer in the struggle is one thing; the end of the struggle is quite another thing. And looking at it in this light I am not disturbed by temporary successes or defeats on the one side or the other; nor am I elated by appearances which seem to promise us any help from man.

This is God's war; he has conducted it upon very remarkable principles; and he will terminate it in his own way and just when he thinks that the ends have been worked out which He designs to fulfill. Let us consider these points before we close.

The two ends which be seems to have had in view in the permission of this terrible war have been the punishment, in a natural way of an arrogant people, who were ascribing their prosperity and their material power, not to his loving kindness and divine mercy, but to their institutions and the liberty upon which they were founded, and then the discomfiture of the short-sighted philanthropists of the world, who conceiving themselves to be wiser and more merciful than God, had determined to blot out of the world all the evils which sin and the curse had laid upon it, and especially the evil of slavery.

Now was the time for this glorious work! The South had laid itself open to their assaults by her secession, and the axe must be laid at the root of the tree. This war, continued now for more than three years with unparalleled bloodshed, is the mode in which God is accomplishing his purposes.

Our punishment is, as I said to you a few Sundays since, a dispensation of death. This war has produced no results but slaughter and bloodshed. God has conducted it upon such principles, as that while death has reigned triumphant, no permanent success has crowned either side. All its great battles have produced no results looking to any settlement of this dispute.

At the first battle of Manassas we gave the enemy a shameful defeat; disgraced and panic stricken he fled to his Capital; and we held victory in our grasp, but it was fruitless in its consequences. Our great defeats in the West, the capture of New Orleans, the overrunning of Louisiana, Arkansas and Mississippi, have in like manner been fruitless in their hands. We have recovered almost every thing which we lost, and all that remains of those bloody fights are the graves which furrow the banks of the Mississippi and the bones which are bleaching upon its plains.

The wheel of fortune again turned in our favor, and Lee's great victories in Virginia, in 1863, were rendered without permanent benefit by our failures on the other side of the

Potomac. We reaped a harvest of death and nothing else. And so will it continue until God's wrath is satisfied, and therefore have I not been disturbed by our recent reverses. They mean blood and death and nothing more. Subjugation is as far off as it ever was and never can take place, for God's other purpose interferes with it, and his purpose must rule.

That other purpose, as I said before, is the discomfiture of the so called philanthropy of the world — its discomfiture by showing it practically how little the slaves care for such freedom as they can offer, and that the tender mercies of such friends are cruel. The bitterest disappointment of this war has been the quiet contentment of the slaves.

They have never gone to our enemies in any numbers; deceit and cajolement have been used in vain; they have had to come to the slave. He has continued in obedience through all the changes of the struggle, and never yet has offered violence to those who have had charge of him. Their quiet has been wonderful even to ourselves, and has caused the world not only to wonder, but to reverse its settled judgment about their treatment and condition.

And how sad has been their fate since they have been beguiled and betrayed into the hands of their so called liberators! The husbands and sons perishing by thousands upon the battle field, and the wives and mothers and little children sinking into inhospitable graves with none to care for them or watch over them. I will venture to say that of the negroes who have fallen under the dominion of the Federal armies, more than one-half of those who have been deprived of the protection of their masters have already perished.

The world even now sees and acknowledges that the slaves have gained nothing by their emancipation, and are beginning to be satisfied that it has made a grievous mistake in attempting to remove these people from their normal condition of servitude.

When these two purposes shall have been effected, our punishment through the dispensation of death, and the overthrow of man's folly and fanaticism, then may we look for peace — and not until then! Therefore is it that I repeat, "Vain is the help of man."

I have no faith in national platforms and Presidential elections; no expectations from European recognition or foreign interference; no trust in the power of cotton, or in the failure of money. I look to God for His help, and in due time it will come. Meanwhile we must be patient and enduring — patient under his chastisements, and enduring while he is making things work together for good to us. As I have said to you, again and again, this war is never to be ended by any victories of ours; God will give us just enough of them to enable us to keep our enemy at bay; it will be ended by his turning their arms inward upon themselves.

In the punishment of Europe for its horrid blasphemy, infidelity, and vice of the last century, that punishment took the same form of a dispensation of death. The French Revolutionists slaughtered their fellow citizens at home until they were glutted with blood, and man could endure no more; then the carnage was carried on still upon themselves, but likewise upon their neighbors, who had abetted their sins, through the wars of Napoleon.

Upon our continent the punishment has been reversed; the people of the Northern States had been trained upon such principles of law and order, that they were not prepared at once, to cut each other's throats; they must first be accustomed to violence through years of bloody war, and grievances must be created great enough to excite their angry passions. The dispensation of death upon this continent, has taken, therefore, a different course; first outward upon us, and then inward upon themselves.

When God is satisfied with our chastisement, and we, in humble penitence and submission have said, "Give us help from trouble; for vain is the help of man," then will He permit our sufferings to cease and theirs to begin. They need not boast that they do not feel the war; they need not exult in their wealth and luxury; they are only fattening in a large place as a lamb for the slaughter. Their feet shall slide in due time.

The election of Lincoln is a necessity for our deliverance; any other result should be disastrous to us. We need his folly and his fanaticism for another term; his mad pursuit of his peculiar ideas. It is he that is ordained to lead his people to destruction; to force them into conflict through the arbitrariness of his decrees.

His re-election will give him fresh courage and additional madness. He will drive all sound and rational men from his side; he will gather around him the radical and the fanatic; he will pursue the war with redoubled fury, until at last satiated with misrule, the sober thinking men of the North will perceive, that submission to him is utter and perpetual ruin.

Then will come the conflict which shall deliver us, when we shall be obliged to confess, (for it may not come until we are in our last extremity); "It is the Lord's doing, and it is marvelous in our eyes." All things are working together for our good. The fall of Atlanta, the victories at Mobile, our reverses of whatever kind, are so many links in the re-election of Lincoln, and therefore, so many links in the chain of our deliverance.

Every thing which gives them confidence, is so much in our favor, because it goads them on in their career of madness. What we have most to fear in our exhausted and depressed condition, is an administration which would come with kindness on its lips, and reconstruction with our ancient privileges in its hand. I fear our people would not have virtue to resist it, and we should be linked once more to that "body of death."

What we require is such fury as Grant's, such cruelty as Butler's, such fanaticism as Sherman's. It is men like these who revive our courage, and reanimate our efforts. We see that we have nothing to look for but degradation and outlawry; that we must fight, or else give up every thing that an honorable man holds dear — not only our property, but our caste — not only our sovereignty, but our personal freedom.

When we realize fully what our future condition is to be, and Lincoln's re-election will make us realize it, then shall we be fairly aroused, and must make the choice between a perpetual resistance, if necessary, and a condition of serfdom, in which we and our children shall be made "hewers of wood and drawers of water," to the paupers of Europe, the negroes of Africa, and last and lowest of all, to the Black Republicans of the North. If any of you are ready for that, I am not, and therefore I cry unto God to help me in trouble, "for He it is who is to tread down our enemies."

The Devout Soldier

Preached by request

to the

Powhatan Troop

at

Emmanual Church

March 6th 1864

by

Bishop Henry Lay Champlin

1864

SERMON

> There was a certain man in Caesarea called Cornelius, a centurion of the band called the Italian band; a devout man, and one that feared God with all his house; which gave much alms to the people and prayed to God always. Acts 10:1-2

Some persons of timid and uninstructed conscience have doubted at times whether the profession of arms is compatible with a just regard to the spirit and the precepts of our holy religion. But the well weighed and mature judgment of Christians has very generally affirmed the position assured by the Church of England in one of her articles "It is lawful for Christian men at the commandment of the magistrate to wear weapons and to serve in wars".

The clearest proof of this proposition is found in the treatment of soldiers mentioned in the New Testament For instance John the Baptist that stern and faithful preacher, received soldiers to his baptism, and admonished them not to forsake their called, but to resist its peculiar temptations to injustice and complaint. "Do violence to no man," he said "neither accuse any falsely, and be content with your wages."

The centurion, or Roman captain whose servant our Lord healed is represented as a man of lovely religious character. Many came to our Saviour to procure healing for their children: but this is the only one we know of who sought this benefit for a servant. Such was his humility and so just were his concessions of Christ's power and goodness as to win from our Lord that singular commendation. "I have not found so great faith, no, not in Israel." That is, this Gentile soldier had a livelier, clearer faith than God's most favored people.

The instance mentioned in the text is equally striking. When the privileged of the church hitherto confirmed to one people, were to be offered to all nations, Almighty God designated a soldier as the first Gentile to whom the Gospel should be preached and Holy Baptism administered. He is described as "a devout man": he made faithful use of those three private means of grace which our Lord commends to us in the Sermon on the Mount, prayer, alms and fasting: "he gave much alms to the people and prayed to God always".

He "was fasting" when the angel appeared to him and bade him send for Peter. And his influence pervaded those around him. He "feared God with all his house": "a devout soldier of them that waited on him continually" was his messenger to Joppa. His kinsmen and near friends were blessed through him, for on all of them the Holy Ghost did fall.

When we remember moreover that the Old Testament worthies are Moses and Joshua, Samuel and David were warrior Saints, as famed for their valor as for other virtues, we have abundant illustration of the truth that the pulses of the Christian heart may beat calmly and earnestly beneath the breast plate of the warrior.

It may be that some one of tender conscience still enquires, how are these things to be reconciled our religion breathes always the accents of gentleness and peace. It forbids bloodshed and violence: it tells us not to resist iniquity and wrong: it bids us love your enemies and pray for them which despite fully use you and persecute you. It sets out for our imitation the sublime example of One, the most cruelly sinned against and outraged of all the martyrs, whose last breath was expended in the entreaty "Father forgive!"

Does it not seem a contradiction for use with the memories of Calvary in my mind, and the cross, badge of patience signed upon my brow, to uplift the weapon of violence against a fellow creature, and to crimson my hands with the blood of the stranger?

To this we answer, that the spirit of revenge, the love of bloodshed, the redressing of individual wrongs at the expense of human life, is expressly forbidden by the precepts of the Gospel. That is no Christian warrior who delights in carnage and who is animated by hate and malevolence.

There are three cases, and I believe only three, in which it is lawful for men to destroy life viz, in self defense, in the protection of the helpless, and at the mandate of the civil power.

We may destroy life in self-defense: for this is a right secured by the law of nature, confirmed expressly by the law of Moses And in nowise taken away by our Saviour. He bids us submit to injuries, but then he specifies the sort of injuries: a buffet on the cheek, the robbery of a garment or such a matter, the imposition of a mile or two of travel —

He does not exact passive submission when the injury proffered is a deadly blow, a desolation of home and substance, a shameful and prolonged violation of personal liberty. Manliness is a part of our religion, and he is no true man who does not defend the life and liberty which God has given him against the violence of the wicked.

The protection of the helpless is not only a right, but a sacred duty. Our religion is not all mercy: it is justice as well as mercy. God himself prompts that generous wrath and indignation, that honest uprising of the soul which good men feel, in the view of pride insulting over helplessness and brute power grinding the faces of the innocent. As Moses smote the Egyptian and delivered his oppressed brother, so is it the duty of every Christian man to oppose the protection of his strong arm between the helpless and the oppressor.

We may also bear arms at the commandment of the magistrate. The Bible everywhere speaks of the civil authority as being God's representative: to it is committed the power of life and death for the preservation of the social order & for the terror of evildoers, and he beareth not the sword in vain.

Without this right to arm its citizens, Society would lie at the mercy of the reprobate: and when Summoned by its authority, the citizen acquires a new character. He is no longer a private man repelling private injuries, but becomes an official of the State, acting under its authority, obeying its mandates and not his own wishes.

We cannot indeed conceive that a Christian man should for revenge or for anger add one pang to the mass of human suffering, or shorten one life brief and sorrowful enough at best. But it is entirely consistent with our sense of right and with the teaching of our holy faith that a man of gentlest nature and tenderest sensibilities, a man the freest from hate and rancor, the fullest of kindness and forbearance, shall yet in a case of inevitable self-defense, or to ward off injury from those who look to him for aid, or at the solemn summons of the country which has given him birth, shall assume the character of the stern warrior, and smite fiercely until the aggressor desists from his injury.

Every conscientious man, my Hearers, ought to define to himself the grounds on which he acts in any serious matter: should be able to give a rational and religious account of his conduct. And surely it is enough for THE CONFEDERATE SOLDIER to rest upon the principles just laid down. He need not enter into speculation as to the nature of government, or touching the origin and causes of the war. It presents itself as a practical matter — what is my duty under God to myself, my neighbors and my country?

Yours is the plea of self-defense. You stand on your soil, next your own hearth-stones, to repel the invasion, not to make aggression. The enemy is here, at your doors in hot and angry pursuit of those who would live at peace; his firebrands are scattered along your border, and the course of the beautiful river may be traced in the darkness by the flame of his incendiary fires.

If conquered you are bereft of property, reduced to social degradation, nay robbed even of your conscience: for submission is not accepted unless you will add perjury to obedience, swearing such oaths and praying such prayers as the conqueror shall dictate. The only mercy for you is the base liberty to crawl dishonored on the earth, and to breathe the common air, so long as you mould into voices that will displease your masters.

You are fighting for the helpless. In this war there are none of these alleviations which knightly courtesy and Christian kindness had grafted on the barbarism of the past.

The unarmed citizen is driven from his home and lodged in the felon's cell. The man of grey hairs and tottering steps is insulted and jeered, while the torch is applied to his unoffending habitation.

The poor widow is surprised as she labors for the bread of her children, and sees every domestic animal slain, every implement of husbandry destroyed that she may be reduced to starvation: and this not occasionally and by a few soldiers, but systematically and by orders from the supreme authority.

Every where throughout our land, innocent and helpless people are weeping bitterest tears, and with hands upraised to heaven exclaim how long O Lord shall the ungodly triumph: how long shall the enemy do me this dishonor! And you under God are their vindicators and protectors.

Nor would I forget another class of helpless persons in whose defense you stand forth. I mean our negroes. That is a low and ignoble view of unworthy of any Christian Southerner, which would regard them as mere animals for labor to be bartered in for profit. There is a nobler sentiment among the good men of the Old Dominion, and of other states as well.

They are an inferior race committed to our guardianship by divine providence for our mutual benefit. They are members of our families, Sharers in our sustenance, often the affectionate nurses of our children, faithful watchers by our beds of Sickness. In prosperous times we have reaped the avails of their labor: now we are called to render them their due, and to protect them against the seductions of the of the crafty, and the refined cruelty of those who first tempt them to betray their masters and then in their distress reply "what is that to us" and leave them to perish.

Alas! how brave they died of want by thousands in every fence corner near their dismantled homes, or shivered and frozen beneath the cold charities of a Northern sky! What ruin of body and soul awaits them, when they exchange kind masters for pretended friends. —

Leaving all other considerations apart, this one alone seems decisive of our duty. This war is in a true and holy sense a war for the negro: and we would be false and craven if we did not stand forth in defense of our dependents and preserve them from demoralization and extermination. But chiefly, my friends, you are fighting for your country, and that word comprehends all.

The commandment of the magistrate or civil power is entitled to be reverenced and obeyed. Its enlistment or commission invests you with rights which a private man has not — Among the Romans it was considered infamous for a man to smite an enemy before he had taken the sacramentum [sic] or military oath: and the public law of later times affirms the principle teaching that while private persons may snatch up arms to defend their homes in case of sudden invasion, none is competent to make war who has not been delegated by the sovereign power and sworn to obey its wishes.

You can readily see how necessary this is to lift war above the level of personal malignity and private revenge. The strife becomes one of principles instead of persons. It is the public enemy you smite and not your own. This view encourages a loftiness and generosity of sentiment along with it, and adds to valor in combat, mercifulness in victory.

It is for your country you are fighting: a fair and lovely land, too fair to be the mere convict settlement of a foreign power. A country which by its heroism and endurance, by its adherence to right and justice, by its noble refusal under every provocation to barbarize itself by imitating the outrages it has suffered, has won already a glorious name. Could our cause be overthrown tomorrow, and three brief years sum up our national history, the exile in any foreign land should never blush to own "I was a soldier of the Confederacy."

I have said this much, not to strengthen your convictions, for that it is not needed: but that in the hope of assisting you to explain to yourself your own motives. Perchance my words may be recalled in some moment of solemn interest when you are to charge upon the ranks of living men, and facing death yourselves to carry it to others.

And surely it will nerve your arm and strengthen your heart to appeal to almighty God for the justice of your motives — that you strike not in wanton aggression, but for the defense of dearest rights" not to carry woe to others, but to avert it from millions of helpless brethren; not with personal malice but as the sworn soldier of an honored country.

I have urged thus far that the military profession in general, and the engagement of the Confederate soldier in particular, are entirely consistent with the Spirit and precepts of our holy religion. And now I invite you to consider another question — what there is in your peculiar circumstances as soldiers to help and what to hinder your religious welfare? It is a practical question and deserves to be weighed.

Some circumstances are in your favor — For instance it cannot be doubted that some of you occupy a much more unselfish position than before the war. And the more elevated are a man's moral sentiments, the more capable is he of readily receiving impressions strictly religious and spiritual. Every young man preparing to enter upon the active duties of life must needs arrange his plans. Shall I remain in Virginia, for instance or remove to the West? Shall I become a farmer, a mechanic, a merchant or shall I prepare myself for one of what are called the learned professions.

Now in deciding these questions you ought to be guided mainly by the consideration that one or another of these paths seems to afford a better opportunity to serve your God and Saviour, to be extensively useful to others, and to promote your own growth in grace and godliness. This ought to be the controlling argument: for whatever inducements any other career may hold out, it will profit you nothing to gain the whole world and lose your own soul. But how few young men do this!

How common is it for our youths to ask this question only, in which of these directions can I soonest get rich, or attain the most reputation, or find the most comfort and enjoyment: and to determine their actions by these considerations only or chiefly. And this when you sift it down is selfishness pure and unmitigated. I do not deny that some place may be allowed for duties to God and man, but they are entirely subordinated. Self stands first: God and man stand far below.

Bodily ease, human praise, increase of wealth are the main objects of life: religion must reconcile its claims with theirs if it can. And thus many a man at the very outset of life makes the terrible mistake of setting his face in the wrong direction.

Now the war has done you good in this regard. It has enlarged the scope of your vision, and lifted you out of your petty selfishness. You have felt there is a debt greater than that due to self. Generous ideas have invaded your minds. You have appreciated the beauty and nobleness of self-sacrifice. You have rallied cheerfully at your country's call. You have resigned your ambitious schemes and consented to endure the hardness while the extortioner and the laggard win the profit.

If you have said world thou must not tempt me: I cannot afford to make money: flesh thou must not murmur: it is in behalf of my country that I endure the weary vigil and the sharp hunger pain. This self-conquest is not necessarily religious in its character — it may be due to inferior motives: but you are better men for it, nobler men: your moral vision is cleared by it so that you can see something of the sublimity of self-conquest.

You are the better prepared to hear of him, that lonely chieftain sublime in his love and in his sorrow, who undaunted stood between the living and the dead until the plague was stayed: who stepped forth with noble boldness and stood patient while there settled on his devoted head that awful curse which would else have sunk us body and soul in hell.

You have borne privation and losses and felt the comfort of them. You are the more accessible to the entreaty come take up the cross and follow me. And oh that this very day you may rise from this mere stepping stone of duty, to the noblest of all: and resolve that you will live all henceforth for Christ, his Church and man's salvation.

Again — There are circumstances in your experience which tend directly to promote religious belief. Do you any of you for instance doubt the doctrine of a Special Providence now?

You have in former days perchance heard some argue that God does not concern himself with everyday matters: that the universe is like some great clock with its movements pre-arranged, wound up once for all, and interfered with only under circumstances of peculiar embarrassment. Such teachers are no longer listened to.

In nothing have the people of this great nation been more unanimously agreed, than in recognizing a Supreme Providence, ever watchful, never idle, working all things according to the counsel of his will.

Standing alone and friendless among the nations we have been led to cry there is none that fighteth for us save thou only O our God — we have ascribed to him the glory of every Success, and acknowledged his chastening hand in every reverse.

All have confessed that the future is too inscrutable for us to predict. The wonderful combination of events has baffled the wisdom of the most sagacious: we have felt our littleness and insignificance as unknowing actors in a drama of wonderful incident and unknown results, and have said with one voice "if the Lord delight in us, then he will save us."

Each of you has some story of special providence to tell: each one of you has in his thought been brought face to face with God, as one on whom you are dependent and with whom you have to do. The hair-breadth escape from danger imminent, the garment pierced by balls which avoided the body, or the strange course of missiles which reached the frame, but travelled curiously as though avoiding each vital part: these and Such like things have brought Divine

Providence home to your thoughts and assisted you to realize that the very hairs of your head are all numbered.

We believe that has been also much in your experience to commend to you Specially the religion of the Gospel. Yourselves exposed to dangers and trials, you need a religion of plain and familiar promises: for yourselves and for the sake of the dear ones at home you need a religion of sympathy: with little time and opportunity for close thought or severe neutral application you need a religion of certain facts and principles easily comprehended. And how do all these characters combine in the Gospel of our Lord and Saviour Jesus Christ!

What a comfort it is, Christian Soldier, to be permitted to look upwards and say, "Our Father which art in heaven" — To remember that you and yours are in the hands of a merciful Saviour who sympathizes with you, who has know by personal experience what it is to hunger and to be weary, to be lonely and persecuted.

A venerable professor of divinity is reported to have said upon his dying bed "My theology is all reduced to this, that Christ Jesus came into the world to save sinners." Ah, my friends, how have you felt that the simple scheme of redemption just meets the need of men anxious and harassed, in peril and in fear.

Vain is the hope to such that they can atone for their misdeeds, and by reformation blot out transgression. That dear word come unto me all ye that travail and are heavy-laden just meets their need: and it is not hard for them to believe that if saved at all, it is as miserable and guilty sinners by the free blood, of the atonement and by the tender mercy of God in Christ Jesus.

But I must not forget that there are many things in a Soldier's life unfriendly to godliness. It is a great misfortune to see separated from home influences: these gentle us and civilize us and tent to keep us pure. Mother and wife and sisters are guardians to us, as a general rule they are more unselfish and heavenly-minded than we are. And little-children with their pure minds and loving hearts are useful preachers to us. It is a misfortune to be separated from all these.

And men gathered in large crowds are apt to become coarse and rough in manners; to lay aside the delicacy and courtesy they observe at home. Unable to avoid unseemly and blasphemous talk, they become familiarized with it and ceases to shock and offend them. Nay, one who seeks to keep himself pure, will sometimes excite prejudice and lay himself open to the charge of pride: a charge by which some seek to destroy every man who preserves his self-respect and refuses to let himself down to the level of the vicious.

How necessary is it for the good soldier to guard against their influences: to resolve that under any and all circumstances he will still be the Christian gentleman, and carry back to his home a heart as pure, hands and tongue as undefiled as when he left it.

And so also of the publicity which attaches to your mode of life, and the irregularity of it, interfering so much with fixed habits of reflection and devotion. Often you have no closet to which you can retire, save the sanctuary of your own heart: you cannot read your bible or say your prayers without interruption and distraction. The day of rest comes with no hallowing influences, and is often occupied with week-day cares and employments that you almost lose the habit of counting it Sacred.

And yet you must keep the thought of Christ and his love fresh in your heart: you must pray without ceasing, you must in heart and mind thither ascend where Christ has led the way — what energy of purpose, what special grace and help to enable you to resist these hindrances and to preserve a religious temper.

We are all apt to think that our peculiar state of life is specially unfavorable to religious improvement: and I suppose it is hard for any one to form a correct and fair judgment. It is enough for you to recognize whatever there is in your state and calling to favor religious endeavor and to use it well: to consider well your difficulties and use every precaution against them.

We trust we have proved to you, however the balance may seem to incline, that a soldier can be a Christian: a devout man, a burning and shining light to those around him. Your own observation has found living examples not unlike those which we have cited from the New Testament days. For the Spirit helpeth our infirmities: He is with us abroad as at home, in war as in peace. He works by means and Seemingly without means. And when a Sinner cries "take not thy Holy Spirit from me", this dove of purity and peace come to nestle in his bosom, even amid the discords of horrid war, and the tumult of the crowded camp.

And now my Hearer, suffer us to ask you plainly what sort of a soldier you are: patriotic, brave, uncomplaining, subordinate to authority — we trust you are all these. The Powhatan troop has won a good report. Among the first to step forth, it has blanched before no duty or danger: it will stand enduring to the end.

But there is a deeper question. Are you such a soldier as Cornelius — a devout man, and one that feared God with all his house, which gave much alms to the people and prayed to God always? Death has already made mournful gaps in your company: Some of you will probably yield up your breath in the hospital or on the field, before another campaign is over. Consider well, that is the devout soldier only: the God-fearing man, the charitable man, the praying man to whom belongs the promise of a better life after death.

Let not any one say that this suggestion discouraged men, and promotes fear and cowardice. For if you have not made your peace with God, or are uncertain of it, still is it better for you to play the man. The post of duty is the place of safety. It is safer for a man to rush up to canon's mouth with only time to say "God be merciful to me a Sinner", than to seek a longer probation by evading his duty as a man and a citizen.

He has no right to hope than such a willful and presumptuous abandonment of his trust, will ever be repented of or forgiven. But to return, You may be fired with generous principles, and win a glorious name, and die an honored death: and yet after all perish for ever. There is mentioned in the Gospel a young man who lived a very upright life, and whom our Lord loved when he looked upon him: he was so amiable and honest. And yet he could not enter into the kingdom of heaven because he would not take up his cross and bear it.

Our hearts yearn over the gallant defenders of their country: God forbid that in so good a cause, spending so much, you should win no more than man's applause; whereas you may so live and die, that at the last God himself: think of it my Hearer: how proud is a private to be praised in General Orders: that God himself shall say to you before an assembled universe "Well done, good and faithful servant!"

What must you do to be saved? The answer is plain and familiar. Believe in the Lord Jesus Christ and thou shalt be saved: repent and be converted that your sins may be blotted out. Do you not know what these precepts mean? Believe in the Lord Jesus Christ.

Do you not know what it is to believe in man? Is there no physician in whose skill and kindness you have such confidence, that you would submit to his prescription without a question? Is there no military leader in whom you so believe that you obey his order gladly as well of necessity, and approve his designs when you least comprehend them?

Now reason upward. Your soul is sick and Christ is the good physician. You are a Soldier in an enemy's land, beset with many dangers, and Christ is the captain of your salvation. Believe in him then: trust him with all, submit to his every commandment: do just what he tells you, follow just where he leads you. Expose your sins to him that he may wash them away in the blood of his cross: bow your neck before him that he may bind upon you his yoke.

Do you not know what Repentance is? Its chief element is Godly sorrow for sin: not mere sorrow, but Godly sorrow: the sorrow that comes when you survey your sins in the light of God and of eternity: when you stand by the cross and see how terrible is the punishment they deserve, how prodigious the mercy that forgives them all.

You have not been sorry because you have been thoughtless and inconsiderate; you have not asked for the help of the Spirit to show you their enormity, to break your hard heart, to give you the grace of grief and tears. But now consider your ways and call to mind your doings: count up your mercies, consider how patient God has been with you, how much Christ loves you, how tenderly he reproaches you for avoiding him, how lovingly he invites you and you will repent. And "be converted".

This you say is my stumbling block: conversion seems to be such a strange something: you associate it perhaps with an unnatural excitement, and transcendent ecstasy, a miraculous and instantaneous release from the bands of Sin and Sorrow. Conversion is nothing of the sort. God's service is a rational service: his ways are heavenly and spiritual, but they unite sobriety with fervor, and good sense with tender emotion. Conversion, Brethren, is properly the outward and visible effect of the inward repentance and faith.

It does not describe the experience of any one moment, but is used to describe that change of mind and will and affection and purpose, which is wrought in us by the Spirit of God, when we come to him according to the terms of the Gospel. Conversion is not something which we must wait to happen to us: it is a duty to be performed at God's command and with his gracious help. Be converted, Christ cries to us all.

We may well express it in military phrase "face right about". You have mutinied against your lawful sovereign, and deserted your standard. You have fought against God, and are rushing to give yourself up body and soul to his enemies. Christ, as a warning angel meets you on the way: with the imperiousness of authority, with the tenderness of love he withstands you.

Repent & be converted he cries: remove your shameful purpose and face right about. And when you see your crime and loathe it, when you recognize the drawn sword in his hand & adore his forbearance when from the depths of a convicted and sorrowful heart you cry "Lord if it displease thee I will get me back again". When you do turn back, and

renew your allegiance, and acknowledge your ill-desert —
This, this my Hearers is conversion.

My Hearers you ought to understand these matters. If yet
in the dark, devout study of God's word and careful
meditation over it, constant and earnest prayer for the help
of the Holy Spirit, whose office it is to open blind eyes, to
teach dull souls & to give heavenly wisdom, that you must
seek to know these mysteries on which your life depends.
And as an additional means I beseech you to use the counsel
and advice of the godly ministers of the Church.

Let not shame or diffidence hinder you from coming to us
and opening your grief. Our holy office has brought us unto
contact with men as erring and as despairing as any of you
can be: and the good physician has furnished us with
medicine for their diseases. The turning point in many a
man's religious history is found often in the moment when he
unburdened his soul to the minister of Christ.

I have said [that] among the Romans no man was allowed
to fight, until he had taken the Sacramentum or military oath.
Hence comes our word Sacrament. The Church caught up the
word and sanctified it for her own uses. If you would fight in
Christ's army and be carried by him into his glory, you must
take his Sacrament. You must Solemnly, in the presence of
his people, swear allegiance to him, and by a vow uttered
with the mouth, announce the purpose formed by his grace
in your heart.

You cannot keep your religious purpose a secret: it is a
rash and presumptuous thing to encounter temptation
without the help offered you in the Church, and without the
spiritual benefits covenanted and conveyed to us in Baptism
& in the Holy Communion. (Note — Confirmation in
Richmond March 20)

Some of you are baptized members of the Episcopal
Church: others are inclined to enter her sacred fold. As her
accredited representation, as the ambassador of Christ, I say
to you one and all, Come thou with us and we will do thee
good. She has many chains upon you. It is the old time
Church planted first in England by Apostolic men, and

brought by our fore-fathers to Jamestown when first they came to Virginia.

It is the Church which teaches the faith as once delivered to the Saints, and as constantly held by all orthodox persons in the ancient creeds. It is a Church of devout ceremonial, of authoritative ministry, of boldest and yet gentlest evangelic teaching. It is the Church which framed the translation of the Bible which we do so highly prize, a Church of many learned doctors and Saintly children and to which have adhered many of the wisest and best leaders of the American revolution and of this young republic. Come with us, my brother and we will do thee good.

Not that we can do good to the careless and impertinent, to the prayerless men who love not the Lord Jesus Christ. For these are condemned already and the wrath of God abideth on them.

But if you are sorry for your Sins: if you are grieved and wearied with the burden of them, and determined by God's help to abjure and forsake them: if you have a thankful remembrance of Christ's death, and are willing to trust your all to his power and goodness, then do the Spirit and the Bride say come, and whosoever will let him come & take of the water of life freely.

Thus, dear friends, have I sought to address to you such affectionate counsel and exhortation as the occasion seems to demand: remembering that we shall never all meet again, until at the bar of God we give our several accounts as preacher and as hearers. May these teachings fall as good seed upon good and honest hearts and bring forth fruit abundantly.

May God almighty set his angels to guard you in all perils and hardships: avert every danger and lighten every sorrow. You carry with you the sympathies and the prayers of families and friends: if you fall in battle, oh let them not experience the bitter grief of those who sorrow without hope: if you return, bring with you a pure mind, an unsullied reputation, a holy heart, a Christian character matured by temptations resisted, inaugurated by unfaltering and manly endeavors.

Sooner or later death must come to all. It matters, much indeed to us, but little to you, whether you be cut off in youth or survive to grey hairs, provided only it may be said at your grave: "He was a devout man, and one that feared God with all his house. He gave much alms to the people and prayed to God always."

POWER

A SERMON

PREACHED AT

ST. PAUL'S CHURCH, RICHMOND

ON THE 13TH NOVEMBER, 1864

BY

REV. CHARLES MINNIGERODE, D. D.

1864

"POWER"

I Cor. 4:20.

IT is a single word to some meditations on which I would invite you this morning, my brethren: POWER. It is found throughout the Scripture, its idea pervades it from one end to the other. It is ascribed to God, and it is ascribed to man; the attribute of God. "Power belongeth unto God;" and by Him, the giver of every good and perfect gift, bestowed upon man, made in his likeness, "it is He that giveth them power." In its highest sense it is pledged to the believer "power to become the sons of God," power "to be like Christ in the world." What is *power*?

In our version it is used in two senses, indeed there are two words for it in the original Greek of the New Testament. The one *(exousia)* is rather the substratum of the other; the possession, the authority and ability (we call that *power)* to put forth that quality, which in its exercise and its effects becomes what in Greek is called "dynamis," *power* in the other sense; or *power* as the. gift, the endowment which is prerequisite to *power* as its manifestation.

We can illustrate the difference in our Saviour's life. Himself the highest revelation of God's power, and hence called, "the power of God," and to whom in his delegated character as the Christ or Messiah "all power is given in heaven and in earth;" he exercises that authority and ability in "his mighty works,? *his manifested power.* "The people glorified God who had given such power (such authority and ability) unto men;" but as he performed them, "power" (in the English version "virtue," in the Greek "dynamis") went out of him." Such authority he delegates and the ability he communicates to his believers.

He gives them power *(exousian)* he bestows it upon them, that they may manifest it in the *life of power,* in its exercise, in *the dynamic force,* which is to influence their own life and the life of the world, which is to produce results according to the ability and the mission entrusted to them. The idea is brought out clearly in those texts, in which power, *its reality*, is opposed to the mere *pretence* or *appearance:* "The kingdom of God is not in word but in power," "having a form of godliness, but denying the power thereof." Just as the Apostle John expresses the same contrast in other words, "let us not love in word, neither in tongue, but in deed and in truth;" and just as St. James opposes the mere hearer to the doer.

Wherever and howsoever the word power is used, this is its bearing, in Mathematics and Mechanics, in Rhetoric, in Natural, in Moral and Mental Philosophy; whatever sense we give it, it involves ability to effect results, to produce changes, power *to do, to* make things, facts, events (hence its Saxon synonym *"might,"* connected with the verbs "may" and "make.")

It is to this life of power we are called. It is the creative, the vital, energizing, motive element of our nature, fraught with consequences both in its use and its neglect, resulting either in good or in evil; and by the kind of power we exercise, by the spirit in which we use our power, we show what spirit we are of, a *power for God* or *a power for the devil.* Surely this is a subject worth our consideration and mate in this pulpit.

The whole problem of our life, the end of all religion is, to exercise power, i. e. the ability and authority given us by God (to use *the talents* entrusted to us) in obedience to his will and according to his design. Herein we find the proof, that we possess it and have been endowed with it by him ("ye shall receive power after the Holy Ghost is come upon you"); therein alone we show, that by his renewing grace we have become "partakers of the divine nature."

Man is created in the image of God, his high and holy calling is to be like God. In the exercise of this power we must tread in the footsteps of God himself.

The power of God! But can we presume to speak of it? What tongue can tell it, what heart conceive — infinite as it is, beginning and end unlimited but by his own immeasurable power?

I. *The power of God in nature.* The heavens declare that power and the firmament showeth its handiwork, but man can only adore, and as the fire and the storm and the earthquake pass before him — tokens of God's might and power — bows to "the still small voice" which comes in the gentle breeze and tells him, that the life-sustaining, want-supplying, order-keeping laws, his mercies new every morning, are but tokens of the same almighty power, which "makes the seraphs veil their faces and charges the angels with folly."

Yes if we could go back to the morning of creation and see world after world roll from his omnipotent hand; if we could travel from star to star and system of stars to system of stars, and count the inmates of created universe and read the laws which bind them in indissoluble order, and trace the forces which make them move as in spheral harmony around his sovereign will; if we could sound the abysses of the deep and decipher the mysteries of the visible creation, and rise to the view of its hidden forces, and cast a glimpse into the ages to come: it would be but the trailing of his garments, the outer sweep of his passing power.

The Scriptures, his own revelation, teach us how to view the manifestations of *His* all-creating, all-sustaining power, whose thoughts are facts, whose words creations — "he spake and it was done, he commanded and it stood fast."

Man too has power. Given him when God himself stood sponsor at his cradle in Eden "to subdue the earth, and have dominion over the fish of the sea and over the fowl of the air, and over every living thing, that moveth upon the earth:" even the fall did not rob him of his birthright. —

Though the ground revolted and brought forth "thorns and thistles," though "in the sweat of his brow" he had to defend and secure his very existence, he asserted his power and entered upon the reconquest of his domain.

For 6000 years the warfare has lasted, and every age has added spoils to the victor's cause. Every province of nature has been invaded; every element — arrayed in hostility against him — has been braved, fought, mastered and at last forced into his service; the height and the deep been laid under contribution, her secret forces traced and watched and seized upon and placed at his command.

He has and exercises and lives by power in the earth, her manor-born king. He steps into the wilderness and the solitary place: and under the labor of his hands and the use of the means gathered in the school of nature and its laws, they obey his bidding, and "the desert rejoice and blossoms as the rose." He stands before the mountain and wills it to be removed and cast into the sea; and with that will goes forth the power of a hundred-handed energy and the appliance of forces taken from nature's own laboratory: and the mountains are cleaved and the hills thrown down.

He digs into the bowels of the earth and brings out her hidden treasures, and bids them work for him, warm him, speed his engines and become his tools: and they obey the word of his power. It opens a pathway for him in the sea, sets distance at defiance as he speeds triumphantly along in his fire-driven chariot, and seizes upon the secret of the lightning to make it the carrier of his thoughts and words as with the speed of omnipresence to the farthest ends of the earth. *Power indeed!*

The peaceful monk, whose curious art brought together the latent forces of explosion and almost paid with his life for setting free a power, which has revolutionized war and changed the whole aspect of the political world; the humble artisan, who first taught time to give notice of its passing hours and tick out its fleeting minutes; the man, who bound the "winged" word in types and became the father of the press; the mechanic, who raised he Southern staple to a royal power by passing it through the gin into the loom; the philosopher, who watched the expansive properties of steam, and calculating its force made it a power in the hand of man; the engineer, filling valleys and leveling mountains, who makes straight the crooked, and the rough places smooth, who hangs his highway over the foaming abyss and forces his tunnel through the everlasting hills,

These and such as these are the leaders of the race in its mighty conquest of the forces of nature and have proved, *that man has power in the earth.* But brethren, *power which acknowledges and glorifies and testifies to the power of God,* of which his is but the reflex; which sits at the feet of the great master who has made and upholds the universe in its everlasting laws, and learns to read those laws and apply the facts of experience in harmony with them and the appointed succession of cause and effect; which traces out the hidden secret of its mechanical and chemical properties and appropriates them to their legitimate uses, and produces changes on the face of the earth, and effects results to increase his wealth and comfort and strength, and lays open ever new resources, to proclaim him the lordly tenant, the vice-gerent of God on earth: even so, for only as he obeys the eternal laws of nature, only as he treads in the footsteps of nature's God, can he exercise this power.

II. But we rise from power in nature to *power in providence.* This is *God's power,* the government of his own world. "The earth is the Lord's and the fullness thereof, the world and they that dwell therein."

From everlasting to everlasting he sits enthroned in his sovereignty and his will ruleth over all. To us is revealed but the brief space of six thousand years that man has existed on the earth; and how little is known to us of them, and of the races that have lived there? What records are left us, what plans revealed? What guide to lead us through the wanderings of its nations, like as his dealings with the elect people?

Ah, we have indeed learned that "he plants his footsteps in the sea and rides upon the storm, "that "the pillar of fire by night and the pillar of cloud by day" follow the children of our race; that "deep in unfathomable mines, with never failing skill, he treasures up his bright designs and works his gracious will;"

We have learned — even though he should marshal his sore judgments, the judgment and the sword and the pestilence, and "we know not what he doeth," to acknowledge his hand and "trust him for his providence:" But who can write the annals of God's government and follow through the ages of his eternal reign? "His thoughts are not as our thoughts, neither are his ways our ways."

No philosophy has yet gone beyond the premises of the passing present. *Faith* only reposes on his promises, which point out to the ark of his Church, midst all the downfall of earthly hopes and calculations, its unfailing and eternal triumph; and in every trying hour, every perplexing visitation, *he* points us to the proofs of his past power and mercy, and bids us rejoice, that "the Lord God omnipotent reigneth."

And man? He too has power! Created in the image of God he steps as actor upon the arena of life, himself an energy, a power, a ruling spirit, and makes a history for his race. Have there not been in all ages "giants in the earth," with might to achieve events that seemed to shape the destinies of the world?

Kings — that would guide the masses and stamp their greatness upon nations? Conquerors — that stretched their sceptre over many lands and gave laws to many tongues? Heroes — that could inspire the feeble with strength, and relieve the oppressed, and break the bonds of thralldom, and bid the swelling tide of despotism stay its fury, and raise above the power of brute force the power of manliness and liberty and truth?

Orators — that could command listening senates and sway the heaving masses, and "with the Olympian thunderbolt upon their lips" dictate peaCe or war by the power of their word? Sages — that pierced as with heaven-born light the night Of darkness and superstition, and molded future generations by the wisdom of their laws, the sight beyond the outward appearance into the depths of man's mind and God's government, the power of their prophetic spirit?

The world's history is made up of such, their influence and power for good or evil, the representative men of their age; or the founders of a new era, who concentrating upon themselves all the acquisitions of the past make them instruments of power with which to march upon the opening future, and write their names upon the progress or the doom of generations yet unborn. It is around their names that the events of history are clustered, and in their lives that this power in man is culminated. —

But a *power,* brethren, *held at God's good pleasure* and controlled by his own omnipotent rule; a power used in his hands to carry out his great designs and bring to pass the purposes of his government. No founder of a nation, no prophet, legislator, hero, ever lived to sketch out its life and progress and end; to project a plan for the government of the race and bid the nations at his call advance and take their part in the drama of the world; and prescribe laws by which they should succeed each other, and prophecy which should be called into action, which carry on the work of the world's civilization or abasement, which crown its days with glory or with shame.

In the heat of action, under the fire of ambition, a world of courtiers or of slaves bowing before them: men may forget that they are but instruments in God's hand and say "my greatness is grown and reacheth unto the heaven and my dominion unto the end of the earth:"

But God stretches out his holy arm, and they learn there is a sovereign above; like Nebuchadnezzar — driven from men and dwelling with the beasts of the field; like Alexander — vainly weeping, that the mighty ocean set bounds to his conquests, but whose vast empire fell to pieces when death overtook him at his drunken revels; like the mighty Cesar — stabbed to the heart in the hour of success; with time only to cover decently his dying form, but with that regal toga were covered also and forever the lofty designs with which he aspired to bless his conquered world; like the exile of St. Helena — doomed in his living death to see the world fall back the hundred years, which his ambition thought to overleap on the wings of his victorious eagles.

A power indeed! but itself *the servant of the Power above!'* and blessed, truly powerful only, when wielded in God's service, in acknowledged submission to his will and the great law of his eternal government, that only "Righteousness exalteth nation, but sin is a reproach to any people."

III. But much as we have dwelled on this, brethren, we have not yet spoken of the highest and most glorious manifestation of power, whether on the part of God or man. — Power in nature rules over inanimate matter; power in providence and the history of the world rules over masses, which however active or passive, however happy or suffering, do but follow — willingly or unwillingly, knowingly or unknowingly — its irresistible march over the world, seemingly of the powerful of the earth, truly of the God of all power and might.

But power is *greatest* when exercised *upon power,* and *upon the highest power conceivable,* the individual himself possessed of intelligence and moral power, *the free agent.*

To come to the point: We know little or nothing of God's power as exercised upon the higher intelligences of his universe, his angels and archangels, the powers, dominions, principalities and thrones of which the Apostle speaks; or upon the powers of darkness and the prince of this world. We only know it is an almighty power, all-wise, just, benevolent and holy Still less do we know of the power of these lofty beings, and their agency upon each other and upon ourselves.

The Apostle lifts the veil a little, when he calls the angels "ministering spirits, sent forth to minister to them that shall be heirs of salvation;" and all the Bible, our Lord, his Prophets and Apostles warn us of the power of evil, evil spirits, spirits of darkness and destruction and malice, which war against our race, to rob us of the power of an endless life and spoil us of the powers of the world to come.

But we do know of *God's power over* man, not only in that sovereignty which extends over all creation: but *over man in his individuality,* as a moral being, free to choose and free to act. We do know of *the power of man over his fellow* — *not* in the influence which moves the masses like pawns on a chess board: but the power of *mind upon mind, soul upon soul, spirit upon spirit,*

God's power over man, who has rebelled against his government and is at enmity with him, yet free to obey or disobey, and bold enough to set the terrors of God's law at defiance and abide the consequences of his rebellion; over man, whose heart must be won if the conquest is to be real, whosse enmity must be overcome — not by brute force and irresistible power (for that would annihilate in him the image of God, his prerogative of free agency:) but *by a power higher than all —*

A power to reach the proud heart and subdue it, induce it cheerfully, voluntarily, eagerly to surrender to Him and lay down its arms, aye give it a new spirit which cannot rest satisfied except in the light of his countenance, "his favor which is life and his loving kindness which is better than life;" a power over the stubborn heart to make it willing; a power over the free agent, to resign himself by an act of free will to the will of God; a power, to change enmity to love, to cut loose the soul from self to which it was anchored by nature, and moor it forever and ever and with all its self determining will, all its might and strength, its affections, hopes and powers in the will and love of God!

Pass through all creation, conceive of all conditions and degrees of force, of constraining laws and binding power — and what power is like this? a change from hate to love, from hell to heaven, from death to life!

A power, to defeat the strong hold of the adversary upon that rebellious heart, to break bonds which have been riveted in our birth, and grown with our growth, and strengthened with our strength; to give up life-long habits, all that was dear and made up life's happiness and aim; to change the principle and practice; to change and renew the heart from sin to holiness, from self to God; *not* as the impossible result of force, of threatening laws, of terrors of vengeance:

The free will must be *won,* it cannot be forced. The speech, the act may be controlled; the intent, the affection is its own. Love, a willing heart ca a never spring from such a source. A higher, a more blessed, more stupendous power must be God's to win this victory. It is the power of *love, God's love,* and this power is revealed in the *gospel "the power of God unto salvation."*

Ah, he could have repressed by one volition the insurrection of his creatures, he could have followed up sin with such immediate and sensible suffering as to make its commission impossible — but that would have been the exercise of force, which would have destroyed free agency and robbed his power of this highest triumph; the victory over the sinful and apostate heart.

He could have swept the rebellious race from the face of his fair world, no more to blast its beauty and mar its happiness, and re-peopled by the at of his word this stray orb with happier and better beings — but God's power passed beyond the power of destruction; he yearned over the lost and fallen race, and came and spoke the word of life and salvation. *The power of love!*

Aye, love, which alone can beget love and win the heart; love, so great, so amazing, so constraining, that the heart to which it is revealed, the heart that trusts to it, *must* turn to him and give up all to Him "who loved us first:"

> Thy love unknown
> Has broken every barrier down

Love! aye, more than what the world calls love; more thin what the pompous rhetoric of the proud philosopher; or the shallow feelings of the dreamy sentimentalist can conceive, who wreathes his brow with the flowers that blossom in his path, and quiets his rising fears with a hope of God's goodness, that would undo his moral government; more than that human standard of God's love, which has never made its prophets yield to the power they sing of, never give up for it one idol of the heart and choose him as the ruler of their lives.

No, *it is not in nature:* for along with all the proofs of his love and benevolence which gladden the face of the earth, there go the tokens of a power fearful in destruction, the yawning ruin of the earthquake, the blighted promise of the harvest, the sturdy oak riven by the bolt of heaven.

It is not in God's glorious government of law: along with his promises to the good and faithful go his fearful threatenings upon the wicked, the inexorable law of vengeance against the disobedient, the certain wages of sin; along with it goes the mysterious discipline of sorrow to his own, which only the power of faith and trust can read.

It is only *the love which brings redemption* and opens heaven to the weary, penitent soul; *his love in Christ,* who took upon him all our sufferings and woes, and atoned for all our sins to set us free, and over the altar on which he died for us holds out the hand of reconciliation and brings the boon of mercy and of grace, the free gift of pardon and acceptance

The self-sacrificing love of God, who "spared not his own son but delivered him up for us all," that "whosoever believeth in him should not perish but have everlasting life" — his love to us "while we were yet sinners, at enmity with him;" *it is there alone* where the heart can rest and find hope and peace.

His love to us, the poor prodigals of his universe, the helpless children of deserved and self-imposed ruin; his love which bears their punishment, and opens to them the everlasting arms; it is this love alone, which has power to win back the heart, rescue it from the fatal grasp of self and reclaim it to eternal life.

Love, with one hand pointing to the cross, and in that mangled, suffering body showing us all our misery and all the doom that was mire, but borne away by his own self, from love unmerited, unsought, unspeakable; and with the other pointing to the inheritance of light and glory which is purchased for us by that agony and sacrifice.

And *pleading,* aye pleading as if his own blessedness was at stake with the perishing sinner, and beseeching him in tones of bleeding, weeping love to be reconciled and live; aye, pleading from the cross, not to let him die in vain; pleading from the seat of glory in heaven, not to rob him of the travail of his soul, the jewels of his crown, souls saved from death and hell, and asking in accents to melt the stoutest heart, "was ever love like mine? Son — give me thine heart!"

Such love — can it be resisted? Is the heart here present that could spurn it, that would not fly to it and give itself, its all to him?

> Were the whole realm of nature mine,
>
> That were a tribute far too small;
>
> Love so amazing, so divine,
>
> Demands my life, my soul, my all

Bear with me, brethren, as I delay you. My subject possesses me. Oh may it possess you, and draw your hearts to open to its power; the love of God!

I pass in review the perfections of the Deity; but love alone, this bleeding, dying, redeeming, self-sacrificing love; which stoops from heaven and empties itself of glory, to speak to the apostate soul the word of life, which surrenders self to save the lost, bearing their sins, suffering their punishment — so great, so unfailing as to wed the rescued soul unto himself for all eternity — this love alone gives me hope and wins my heart.

God's omnipotence — *it* is but his arm of strength, not his heart. *God's eternity* — 'tis as the boundless waste of the ever moving sea, no rest for the longing soul, for the mind gazing into endless ever-growing distance. *God is holy, just, omniscient* — 'tis the very sword of the cherubim, "the sword turning every way to guard the way of the tree of life" from the approach of the sin-convicted soul. *God is all-wise* — *his* thoughts as high above ours as the heavens above the earth. I stand amazed, bewildered, but cannot understand him, cannot find him.

But God is love. Love! brethren — the brightest jewel in his crown of perfections, the essence of his nature, in which all his perfections unite, to which all his perfections do service. Omnipotence — I adore in silent awe! Eternity — I reel in giddiness as I attempt to scan the height and depth, the length and breadth! Justice — I tremble in my conscience-smitten soul! Wisdom I must bow to thy decrees and be resigned! But love! love! I give myself to thee, I surrender myself, my all, my soul and spirit, my hopes for time and my eternity to love!

> Now to be thine, yea thine alone,

O God of love! O Lamb of God, that has revealed, that has ensured, that hast won and sealed and pledged that love to me, and proved it in thy sufferings and agony and dying groan

O, lamb of God — I come I

This is the power of God.

And brethren, *of like kind is the power of* man, made in his image.

We all know there is a power in man, from mind to mind, from soul to soul, and all life is made up of the passing and repassing of these influences. *A fearful power,* brethren: For does not all experience prove, it may be for evil as well as for good? And more readily for evil? Oh for the influence of example, the influence of a strong mind, the influence of authority or affection; how constantly do we see it abused in the service of sin and the world!

No ruined soul in hell, but can trace that ruin to such power in others. Oh God, perhaps parents, brothers, husbands, friends, who have done the devil's work and led the soul placed under their power, led the soul trembling under the fascination of their influence and example, to eternal misery and not to heaven! Brethren, how parents, how lovers, how friends can be anything but Christians, when the eternal issues of those given in the power of their own are at stake, it passes comprehension!

I shudder at the thought, yet the thought which daily experience brings up constantly. We have souls in our charge, I and you, yea all, and God will hold us responsible for them; eternity is before them and you. Oh use your power, use it for their and your everlasting good! For whom shall those hearts be won, to whom subdued? God or the devil?

Believe me, it is only the love of God, which can guide us aright. Our own souls must first be His, and then a power shall spring up and an influence be wielded, which shall make the heavens shout with joy; if not, it is hell that rejoices, and devils which applaud. It is only the-power of God's love in the heart, which gives power to gain this victory on earth.

There are souls all around us, and power is given us — this principle alone can make it a saving power.

1. Brethren, *our own souls, power over ourselves!* Oh, do we not know, that this is a victory greater than all which can be won on earth; that "he that subdueth his own heart is greater than he that taketh a city." And it is only through the love of God, through the new and better and stronger affection for Him, we can drive out the love and affection for the idols that dwell there.

It is easy, to put it to the test. Have we that power? Is self cast out? Is our life elevated.? Has that step from death to life been taken which changes the heart from sin to holiness? Are *we* changed, our hearts freed from the dominion of sin? Has the impure mind been cleansed so that it has come again like the mind of a little child? Has the grasp of the miser been relaxed and the avaricious learned to spend and be spent for God and Christ, and holiness and every righteous cause? Has that ambition been cast out and the soul been taught to kneel to God?

> Make me little and unknown,
>
> Love and prized by Thee alone!

Is that spirit of revenge gone, that evil eye, that passionate temper, that, selfish fretfulness — and have we learned to "look not on our own things but also on the things of others" and "to esteem others better than ourselves?" and, like Christ, to be lowly and meek and pure, and self-denying, self-sacrificing, kind and gentle?

This power, is it ours? greater than the power to do mighty works, work miracles, remove mountains, and chain the forces of nature to our service? This *power over self,* greater than the cutting off of the right hand and the plucking out of the right eye — is it ours? This change, aye, this radical change, has it been accomplished, greater than all the changes wrought on the surface of the earth, in the society of man? "Has the leopard changed his spots and the Ethiopian his skin?" and yet, it must be so, or we are lost, none of His who has called us to this conquest of self, and given us power "to become the sons of God."

2. *Power over others.* We have it surely; but power over others, for their good, their eternal good! Have we won them over by precept and example, by a Christ-like walk and purity, by love and devotion and unselfishness? By the manifestation of the power which grace has given us over our own spirits? Do we exercise such power over them? Do we lead their souls with ours to heaven?

Oh, let us flee to Christ and get power of Him, the power of a divine and Christ-like spirit and life I Ours must be either a crown in heaven of souls saved, or a crown of fire in hell of souls lost — by us, by our blessed or baneful power. Mothers, Fathers, Christians! What an alternative I How high, how holy, how fearful your calling!

It is the power of love, of self sacrifice by which God gains the victory over the will and wins the heart of man.

It is the same *love and self-sacrificing spirit,* which shall give *us* power over human hearts. To this power we are called, beloved; and should it be *the power of suffering,* which is involved in self-sacrifice. All history sets its seal to this power. Men in all ages have felt for it, hoped for it. There is no mythology but the fabled saviour-god passes through suffering; no legendary period of any nation, but it sings of heroes that proved themselves saviours and benefactors by suffering for the good of all.

What is this, but the groping of the natural mind, its dim anticipation of the great truth, that redemption demands sacrifice; its intuitive longing for the revelation of the true Saviour, who through suffering and death should work out the salvation of the world? But is it not the noblest ambition, to have this Christ-like power, and be his missionary in the world?

Is there a greater reward — "he that converteth the sinner from the error of his way shall save a soul from death, and shall hide a multitude of sins?" Is there a higher life — like Christ, by example, by bearing, by charity, by constraining love, by self sacrifice, to be a *power in the earth for God and heaven?* To stand in this world and meet its evil and its evil power; and by the power of a godly life to change the moral desert into an Eden of God; by the power of faithfulness and perseverance in God's service to remove the difficulties, and level the mountains, which the power of the world has raised in the way of the triumphant march of Christ and his Church?

To stand in this world and meet its enmity and its sorrows with this power, and bid the weary rest and the mourning rejoice, allay strife and woo the heart by love, relieve suffering and do God's heavenly work on earth "wiping away the tears from their eyes?"

Behold the power of the Gospel! By nature we are a power against God, and thus a power of destruction to ourselves and our fellows. The Gospel, the might of God's converting love, makes us *a power for God and thus for good in the world.*

It gives us such power in our intercourse with others, our social influence, in our public and our private life, Power to leaven the laws of the country and elevate the spirit of the people, and lay the groundwork for a better future; power in us now, to lay the foundation of our new empire upon the everlasting premises of truth and godliness, to make it a power in the earth for good, a blessing to ourselves, to our children's children and the nations of the world — worthy the sacrifice it cost.

Power in our private life, to lay the foundation of true and lasting happiness in the sacred circle of the family, and make every relation of life its channel and every duty its instrument; which from there shall spread in ever widening circles, and whose influence upon the happiness of others and the world at large, eternity alone shall fully unfold.

A power for all — not the monopoly of a privileged few — for all, in every condition of life, every class of men; for the rich who are God's stewards, for the poor who yet can give "the cup of cold water in the name of a disciple." A power, that commands all circumstances, that turns trials into blessings, that robs death of its sting and rises victorious over the grave!

Yes, *this is power;* power which lodged in the heart by God himself, goes out and blesses the family, the friendly circle, the community, the state, the world, the living and the corning generations; which goes on conquering and to conquer, and to accomplish the purposes of God's gospel, "peace on earth and good will towards men," and to change the kingdoms of the world into the kingdom of the Lord; power which reaches the very heavens, and ascends to God himself — for

3. *There is power in man with God!* Not with man only, from mind to mind and spirit to spirit, but with *God;* not only *for* God and his kingdom, but *with God.* Aye, in prayer to prevail with him, like Israel of old, and draw his saving power down upon ourselves and others; like Abraham to stay the sentence of his justice and intercede with him for perishing sinners; like Christ himself to ask forgiveness for his murderers and power for his tempted followers, to claim the life of his redeemed: "Father, I will that those whom thou halt given me be with me where I am."

With God who will he entreated and invites the violence of earnest, constant prayer, that takes no refusal; *who feels the power* which he gives us over others, for he saith "inasmuch as ye have done it unto one of the least of these my brethren, ye have done it unto me," *who yields to this power* when he hears our prayers, when he gives the Holy Ghost to those that ask him; who himself *gives* this power, and *uses this* power, to hasten on the advent of his kingdom and reveal his glory!

Surely man *has power.* But as certain as God has given us power, so certain its exercise in his service and to his glory becomes our duty, our responsibility.

Have we this power? This power of faith and love, in faithfulness which endures unto death, perseverance which disarms every difficulty, in the conscientious use of every means given, which proves our earnestness and loyalty and is the pledge of success? The power of prayer which reaches the heart of God, of godliness which glorifies him before men? The power of a holy lite on earth which is the earnest of the blessed life above? The power to walk with God and be his ministering spirits in the world, the sons of God and heirs with Christ of his glory?

Brethren — may Almighty God accompany what has been said with his blessing and give us this power to the praise and glory of His holy name! Amen.

FUNERAL SERVICES

AT THE BURIAL OF THE

RIGHT REV. LEONIDAS POLK, D.D.

TOGETHER WITH THE SERMON

DELIVERED

IN

ST. PAUL'S CHURCH, AUGUSTA, GA

ON JUNE 29, 1864

BEING THE FEAST OF ST. PETER THE APOSTLE.

They that sow in tears, shall reap in joy. — Psalm 126:6.

1864

COLLECT FOR FOURTH SUNDAY AFTER TRINITY.

O God, the Protector of all that trust in Thee, without whom nothing is strong, nothing is holy: Increase and multiply upon us Thy mercy; that Thou, being our ruler and guide, we may so pass through things temporal, that we finally lose not the things eternal. Grant this, O heavenly Father, for Jesus Christ's sake our Lord. Amen.

OCCASION OF HIS DEATH

On Tuesday morning, June 14th, General Johnston, Lieutenant Generals Polk and Hardee, and Brigadier General W H. Jackson, accompanied by members of their respective staffs, visited Pine mountain, an elevated position lying beyond the Confederate lines, and some six miles from the Town of Marietta, for the purpose of making a military reconnaissance.

Leaving their escorts and horses behind the hill, they proceeded to the top on foot. Their observations having been completed, they were about to return, when a shot from a Federal battery, striking the ground a short distance in front of their position, warned them that their presence had been discovered by the enemy.

The group at once separated: Generals Johnston and Polk passing along the brow of the hill, still farther to the left, while the other officers withdrew toward the right and rear. After finishing their survey in that direction the two parted — the former moving around the hill to rejoin his escort, and the latter leisurely retracing his course across the summit.

Upon reaching a commanding, point he paused for a moment, either to make a final examination of the scene before him, or, as is more probable, to spend a short interval in silent communion with his God.

As he stood thus occupied, his arms folded upon his breast, and his face wearing the composed and reverent look of an humble and trusting worshipper, a second shot was heard, and the cry arose that General Polk had fallen.

Colonels Jack and Gale, members of his staff, at once returned to the spot, but life was already extinct. His body, badly torn, was lying upon the ground at full length, with the face upturned, and retaining its last expression of prayerful faith, and the arms, though broken, still crossed upon the breast.

The enemy's battery was by this time shelling the hill with great rapidity and precision, and the remains were borne to a place of safety in the rear under a heavy fire.

In the left pocket of his coat was found his Book of Common Prayer, and in the right four copies of a little manual entitled "Balm for the Weary and Wounded." Upon the fly-leaf of three of these had been written the names respectively of "General Jos. E. Johnston," "Lieutenant-General Hardee," "Lieutenant-General Hood," "with the compliments of Lieutenant-General Leonidas Polk, June 12th, 1864." Upon that of the fourth was inscribed his own name. All were saturated with his blood.

The General-in-Chief at once made known the great loss which his army had sustained, in the following order:

"HEAD-QUARTERS ARMY OF TENNESSEE,

In the Field, June 14, 1864."

General Field Orders, No. 2.]

"COMRADES! You are called to mourn your first captain, your oldest companion-in-arms. Lieutenant-General Polk fell today at the outpost of this army — the army he raised and commanded — in all of whose trials he has shared — to all of whose victories he contributed.

"In this distinguished leader we have lost the most courteous of gentlemen, the most gallant of soldiers.

"The Christian, patriot, soldier, has neither lived nor died in vain. His example is before you — his mantle rests with you.

J E. JOHNSTON, General.

"Official: KINLOCH FALCONER, A.A.G."

The members of his military staff not feeling at liberty to determine upon the place of his interment without consultation with his family and friends, sent telegraphic dispatches to his eldest son, then in Montgomery, Ala., and to Bishop Elliott, at Savannah, to meet the body at Augusta, as it was their intention to proceed with it to that point.

On reaching Atlanta the body was received by a committee appointed for the purpose by the Mayor of the city, and taken directly to St. Luke's Church. It continued lying in state for several hours, and then, after appropriate religious services and an impressive eulogy pronounced by the Rev. Dr. Quintard, Rector of the Church and Chaplain attached to the staff of General Polk, was conveyed to the depot under a proper military escort, attended by a large concourse of sympathizing citizens.

A car having been provided expressly for their use, the immediate attendants proceeded with it to Augusta, and upon their arrival, early the following morning, were met by the Rectors, Wardens, and Vestrymen of St. Paul's Church and the Church of the Atonement. The remains were reverently conveyed to St. Paul's Church, where a guard of honor had been stationed to receive them by the Commandant of the Post.

Upon consultation at Augusta with such members of General Polk's family as could be gathered at the spot, and with Bishop Elliott, it was decided to be most appropriate to commit his remains to the keeping of the Diocese of Georgia, whose Bishop had now become the Senior Bishop of the Church in the Confederate States, until the Church of Louisiana should claim them as her rightful inheritance. The following invitation was accordingly issued:

"The Bishops, Clergy, and Laity of the Protestant Episcopal Church in THE CONFEDERATE STATES, the officers of the Army and Navy OF THE CONFEDERATE STATES, and the citizens generally, are invited to attend the funeral services of the Rt. Rev. Leonidas Polk, D.D., from the City Hall of Augusta, Georgia, on Wednesday, the 29th of June. The procession will move from the City Hall to St. Paul's Church. His remains will be deposited in the church-yard of St. Paul's until the war closes.

" STEPHEN ELLIOTT,

"Senior Bp. of Prot. Epis. Ch. in C. S. A."

After remaining two days in St. Paul's Church, the body, by the direction of Col. Geo. W Rains, commanding the Post, was enclosed in a leaden coffin and placed in an apartment of the City Hall tendered for the purpose by the city authorities, where it was left under a proper guard until the morning of June 29th.

FUNERAL SOLEMNITIES

Upon the day appointed — being, by a happy coincidence, the Feast of St. Peter the Apostle — the local military force of Augusta, consisting of one full regiment of infantry, a battery of light artillery, and a company of cavalry, was drawn up on Telfair St., in the rear of the City Hall, at half-past nine o'clock, A. M. The case enclosing the remains was brought and placed within the hearse by soldiers detailed for the purpose. The hearse was draped IN THE FLAG OF THE CONFEDERATE STATES, with its broad folds of white and its starry cross of Trust and Truth upon a field of blood, and surmounted with wreaths of bay and laurel, and a cross of evergreen and snow-white flowers.

The military escort, under Major I. P Girardey, headed by the Palmetto Band, began its solemn march, the Colonel commanding the Post and His Honor the Mayor of the city on horseback, immediately preceding the hearse. Wardens and Vestrymen, representing St. Paul's Church, Augusta, St. John's, Savannah, and the Church of the Atonement, Augusta, accompanied the remains on either side as pallbearers. After them, under the direction of Captain C. A. Platt, the remainder of the funeral cortege was arranged in the following order:

> The Military Family of General Polk,
> with the Clergy and
> Citizens of Louisiana.
> The Reverend Clergy.
> Officers of the Army and Navy.
> Members of the City Council.
> Civil Officers of the Confederate Government.
> Members of the Medical and Legal Professions.
> Other Citizens.

While the imposing procession was passing along the principal streets of the city, houses and balconies and walks were thronged with multitudes who had come out to pay the respects of loving homage to the departed Christian soldier. All places of business were closed. The band played appropriate dirges, and the bell of St. Paul's Church was tolled at intervals.

As it came down Reynolds street, approaching the church, the Bishops of Georgia, Mississippi, and Arkansas, in their robes, attended by a company of surpliced Priests, moved from the vestry-room, and took their station in front of the church near the entrance-gate, while the company of Silver Greys was detached from the regiment and drawn up on either side of the avenue as a special guard of honor.

The Bishops and Clergy having met the corpse, went before it into the church, the Senior Bishop repeating the words, "I am the Resurrection and the Life, saith the Lord," etc.

The three Bishops, with the Rector of St. Paul's, entered the chancel, while the attendant Priests occupied places assigned them on either side without the rail. The anthem, "Lord let me know my end," was chanted by the choir, with a solemn and effective accompaniment upon the organ.

The Bishop of Arkansas read the Lesson; after which the choir and congregation united in singing the first three stanzas of the familiar hymn, "I would not live alway."

The Senior Bishop then delivered, in the presence of a vast assemblage gathered within and around the church, the

FUNERAL ADDRESS

ST. JOHN'S GOSPEL, chapter 11, verse 28. — *The Master is come and calleth for thee.*

God hath made everything beautiful in his time, and nothing is more beautiful than Death, when it comes to one who has faithfully fulfilled all the duties of life, and is ready for its summons. To such an one the solemn message, "The Master is come and calleth for thee," has no terrors. It is but the long-expected announcement of rest — but the long-desired ending of the toil of life. The battle has-been fought, the victory won, and the war-worn veteran is heralded by his vanquished enemy to his crown of righteousness.

And it makes no matter to the faithful servant under what shape that summons comes. In the history of the Church of Christ the death of its most illustrious saints has taken the revolting form of violence.

Some have gone to glory imitating Christ in the shame and agony of the Cross. Others have ascended to the gates of Paradise in chariots of fire. The spirit of the Martyr Stephen passed away amid the curses of an infuriated mob; and the gentle James was smitten with the sword of ruthless tyranny.

Why, then, stand appalled that, in these latter days, our brother should have died by the hand of violence? Has human nature changed? Has fanaticism learned any mercy? Does the fire which is lighted from hell ever cease its fury against the children of the Most High?

We have been plainly told in Holy Writ that, in the latter days, perilous times should come, and come they have to us. Instead of being appalled, Bishops of the Church of Christ, let us rather prepare for what may be our own future fate!

Do ye not hear the voices of your own brethren, Ministers and Bishops, hound-mg on these hordes of lawless men to the desolation of our homes, our altars, our families ourselves? The body which lies before us is the last, but not the only one, of our martyred Bishops.

The heart of the gentle, loving Cobbs. was broken by the vision of coming evil which he foresaw. The lion-hearted Meade died just when the hand of destruction was laid upon his quiet home, and its sacred associations were scattered to the winds. Otey, the high-souled, the honest-hearted, the guileless, expired a prisoner in his own home, his closing eyes looking upon a desolated diocese, a scattered and ruined people, an exiled ministry — all the work of his life in ruins.

The mangled corpse of our beloved brother closes, for the present, the succession of our Episcopal martyrs. Who shall come next? I, in the proper order of succession. God's will be done. My only prayer is, that, if He sees necessary, I may die in defense of the same holy cause, and with the like faith and courage.

Our brother fills the grave of a Christian warrior! Although a minister of the Prince of peace and a Bishop in the Church of God, he has poured out his life-blood for us upon the field of battle. Some, even of those for whom this precious blood is shed, have cavilled at it. Many, even of those who are stirring up this hellish warfare, have found a mote in their brother's eye.

As he has given his life for us, our duty is not only to honor his ashes, but to place his noble life, and still nobler death, beyond the reach of human calumny. His judgment is with his God, whom he loved so earnestly, whom he served so faithfully. His aster has come and called for him, and with him we leave his cause gladly, joyfully, in unswerving confidence.

That we may form a just estimate of a man's life, we must keep with us the great principle which is its pervading influence; and we must consider it in connection with the natural temperament of the individual whose life we are examining. The sun does not change by his beams the outlines of the landscape upon which he shines. They remain ever the same, stern or soft, rugged or gentle, as they came from the hand of their Creator.

The sun only bathes this natural arrangement in its flood of light, and clothes it with its robes of purple and of gold: And so with divine grace. It does not alter the great characteristics of a man's natural temperament. It only softens it, and illumines it, and makes it glorious to all who look upon it, and fills it with the fullness of God's divine spirit.

St. Peter was by nature bold, impetuous, full of ardor and devotion, and in him the spirit of Christ found materials for a grandeur of design and a high-souled energy which made him foremost in all the acts which illustrated the earth-life of our Saviour and the annals of the Apostolic Church. Is any one inclined to disparage Peter because he was not the same gentle, loving spirit as John, or to quarrel with him because his fervent temper and burning zeal made him sometimes liable to rebuke?

God raises up instruments in his Church for his own purposes, and moulds them according to his own predetermined counsels.

A man can not be ardent, uncompromising, single-minded, full of a grand ideal of religion, without being a mark for the criticism of the Church as well as of the world. Such men have been filled with a divine afflatus of which lookers-on know nothing. They seem, in the fullness of their zeal and ardor, to be carried away by a spirit which is mistaken for the spirit of the world. It is not indeed the spirit of the world; it is only that they are fighting the world with the world's own fearlessness.

"The children of this world," said our Saviour, "are wiser in their generation than the children of light." Such men as these — men specially raised up — do not permit the children of this world to assume this superiority. They meet them face to face — use different weapon, tis true, but use them alike — hurl at their adversaries the armor of the Lord, in the like spirit of zeal in which the armor of the world is hurled against them; and God means them to do it.

There are times and occasions when such a spirit is not only right, but glorious, in the sight of the Lord. Look at our Saviour himself, when he lashed from the temple those who were dishonoring his Father's house! See him raging, like a man of war, among the money-changers and the hucksterers, overturning their tables, and casting out their merchandise!

Hear that same Saviour when he burst forth in indignation against the Scribes and Pharisees, hypocrites, using such language as a weak Christianity would now find fault with. "Ye serpents, ye generation of vipers, how can ye escape the damnation of Hell?"

Hear St. Stephen, when he stood in the midst of the infuriated multitude and said: "Ye stiff-necked and uncircumcised in heart and ears, ye do always resist the Holy Ghost; as your fathers did, so do ye. Which of the prophets have not your fathers persecuted? And they have slain them which showed before of the coming of the Just one; of whom ye have been now the betrayers and murderers."

Hear St. Paul, when he was withstood by Elymas the sorcerer "O full of all subtlety and all mischief, thou child of the devil, thou enemy of all righteousness, wilt thou not cease to pervert the right ways of the Lord?"

Recalling instances like these, tell me if you can not perceive, mingled with the grace and the love of the Gospel, a spirit of fiery indignation, rising and swelling in the bosoms of the Apostles, and Martyrs, and Saints, and even of our Lord himself, which should make us careful how we judge and condemn our brethren who may differ from us in spirit and in action.

God raises up his own servants for his own use; elects them, calls them, prepares them, places them where they shall be ready for action, and in due time gives them their work to do. It rises up so plainly before them, that they can not avoid it. It sweeps up to their feet; it involves them in its current. They oft times struggle against it, but it overpowers them by its irresistible circumstances, until at last they find themselves mere instruments in God's hands, doing His will, driven on by His spirit, supported by His strength, dying as His martyrs! Let us apply these principles to the life and conduct of him whose murdered body now lies before us.

In the year eighteen hundred and twenty-six we find, in the military school of the United States, a young man of heroic lineage, with the fiery blood of the Revolution coursing in his veins, of independent fortune, of chivalric tone, of high and noble impulses, preparing himself for the service of his country.

He had every qualification to ensure him success as a military man; every prerequisite for carrying him up to lofty reputation. No one doubts, for a moment, that had he followed the beck of ambition, he might have risen, as a soldier, to the very proudest rank in the army of the Union. His most fastidious critic has never doubted that he had military traits in his character of the very highest order.

If personal courage, comprehensive views, quick perception, rapid combination, prompt decision, great administrative capacity, with the faculty of commanding men, and at the same time of attaching them to him, are the qualities which make a great military leader, then we, who knew him best arid have longest acted with him, can bear our testimony to his possession of these qualities in a most eminent degree. They were his characteristics in everything he did — the qualities which have made him illustrious in every phase of his life.

Upon this young man, thus preparing for the service of the world, Christ laid the touch of His divine spirit, and transformed him into a soldier of the Cross. He had work for him to do in his Church. He had use for those very qualities which would have fitted him for a glorious service of the world. The Church needed a bold and fearless man, full of youth and nerve, to plunge into the great wilderness of the

Southwest, teeming, as it then was, with the young and vigorous life of the republic, swelling and surging under the rushing tide of emigration, and consecrate it to her service; and she found that champion in this youth of military training.

The Church needed a man of high social position, with the carriage and manners of a gentleman, with the courtesy and grace of a well-bred Christian, to commend her to the consideration of men of hereditary wealth, of great refinement, of cultivated accomplishments. For in the vast country over which he was appointed to establish the Church, extremes were meeting — extremes of established position, and of struggle for position — of old settled landholders and of needy adventurers — of men with all the polish of foreign refinement, and of men with all the strength of unpolished intelligence.

The Bishop who should go forth to conquer that country for the Church must possess manners as well as energy — cultivation as well as Christian courage — and the Church found such a combination in this young soldier, who had been snatched from the flatteries of the world. The Church needed a large slaveholder, who might speak boldly and fearlessly to his peers, as being one of themselves, about their duty to their slaves, and. might teach them, by his living example, what that duty was, and how to fulfill it; and she found it in this young disciple.

He combined in himself just the natural qualities and the accidental circumstances which fitted him for the work to which he was called; and when these had been sanctified by the Spirit of Christ, and constraint was laid upon him to preach the Gospel, he went forth in the power of the Holy Ghost to the earnest fulfillment of his bishopric. And who shall dare to say that the foreknowledge and election of the Head of the Church ended at this point?

Who shall presume to say that Christ did not prepare this glorious servant for the final work of his life? It all depends upon the stand-point from which we view this conflict.

If we consider it a mere struggle for political power, a question of sovereignty and of dominion, then should I be loath to mingle the Church of Christ with it in any form or manner. But such is not the nature of this conflict. It is no such war as nations wage against each other for a balance of power, or for the adjustment of a boundary.

We are resisting a crusade — a crusade of license against law — of infidelity against the altars of the living God — of fanaticism against a great spiritual trust committed to our care. We are warring with hordes of unprincipled foreigners, ignorant and brutal men, who, having cast off at home all the restraints of order and of belief, have signalized their march over our devoted country by burning the Churches of Christ by defiling the altars upon which the sacrifice of the death of our Saviour is commemorated, by violating our women, by raising the banner of servile insurrection, by fanning into fury the demoniac passions of the ignorant and the vile!

For active personal resistance to such an invasion might Christ well have fitted and prepared a servant, even though that servant should meanwhile have worn the miter of a bishop. It is a wonderful coincidence (to say the least of it) that he who, in his young manhood, consecrated his sword as an offering to the Lord, should, in the ripeness of his old age, have resumed that sword to do the battles of Religion and the Church! Who knows the communings of a spirit like his with his Master?

Up to that moment he had commended himself to the Church as a self-sacrificing, self-devoted servant and bishop. He had laid down everything at the foot of the Cross. He had stripped himself and his family of riches and of home. He had wandered with them, delicately trained and delicately nurtured, from resting-place to resting-place, until they felt that they were pilgrims and strangers, and had no sure abiding place.

He had laid aside, for the Church's sake, the comforts of domestic life — being separated for months from wife and children — until at times he was, as Job says, strange to them. He had his mind, his heart, his soul teeming at all times with great ideas for her advancement and glory, so that his noble, generous soul was well-nigh bursting with its exuberant riches; and can you believe that all this was suddenly changed into a vain and paltry ambition of winning renown upon the battle-field? Why, his views were as much above all such littleness as the heavens are above the earth!

I speak what I do know when I affirm that the complexion Which this war was to assume was known to him long before it burst upon our country. We had studied together for years the gathering elements; we had analyzed them; we had seen in them the ripening germs of irreligion, of unbelief, of ungodliness, of corruption, of cruelty, of license, which have since distinguished them, and we came' long since to the deliberate conclusion that it was a struggle against which not only the State but the Church must do her utmost.

Not merely the layman, but the priest. And this conclusion was not confined to our own breasts. Others of our brethren coincided with us in our views, and even the gentle, loving Cobbs told us, again and again, that when the moment came, old and infirm as he was, he should shoulder his musket and march to the battle-field' And when at last this great responsibility was laid upon him unexpectedly, it met him in the strict performance of his duty.

During the first year of the war when our armies were in the peninsula of Virginia, he left his diocese upon an episcopal visitation to the soldiers from Louisiana, who then thronged those armies. Having fulfilled that mission, he returned to Richmond just when the Federal armies were preparing to sweep down the valley of the Mississippi and blot out its civilization.

A committee of gentlemen from that valley was then at Richmond beseeching the President to appoint some man in whom the people of that vast region could have confidence, and around whom they might rally for its defense and preservation. Sidney Johnston, upon whom the President had relied as the commander of the forces of the Southwest, had not yet arrived from California.

Beauregard and Joe Johnston were in command in Virginia. Magruder was in the peninsula. Jackson and the

Hills and Longstreet had not yet exhibited their military skill, and were unknown in the valley of the West. The incomparable Lee was engaged in defending the frontiers of his own native state. Hardee was in the service of the State of Georgia.

The emergency was great, for the Northwest was gathering all its clans to open the course of the Mississippi, the point which most nearly touched its interests. The people of Mississippi, Arkansas, and Louisiana were clamoring for a leader, and, unless one was furnished them, might abate their enthusiasm and make but faint resistance to invasion.

At this critical moment the President bethought him of this man, whom he remembered as a young soldier of the academy, whom he knew as a bishop of the Church, whose lofty qualities he had marked all through life, and whose wide and commanding influence in the valley of the Mississippi he well understood. An unusual sphere in which to seek for a general; but, with his usual promptness and sagacity, he marked his man, and asked the commissioners if Bishop Polk would meet the wishes of the people of the valley. The reply was as prompt as the nomination.

The very man; no one whom you could name of all at your command, would be so acceptable. Then arose the important question —

"Can he be persuaded, in this moment of his country's peril, when all eyes are turned upon him, and all hearts are yearning for him; when his home, his diocese, his Church, the sheep entrusted to his keeping and for whom Christ had died, are threatened not only with temporal but with spiritual destruction; when hordes of infidel foreigners, spawned upon our shores from their hotbeds of infidelity and ungodliness, are coming to preach blood and license to the slaves he was laboring to humanize and Christianize; can he be persuaded, was the interesting question, to resume the sword which he had laid in youth upon the altar of God, and use it in their defense?

There it lay, where he had placed it in the prime of life, a virgin and unsullied sword. Not a stain had dimmed its brightness; not a drop of blood had ever marred its purity! It was consecrated to his Saviour — a votive offering which he had made in the days of his early love. Can it be resumed with honor to his Church — with safety to his soul?

For vain ambition, no! For worldly distinction, no! For the preservation of property, or even life under ordinary circumstances no! But for the defense of his Church, the spouse and bride of Christ, for the purity of the altars to which he had been bound as a sacrifice, for the care of the sheep bought with Christ's death and committed to his charge, for the maintenance of the sacred trust of slavery, yes! — a thousand times yes!

That sword had been laid upon that altar for the glory of God, and for the glory of God it might be resumed, and for the glory of God it was resumed, and has flashed with a celestial brightness in the eyes of the adversary, dazzling and confounding them. And God has blessed that sword upon every occasion of its use.

No matter what was the fate of the rest of the army, wherever that sword was wielded, there was victory. He never knew a defeat. He never received a wound. He moved unharmed through all the perils of the battlefield. Until his work was accomplished upon earth and God would call him to his rest, no weapon that was directed against him ever prospered.

The mode in which Bishop Polk accepted the responsibility which was laid upon him was eminently characteristic of him. When he had determined to assume the military rank with which the President thought fit to invest him, he wrote to me to inform me of the step.

"I did not consult you beforehand (were his words), for I felt that it was a matter to be decided between my Master and myself. I knew how it would startle the Church; how much criticism and obloquy it might fetch down; and I determined that all the responsibility should rest upon myself. When I had fully made up my mind to the step, I went to the valley and paid a visit to our venerable Father Meade, feeling it to be my duty to let him know, as the presiding bishop of our flock, what I had determined upon. I told him distinctly that I had not come to consult him; I had come to communicate a decision and to ask his blessing.

His answer was, "Had you consulted me, I might not have advised you to assume the office of a general; but knowing you to be a sincere, earnest, God-fearing man, believing you to have come to your decision after earnest prayer for light and for direction, I will not blame you, but will send you to the field with my blessing." What our brother did he always did boldly, fearlessly, openly, in the face of God and of man. The act was always his own; the responsibility he never laid upon the shoulders of another.

There was in Bishop Polk's character an earnestness of purpose and a concentration of energy which distinguished everything he did. Whatever Christian work he took in hand, he labored at it with all his heart and soul. His early missionary work, his later diocesan supervision, his interest in the advancement of the slave, his grand university scheme, his military career, were all marked by a like intense devotion and absorption. And this characteristic of the man caused him sometimes to be misunderstood.

He appeared to be so wrapped up in what he had in hand, that superficial observers supposed him to be neglecting concurrent duties, and even his own spiritual discipline. But never was there a greater mistake in the judgment of a man's character.

During his conception and conduct of that glorious scheme of education which will remain as his enduring monument, I was his chosen colleague and constant companion. For months together we lived under the same roof, often occupying the same chamber, and interchanging, as brothers, our thoughts and feelings. During that period of three years he seemed, to those who saw only his outer life, to be entirely absorbed in the affairs of the university — to have no thought or care for anything else.

But I, who was with him in his moments of retirement as well as of business, know better, and testify that I do know. At the very time when he was putting in motion every influence which might advance his gigantic enterprise, he was conducting a parish church in the City of New Orleans with the entire love of his people; he was managing a diocese which felt no neglect because of his other occupations; he was keeping up a correspondence with literary and scientific men coextensive with the limits of the republic. His pen knew no rest.

Midnight often found him at his desk, and early morning saw him resume his work with unflagging energy. He left nothing undone to ensure the success of his undertaking, and his enthusiasm and self-devotion were contagious. They spread to every one whom he approached, until his impulses animated all about him.

Cold indeed was that nature, and selfish that heart, which he could not awaken to some generous and liberal emotions. Very fascinating were his manners, and that not from any art or design, but from the high-toned frankness of his nature, and the noble feelings which welled up from his soul as from a fountain of truth and of purity.

And during all this time, while he was so absorbed in his great purpose of linking education to the chariot-wheels of the Church, he never forgot the fresh spring of his conception, the author and designer of his plan. God was ever in his thoughts; Christ, the head of the Church, was ever upon his lips; the Holy Ghost, the enlightener of the understanding of men and the controller of their wills, was unceasingly invoked.

Never was any step taken in this great work which was not preceded and accompanied by constant prayer. Never was any man approached whose cooperation was important, unless prayer preceded that approach. Every morning, ere he sallied forth upon his work, was the power of Christ called down to bless and forward his plan. Never was any enterprise more bedewed with the spirit of prayer.

At the same time that he was busy among men, enlisting the power of the press, securing the sympathies of the wise, opening the purses of the rich, bringing into harmonious action minds and interests of the most diversified nature —

seeming only to be employ-big human means and human appliances — he was likewise busy in his closet invoking upon these efforts the blessing of the Most High.

And as it was in his connection with his university plans, so was it likewise during his. military career. He entered upon that with the like concentration of energy and of will, because he believed it to be, for the time, his highest duty toward God and his Church.

The duties of his episcopal office he laid down during his military career, in imitation of his Master, who put aside the glory which he had with the Father ere the world was, during his humiliation upon earth. For he felt his change to be an humiliation — such an humiliation as all God's children and servants are forced to pass through in .-their discipline upon earth.

When some one, who did not understand the spirit of his act, was foolish enough to congratulate him upon the high honor which the President had conferred upon him, his indignant reply was: Honor, sir! there is no honor upon this earth equal to the honor of being a Bishop in the Church of God." And never did he depart from this proper feeling.

He felt his military character to be a burden to him, and again and again, as opportunity offered, did he pray to be released from its trammels. But the same necessity which called for his appointment required the continuance of his services, and our highest civil magistrate, the power which we believe to be ordained of God, denied his request.

At Harrodsburgh, Kentucky, after the bloody field of Perryville, he said to Dr. Quintard, who accompanied him all through that campaign, with the deepest emotion, "Oh, for the days when we went up to the House of the Lord and compassed his altar with the voice of prayer and of thanksgiving!"

Whenever it was possible, during his military career, be surrounded himself with all the appliances of his priestly office, and rejoiced in them to the bottom of his soul. Two days before his death — a Sunday of storm and darkness —

he said to one of his aides: "Everything is dark in nature without, but all is peace within this house. Call all my military family together, and let us have the precious service of the Church." "And never," said he, "did I hear him more fervent, or see him more absorbed." He was being anointed for his burial.

Who can estimate the influence of such an act as that of our brother upon the cause which is so vital to every one of us? What could invest it with a higher moral grandeur than that a bishop of the Church of God should gird on the sword to do battle for it? A faction of the Northern. Church pretended — some of them engaged in acts infinitely more derogatory to the glory of Christ's Church — to be shocked at it; but it, nevertheless, filled them with dismay.

They saw in it an intensity of feeling and of purpose at which they trembled, and when they found no echo of their pious horror from the Church of England, they ceased their idle clamor. And our brother thus became, before even he had drawn his sword, a tower of strength to the Confederacy. And who can say how much of the religious influence which has diffused itself so remarkably among the officers of the army of the West may not have reached their hearts through the silent power of his example and his prayers!

Bishop Polk did not think the public exercise of his ministry a proper accompaniment of his military career, and in that I think he acted most wisely; but his dignified and irreproachable life was a perpetual sermon, and his private communion with God was his spiritual power.

It is a very striking fact that every officer of high rank in that army — the army which, in the language of Gen. Johnston, he created, and had always commanded — has become a professed disciple of the meek and lowly Jesus; and that the last act of our warrior-bishop was the admission into the Church of his Saviour and Redeemer, through the holy sacrament of baptism, of two of its most renowned commanders. He lived long enough to see Christ recognized in its councils of war; and, his work on earth being done, he obeyed the summons of his Master, and passing away from earth, his mantle rests upon it.

Time does not permit me to enter into any detail of his long and useful career as a bishop in the Church of God, That must be left for the biographer, who shall, in moments of leisure and of peace, gather up the threads of his most eventful life and weave them into a narrative which shall be strange as any fiction.

The vicissitudes of that life have been as wonderful as those which have distinguished the annals of so many princely families during the last eighty years. Born to large hereditary estates, and increasing that fortune by intermarriage with the noble woman whom he had loved from boyhood, and who has cheerfully shared with him all his Christian pilgrimage, he has died leaving his family without any settled dwelling-place, wanderers from the pleasant homes which knew their childhood and their youth.

Trained as a man of the world and a man of pleasure, he has lived a life of almost entire self-denial, a servant of servants, and has died a bloody death upon the battle-field.

Destined, in his own intention, to mount to earthly glory by the sword and his own brave heart, he has mounted to heavenly glory by the crook of the Shepherd and the humiliation of that heart.

Full of heroic purposes as he leaped into the arena of life — purposes always high and noble, even when unsanctified — he has been made, by the overruling hand of God, to display that heroism in the fields which Christ his Master illustrated, teaching the ignorant, enlightening the blind, gathering together the lost sheep of Israel, comforting the bedside of sickness and affliction, watching long days and nights by the suffering slave.

Oh! how many records has he left with God of heroic self-devotion, of which the world knows nothing; records made up in silence and in darkness, when no eye saw him save the eye of the Invisible! The world speaks of him now as a hero! He has always been a hero; and the bloody fields which have made him conspicuous are but the outburst of the spirit which has always distinguished him.

Battles which he fought long since with himself and his kind; which he waged against the pomps and vanities of the world and the pride of life; which he contested with the pestilence that walketh in darkness and the destruction that wasteth at noonday — were far more terrific than Belmont, or Shiloh, or Perryville.

These required qualities which were natural to him — those qualities which came from the grace, of God and the spirit of Jesus. If, as the wise man says, "Greater is he that ruleth his spirit than he that taketh a city," then was he truly great — for he had a Spirit hard to rule, and Christ gave him the mastery over it.

But his work is done, and now he rests from his labors! That brave heart is quiet in the grave — that faithful spirit has returned to its God. "The beauty of Israel is slain upon the high places. The mighty is fallen in the midst of the battle. I am distressed for thee, my brother — very pleasant hast thou been unto me." And thou hast come to die at my very door, and to find thy burial amid my pleasant places.

Welcome in death, as in life; welcome to thy grave as thou hast ever been to my home and to my heart. Thy dust shall repose under the shadow of the Church of Christ. These solemn groves shall guard thy rest; the glorious anthems of the City of God shall roll over thy grave a perpetual requiem.

And now, ye Christians of the North, and especially ye priests and bishops of the Church who have lent yourselves to the fanning of the fury of this unjust and cruel war, do I this day, in the presence of the body of this my murdered brother, summon you to meet us at the judgment-seat of Christ — that awful bar where your brute force shall avail you nothing; where the multitudes whom you have followed to do evil shall not shield you from an angry God; where the vain excuses with which you have varnished your sin shall be scattered before the bright beams of eternal truth and righteousness.

I summon you to that bar in the name of that sacred liberty which you have trampled under foot; in the name of the glorious constitution which you have destroyed; in the name of our holy religion which you have profaned; in the name of the temples of God which you have desecrated; in the name of a thousand martyred saints whose blood you have wantonly spilled; in the name of our Christian women whom you have violated; in the name of our slaves whom you have seduced and then consigned to misery; and there I leave justice and vengeance to God.

The blood of your brethren crieth unto God from the earth, and it will not cry in vain. It has entered into the ears of the Lord God of Sabaoth, and will be returned upon you in blood a thousand-fold. May God have mercy upon you in that day of solemn justice and fearful retribution!

And now let us commit his sacred dust to the keeping of the Church in THE CONFEDERATE STATES until such time as his own diocese shall be prepared to do him honor.

That day will come; I see it rise before me in vision, when this martyred dust shall be carried in triumphal procession to his own beloved Louisiana, and deposited in such a shrine as a loving; mourning people shall prepare for him. And he shall then receive a prophet's reward! His works shall rise up from the ashes of the past and attest his greatness

! A diocese rescued from brutal dominion by the efficacy of his blood! — a Church freed from pollution by the vigor of his counsels! — a country made independent through his devotion and self-sacrifice! — an university sending forth streams of pure and sanctified learning from its exuberant bosom — generations made better and grander from his example and life, and rising up and calling him blessed!

At the close of this address, the coffin, under the escort of the Silver Greys, preceded by the bishops and clergy, was carried to the grave prepared for it in the rear of the church, immediately behind the chancel window, the family and near friends of the departed. accompanying it. While it was made ready to be laid into the grave, the senior bishop pronounced the sentences, "Man that is born of a woman," etc., and the form of committing the body to the ground, and the sentence, "I heard a voice from heaven."

As he uttered the words "Earth to earth, ashes to ashes, dust to dust," earth was cast upon the body by the Bishops of Mississippi and Arkansas, and Lieutenant-General Longstreet, of the Army of Virginia; and the last military honors were paid by a salvo from the battery of light artillery, stationed for the purpose, at the foot of Washington street.

The Bishop of Mississippi concluded the solemn services by offering the "Lord's Prayer"; the first prayer in the order for the burial of the dead; the prayer, "O God, whose days are without end"; the prayer for persons in affliction, and the apostolic benediction.

DEATH OF LIEUT. GEN. LEONIDAS POLK.

The entire community have been thrown into gloom by the publicity of the official announcement that Lieutenant-General Leonidas Polk, of the Army of Tennessee, was killed by a cannon-shot, in the early part of Tuesday, while engaged with his associates in command in making observations at the immediate front.

Lieutenant-General Polk was born in Raleigh, N. C., in 1806, from whence, at an early age, he emigrated to Tennessee, in which state the greater portion of his life was spent. At the age of seventeen he entered West Point as a cadet, in the same class with General Albert Sidney Johnston. While at West Point, under the teachings of Right Rev. Bishop McIlvaine, of the Diocese of Ohio, then chaplain of the post, he was received into the Protestant Episcopal Church by holy baptism, in the presence of the whole corps of cadets.

He subsequently ratified his baptismal vows, and was confirmed by Bishop Ravenscroft, of the Diocese of North Carolina. He was ordained a deacon in the Church by the venerable Bishop Moore, of Virginia, in 1830, and was endowed with the priesthood by the imposition of the same apostolic hands in 1836. He was consecrated to the episcopate in 1838, and exercised his varied functions in the Diocese of Louisiana with great credit to himself and usefullness to the Church, until the commencement of our present struggle for liberty, when he entered the field in which he was engaged at his death.

A divine and chieftain has fallen, and .at an inopportune hour. The Church will mourn the demise of one of its brightest ornaments, while the whole country sustains a loss that can be ill afforded. But to other pens we leave the duty of recording the virtues and services of the deceased. His history is that of his Church and country, and both will acknowledge his worth and revere his *memory*. — *Atlanta Appeal.*

A SERMON

PREACHED BEFORE

Brig. Gen. Hoke's Brigade

AT KINSTON, N.C.

ON THE

28th OF FEBRUARY, 1864

BY

Rev. JOHN PARIS

CHAPLAIN FIFTY-FOURTH REGIMENT N. C. TROOPS

UPON THE DEATH OF TWENTY-TWO MEN
WHO HAD BEEN EXECUTED IN THE PRESENCE
OF THE BRIGADE FOR
THE CRIME OF DESERTION

1864

NOTE

On the morning of the first of February, Brig. Gen. R. F. Hoke forced the passage of Batchelor's Creek, nine miles west from Newbern; the enemy abandoned his works and retreated upon the town. A hot and vigorous pursuit was made, which resulted in the capture of a large number of prisoners, and the surrender to our forces of many others, who were cut off from escape by the celerity of the pursuit, and our troops seizing and holding every avenue leading into the town, near the enemy's batteries.

Among the prisoners taken, were about fifty native North Carolinians, dressed out in Yankee uniform, with muskets upon their shoulders. Twenty-two of these men were recognized as men who had deserted from our ranks, and gone over to the enemy. Fifteen of them belonged to Nethercutt's Battalion. They were arraigned before a court martial, proved guilty of the charges, and condemned to suffer death by hanging.

It became my duty to visit these men in prison before their execution, in a religious capacity. From them I learned that bad and mischievous influences had been used with every one to induce him to desert his flag, and such influences had led to their ruin. From citizens who had known them for many years, I learned that some of them had heretofore borne good names, as honest, harmless, unoffending citizens.

After their execution I thought it proper, for the benefit of the living, that I should deliver a discourse before our brigade, upon the death of these men, that the eyes of the living might be opened, to view the horrid and ruinous crime and sin of desertion, which had become so prevalent. A gentleman from Forsyth county, who was present at the delivery of the discourse, solicited a copy for publication, which has been granted.

For the style and arrangement, as it was preached as well as written in the camp, no apology is offered. Having no pecuniary interest in its publication, it is respectfully submitted to all who go for the unqualified independence of the Southern Confederacy.

J. PARIS,

Hoke's Brigade, April 1st, 1864.

SERMON

MATTHEW 27:3-5

3. Then Judas which had betrayed him, when he saw that he was condemned, repented himself, and brought again the thirty pieces of silver to the chief priests and elders,

4. Saying, I have sinned in that I have betrayed the innocent blood. And they said, what is that to us? See thou to that.

5. And he cast down the pieces of silver in the temple, and departed, and went and hanged himself.

You are aware, my friends, that I have given public notice that upon this occasion I would preach a funeral discourse upon the death of the twenty-two unfortunate, yet wicked and deluded men, whom you have witnessed hanged upon the gallows within a few days.

I do so, not to eulogize or benefit the dead. But I do so, solely, for the benefit of the living: and in doing so, I shall preach in my own way, and according to my own manner, or rule. What I shall say will either be true or false. I therefore request that you will watch me closely; weigh my arguments in the balance of truth; measure them by the light of candid reason, and compare them by the Standard of Eternal Truth, the Book of God; what is wrong, reject, and what is, true, accept, for the sake of the truth, as responsible beings.

Of all deserters and traitors, Judas Iscariot, who figures in our text, is undoubtedly the most infamous, whose names have found a place in history, either sacred or profane. No name has ever been more execrated by mankind: and all this has been justly done.

But there was a time and a period when this man wore a different character, and had a better name. A time when he went forth with the eleven Apostles at the command of the Master to preach the gospel, heal the sick and cast out devils. And he, too, returned with this same chosen band, when the grand, and general report was made of what they had done and what they had taught.

But a change came over this man. He was the treasurer of the Apostolic board; an office that warranted the confidence and trust of his compeers. "He bare the bag and kept what was put therein."

Possibly this was the grand and successful temptation presented him by the evil One. He contracted an undue love for money, and Holy Writ informs us "the love of money is the root of all evil;" so must it ever be when valued above a good name, truth or honor. Now comes his base and unprincipled desertion of his blessed Master.

He goes to the chief priests. His object is selfish, base and sordid, — to get money. He enters into a contract with them, to lead their armed guards to the place to which the Saviour had retired, that they might arrest him. Thirty pieces of silver is the price agreed upon, — about twenty-two dollars and fifty cents of our money. A poor price, indeed, for any man to accept for his reputation, his life, his soul, his all.

When Judas saw that the Saviour was condemned, it is stated in the text that "he repented himself, and brought again the thirty pieces of silver to the chief priests and elders, saying, I have sinned in that I have betrayed the innocent blood." "And he cast down the thirty pieces of silver in the temple, and departed and went and hanged himself."

The way of transgressors is truly hard. As sure as there is a God in heaven, justice and judgment will overtake the wicked; though he may flourish as a green bay tree for awhile, yet the eye of God is upon him and retribution must and will overtake him.

Let us now consider what this man gained by his wicked transaction. First, twenty-two dollars and fifty cents. Secondly, a remorse of conscience too intolerable to be borne. An immortality of infamy without a parallel in the family of man. What did he lose? His reputation. His money. His apostleship. His peace of conscience, his life, his soul, his all.

Well may it be said that this man is the most execrable of all whose names stand on the black list of deserters and traitors that the world has furnished from the beginning until now. — Turning to the history of our own country, I find written high on the scroll of infamy the name of Benedict Arnold, who at one time stood high in the confidence of the great and good Washington. What was his crime? Desertion and treason.

He too hoped to better his condition by selling his principles for money, to the enemies of his country, betraying his Washington into the hands of his foes, and committing the heaven-insulting crime of perjury before God and man. Verily, he obtained his reward; an immortality of infamy; the scorn and contempt of the good and the loyal of all ages and all countries.

Thus, gentlemen, I have brought before you two grand prototypes of desertion, whose names tower high over all on the scroll of infamy. And I now lay down the Proposition, that every man who has taken up arms in defense of his country, and basely deserts or abandons that service, belongs in principle and practice to the family of Judas and Arnold.

But what was the status of those twenty-two deserters whose sad end and just fate you witnessed across the river in the old field? Like you they came as volunteers to fight for the independence of their own country. Like you they received the bounty money offered by their country. Like you they took upon themselves the most solemn obligations of this oath:

"I, A. B. do solemnly swear that I will bear true allegiance to THE CONFEDERATE STATES OF AMERICA, and that I will serve them honestly and faithfully against all their enemies or opposers whatsoever, and observe and obey the orders of THE CONFEDERATE STATES, and the orders of the officers appointed over me, according to the rules and articles for THE GOVERNMENT OF THE CONFEDERATE STATES, so help me GOD."

With all the responsibilities of this solemn oath upon their souls, and all the ties that bind men to the land that gave them birth, ignoring every principle that pertains to the patriot, disowning that natural as well as lawful allegiance that every man owes to the government of the State which throws around him the aegis of its protection, they went, boldly, Judas and Arnold-like, made an agreement with the enemies of their country, took an oath of fidelity and allegiance to them, and agreed with them for money to take up arms and assist in the unholy and hellish work of the subjugation of the country which was their own, their native land!

These men have only met the punishment meted out by all civilized nations for such crimes. To this, all good men, all true men, and all loyal men who love their country, will say, Amen!

But who were those twenty-two men whom you hanged upon the gallows? They were your fellow-beings. They were citizens of our own Carolina. They once marched under the same beautiful flag that waves over our heads; but in an evil hour, they yielded to mischievous influence, and from motives or feelings base and sordid, unmanly and vile, resolved to abandon every principle of patriotism, and sacrifice every impulse of honor; this sealed their ruin and enstamped their lasting disgrace.

The question now arises, what are the influences and the circumstances that lead men into the high and damning crimes, of perjury and treason? It will be hard to frame an answer that will fit every case. But as I speak for the benefit of those whom I stand before today, I will say I have made the answer to this question a matter of serious inquiry for more than eighteen months.

The duties of my office as Chaplain have brought me much in contact with this class of men. I have visited twenty-four of them under sentence of death in their cells of confinement, and with death staring them in the face, and only a few short hours between them and the bar of God.

I have warned them to tell the whole truth, confess everything wrong before God and man, and yet I have not been able to obtain the full, fair and frank confession of everything relating to their guilt from even one of them, that I thought circumstances demanded, although I had baptized ten of them in the Name of the Holy Trinity.

In confessing their crimes, they would begin at Newbern, where they joined the enemy, saying nothing about perjury and desertion. Every man of the twenty-two, whose execution you witnessed, confessed that bad or mischievous influences had been used with him to influence him to desert. All but two, willingly gave me the names of their seducers. But none of these deluded and ruined men seemed to think he ought to suffer the penalty of death, because he had been persuaded to commit those high crimes by other men.

But gentlemen, I now come to give you my answer to the question just asked. From all that I have learned in the prison, in the guard house, in the camp, and in the country, I am fully satisfied, that the great amount of desertions from our army are produced by, and are the fruit of a bad, mischievous, restless, and dissatisfied, not to say disloyal influence that is at work in the country at home.

If in this bloody war our country should be overrun, this same mischievous home influence will no doubt be the prime agent in producing such a calamity. Discontentment has, and does exist in various parts of the State. We hear of these malcontents holding public meetings, not for the purpose of supporting the Government in the prosecution of the war, and maintenance of our independence, but for the purpose of finding fault with the Government.

Some of these meetings have been dignified with the name of "peace meetings;" some have been ostensibly called for other purposes, but they have invariably been composed of men who talk more about their "rights," than about their duty and loyalty to their country.

These malcontents profess to be greatly afflicted in mind about the state of public affairs. In their doleful croakings they are apt to give vent to their melancholy lamentations in such words as these: "The country is ruined!" "We are whipt!" "We might as well give up." "It is useless to attempt to fight any longer!" "This is the rich man's war and the poor man's fight;" &c.

Some newspapers have caught the mania and lent their influence to this work of mischief; whilst the pulpit, to the scandal of its character for faith and holiness, has belched forth in some places doctrines and counsels through the ministrations of unworthy occupants, sufficient to cause Christianity to blush under all the circumstances.

I would here remark, standing in the relation which I do before you, that the pulpit and the press, when true and loyal to the Government which affords them protection, are mighty engines for good but when they see that Government engaged in a bloody struggle for existence, and show themselves opposed to its efforts to maintain its authority by all constitutional and legal means, such a press, and such pulpits should receive no support for an hour from a people that would be free. The seal of condemnation should consign them to oblivion.

Such sentiments as we have just alluded to, are sent in letters to our young men in the army, by writers professing to be friends; often with an urgent and pressing invitation to come home; and some have even added that execrable and detestable falsehood, the quintessence of treason, "the State is going to secede."

Letters coming into our camps on the Rappahannock and Rapidan sustain this position. What are the effects produced upon our young men in the ranks? With the illiterate, they are baleful indeed. The incautious youth takes it for granted that the country is ruined and that the Government is his enemy.

The poisonous contagion of treason from home gets hold in his mind and steals into his feelings. This appeal from home has overcome him. The young man of promise and of hope once, now becomes a deserter. Is guilty by one false step of the awful crimes of perjury and desertion. The solemn obligations of his oath are disregarded; he takes to the woods, traverses weary roads by night for days, until he reaches the community in which he claims his home; but for what? To engage in any of the honorable vocations of life?

No, gentlemen. But to he hidden from the face of all good, true and loyal men. But for what purpose? To keep from serving his country as a man and a citizen. To consume the provisions kept in the country for the support of the women and children, families of soldiers who are serving their country, indeed; and lastly, to get his living in part, at least, by stealing and robbing.

And here allow me to say, I am not sufficiently skilled in language to command words to express the deep and unutterable detestation I have of the character of a deserter. If my brother were to be guilty of such a high crime, I should certainly make an effort to have his name changed to something else, that I, and my, children after me, might not feel the deep and lasting disgrace which his conduct had enstamped upon it.

I hold, gentlemen, that there are few crimes in the sight of either God or man, that are more wicked and detestable than desertion. The first step in it is perjury. Who would ever believe such an one in a court of justice again? The second, is treason. He has abandoned the flag of his country; thus much he has aided the common enemy. Those are startling crimes, indeed, but the third is equally so. He enstamps disgrace upon the name of his family and children.

From amidst the smoke and flames of Sinai God has declared that He "is a jealous God, visiting the iniquities of the fathers upon the children unto the third and fourth generations of them that hate me." The infamy that the act of disloyalty on the part of a father places his children in after him, is a disability they cannot escape: it was his act, not theirs; and to them it has become God's visitation according to the text quoted above. The character of infamy acquired by the Tories of the revolution of 1776, is to this day imputed to their descendants, in a genealogical sense. Disloyalty is a crime that mankind never forgets and but seldom forgives; the grave cannot cover it.

Many cry out in this the day of our discontent, and say, "we want peace." This is true, we all want peace, the land mourns on account of the absence of peace, and we all pray for peace. You have often heard me pray for peace, but I think you will bear me witness today that you have never heard me pray for peace without independence. God forbid that we should have a peace that brought no independence.

But how are we to obtain peace? There are but two modes known by which to obtain this most desirable boon. First: to lay down our arms, cease to fight, and submit to the terms of our enemy, the tyrant at Washington. Fortunately for us, we already know what those terms are. They stand recorded in his law books, and in his published orders and edicts, — and constitute with our enemies, the law of the land, so far as we are concerned.

1. The lands of our citizens are to be sold for the purpose of paying the enormous public debt of the Yankees. This part of the program has already been put into operation at points held by the enemy, as in Fairfax county, Va., and Beaufort, S. C. In the latter place, the lands have been laid off into thirty acre lots, and bought mostly by negroes.

2. The negroes, everywhere, to be declared free, and placed upon a state of equality with the whites.

3. Every man who has taken any part in the war, denied the right of voting at the polls.

4. Our Governors and Judges appointed by the Federal Government at Washington, and sent to rule over us at his pleasure.

5. Even the men selected to administer to us in holy things at the altars of our God, must be men approved and appointed by his military authorities; as it is now done in Norfolk and Portsmouth, where I am acquainted.

In addition to this, Gentlemen, we of course will have to endure the deep and untold mortification of having bands of negro, soldiers stationed in almost every neighborhood, to enforce these laws and regulations.

These things would be some of the "blessings," we would obtain by such a peace. Tell me today, sons of Carolina, would not such a peace bring ten-fold more horrors and distress to our country than this war, has yet produced? Can any people on the face of this earth, fit to be freemen, ever accept a peace that will place them in such a condition? Never! never! never!

The great and good Stonewall Jackson, a few weeks before his death was talking with a friend about the probable issue of the war; the conversation turned upon the possibility of the Confederate States being brought again under the rule and authority of the United States; when our illustrious chief remarked, that if he could have his choice in view of such a contingency, he would prefer the grave as his refuge. What patriot would not? What soldier would not? What freeman would not? This was the noble sentiment of a man whom we all believed to be fit to live, or fit to die.

The other mode by which to obtain peace, is to fight it out to the bitter end, as our forefathers did in the revolution of 1776, and reduce our enemies, by our manly defense, to the necessity of acknowledging our independence, and "letting us alone." We are involved in this bloody war, and the question before us is, not how did we get into it, but how shall we get out of it?

Many tell us the war cloud looks dark and impenetrable to mortal vision. This is all true. But are we not men? Have we not buckled on the armor, putting our trust in the Lord of hosts, as the arbiter of our destiny as a nation? Shall we then lay down our arms before we are overthrown? God forbid!

Sons of Carolina, let your battle-cry be, Onward! Onward! until victory shall crown the beautiful banner that floats over us today with such a peace as freemen only love, and brave men only can accept. We are engaged in a mighty work, the establishment of an empire, which we trust by the blessing of God will become the freest, the best and the greatest on the face of the earth. Every man must act his part in this great work.

Let us then look to the manner in which we perform the part which duty assigns, that there may be no regrets or heart-burnings hereafter. For just as sure as this cruel war began, it will have an end, and that end is nearer now than when it began. And when the sweet and lovely days of delightful peace return to cheer us, and friend meets with friend, and talk over the trials, the perils and sufferings we have endured in freedom's cause; with what emotions of pleasure shall we speak of the soldier ever true and faithful who stood by us, faithful alike both in the sunshine and storm of war.

But what will then be said of the miserable skulker? May God give him a better heart that he may become a better man and a better soldier.

From the position which I occupy, I have been enabled to notice deserters and skulkers closely, and I have made it my business to inquire into their history, and I am happy to say for the credit of Christianity, that among the multitude I have known guilty of desertion, only three of that number professed to be members of any Church, and they had been no credit to the religion they professed, as it lived only upon their lips and was a stranger in their hearts.

The true Christian is always a true patriot. Patriotism and Christianity walk hand in hand. When perils and dangers gather around the country that protects him, he then belongs to no party but his country's party; his loyalty must stand unquestioned and unquestionable.

As one that fears God, he knows that, if a man is not for his country, he is against it. Hence, there is no neutral ground or position for him to occupy; but to stand by his country as its fast, unwavering friend, that its triumph may be his triumph, and its destiny his destiny. There is no toryism in a Christian's heart. The two principles cannot to dwell together.

War is the scourge of nations. God is no doubt chastising us for our good. When the ends of His providence are accomplished, He will no doubt remove the rod. But the ways of His providence are generally dark to mortal vision. Yet he is able to bring light out of darkness. We are only drinking now from a cup, from which every nation upon the face of the earth have drank before us. We have walked the bloody road of revolution for three years; and still we face the foe. Our fathers trod it for seven, and in the end were successful.

The pious Dr. Watts tells us in one of his beautiful hymns, that,

> "God moves in a mysterious way,
>
> His wonders to perform;
>
> He plants his footsteps in the sea,
>
> And rides upon the storm."

His ways with the nations of the earth are deeply mysterious to mortal vision and whilst they are the exhibitions of His majesty and power, we should regard them likewise as the evidence of his goodness and mercy towards fallen man. As He deals with individuals, so does He deal with nations. He lifteth up one and putteth down another; but all this is done for the good of the whole. Righteousness exalteth a nation, but sin is a reproach to any people, is the doctrine laid down in Holy Writ.

Proud Egypt, the cradle, of the arts and sciences, has sadly fallen from her ancient glory and splendor. Ezekiel, speaking as the oracle of God, and accusing her of her sins, declared "she shall become the basest of the kingdoms," and the words of the Seer have become verified to the letter. For transgression, the chosen people of God, the Israelites, were compelled to wander forty years in the Arabian desert, thus suffering the chastisement of the disfavor of offended Deity. And when they were permitted to cross over Jordan into the land of promise, they were required to do a strange and wondrous work; namely, to destroy the nations of this goodly land and possess it for their own inheritance.

The sins of these nations had cried unto heaven, and Israel became the instrument in the hand of God by which the judgments of offended Justice was meted out to the guilty nations. Jerusalem, the lovely, queenly Jerusalem, whose beautiful temple was the glory of the whole earth, in which the presence of the Eternal Shekinah was visible annually to mortal eye, and where Solomon in all his glory once reigned — sinned with an high hand against God; she knew not the day of her visitation, the cup of her iniquity was full; the judgment of offended heaven overtook her; her glory departed; the besom of destruction swept over her, and she is now trodden down by the gentiles — a crumbling monument of her departed greatness.

Babylon, once the proud mistress of the East, whose spacious walls, hanging gardens, and lofty temples stood as the wonders of the world, and Daniel, the prophet, robed in the vestments of royal honors, once spake, and wrote by heaven's prompting of things to come has fallen; her greatness is lost; her walls have perished; her palaces have crumbled; her temples are entombed, and the wandering Arab now nightly pitches his tent over spot where Belshazzar held his impious feast.

Where is the Nineveh? The mighty Nineveh? And Tadmor, and Persepolis, and hundred-gated Thebes? They belong only to the past, the silence of death has spread its sepulchral pall over them, and the relics of fallen greatness alone remain to mark the spot where they lie entombed. Sparta has departed from the map of nations, and Athens is but the tomb of the Athens that was. These have all sinned, and "there is a God that judgeth in the earth."

Four years ago, THESE CONFEDERATE STATES formed an integral part of the United States. Perhaps no nation of people ever sinned against more light, and abused more privileges than the United States. The Northern pulpits hatched and fostered the spirit that produced this cruel and bloody war: but cruel and bloody as it is, I believe in God, today, that great good to us of the South as a people, if we will only depart from our sins and lean upon the Almighty Arm.

If He be for us, who can stand successfully against us? He gave to our fathers a Washington, a man who feared God, to guide them through the revolution of 1771. He has given to us a Lee, a man of like faith and of like hopes, to be our leader in these dark days of trial, and we all love to follow where he leads.

He lent to us a Jackson, that bright and shining light of Christianity, whose ardent piety and strong faith always presented the same beauties, in the halls of science, at the altars of God, around the camp-fires, or on the battle-field. Oh, what a model of a Christian soldier!

Well do I remember how his presence, cheered us as he rode along our line on the morning of the first battle of Fredericksburg, after the artillery began to roar heavily. His very appearance seemed to be the presage of victory. He seemed like one sent by God. But God has seen proper in His providence to take him away, and whatsoever He doeth is right. Let us then bow, to the hand that afflicts in such dispensations as this, take courage and press onward.

Let us then humble ourselves before God as a people, confess our sins, and implore His protecting power to guide us through this mighty struggle to a successful issue. He has certainly done great things for us as a people, whereof we should be glad.

I think you will bear me witness that I have never been hopeful of an early peace in my intercourse among you. But today I fancy that I can discover a little cloud, in the political heavens as large as a man's hand at least, that seems to portend peace. Take courage, then, companions in arms. All things around us today bid us be of good courage.

History fails to tell us of ten millions of freemen being enslaved, who had determined to be free. A braver or more patriotic army than we have, never followed their chief to victory. Their endurance challenges the admiration of the world. When I have seen our brave men in winter's cold and summer's heat, marching from battle-field to battle-field, bare-footed as they were born, and without a murmur, I could not doubt our final success. Such men as these, were never born to be slaves.

Again when I have turned my eye homeward from the camp, and witnessed the labors of our fair country women, in preparing clothing to meet the wants of the suffering in the field, and witnessed their untiring devotion to the relief of the sick and wounded in the hospitals, I knew that the history of no country, and of no age afforded anything like a parallel, and my faith assured me we never were born to be slaves of the Yankees. Then let your trust today be strong in the God of nations.

Surely, then, no man can be found in all our land who owes allegiance to his country, that is so lost to himself, and to all that is noble and patriotic, as to say, "I am for the Union as it was." Such an one could only merit the good man's scorn, and desire the Tory's infamy for himself, and disgrace for his children.

Gentlemen, I have followed your fortunes for twenty months, leaving wife and children far behind me. I have rejoiced in your prosperity, and mourned over your adversity. Marches, battles, sufferings are before us still. By the help of God I am with you, and hope still to be with you to share in your triumphs, your sufferings and your joys. If these be the days to try men's souls, for my country's sake I am willing to be tried, by bearing my humble part in this mighty struggle.

For, standing before you today, you must permit me to say in the language of a noble patriot, "I am for my country right, yea, for my country wrong." My loyalty to her is unqualified, and without any conditions. Her cause is always my cause. If her cause be right, she shall have my free support; if it be wrong she shall have my unqualified support. Therefore, when I shall sleep in the dust, you must not say to my children, "your father was a conservative, (or any other name,) when his country was engaged in a bloody struggle for existence." Then you would do me wrong, and do them wrong also.

I belong only to my country's party. But it may be said, that I can afford to use strong language when I am not required to take position in the front ranks on the battlefield. The duties of my office require me, as you are aware, to take position in the rear, to assist with the wounded, but yet at Fredericksburg, Williamsport, Mine Run, and Batchelor's Creek, I was under the fire of both artillery and musketry, and I will here add that if ever my country calls upon me to fall into ranks in her defense with a musket on my shoulder, my answer shall be, "here am I."

Then, today, in the light of this beautiful Sabbath sun, let us take courage, and with renewed trust in God, resolve to do our whole duty as patriots and soldiers, and leave the event to the Arbiter of nations. Amen!

1865

He That Believeth Shall Not Make Haste

A SERMON

PREACHED

ON THE FIRST OF JANUARY, 1865

IN

ST. PAUL'S CHURCH, RICHMOND
BY THE RECTOR

REV. CHAS. MINNIGERODE, D. D.

1865

SERMON

HE THAT BELIEVETH SHALL NOT MAKE HASTE. — *Isaiah* 28:16

MANY and glorious things are said of faith. It is the theme of the Christian pulpit, a subject which cannot be exhausted. It tells upon all the relations of life and gives character to every believer, whatever the circumstances be in which he may be placed. His whole life in its every manifestation, in thought, word and deed, in the inner sanctuary of his feelings and aspirations, in his outward bearing in the world and towards others, is developed from his position as a believer.

At peace with God through faith in Jesus Christ, he leans on the arm of Omnipotence and reposes on the bosom of Infinite Wisdom; and from these two premises follow, as their legitimate and blessed results, the two cardinal characteristics of the Christian: *humility* and true, calm, fearless *manliness*.

As he looks up to God, he finds a Father, a Father's love, a Father's faithfulness, a Father's home, and feels "the everlasting arms are underneath;" and trustfully, humbly he commits himself and all to Him to whom he has committed his highest, his eternal interests. Secure in that guardian care and covenanted love, he then descends into the relations of ordinary life, and enters cheerfully and zealously upon his daily duties and trials.

Supported by the promise, which for the real believer matures into fruition, of Christ's presence and ever-active sympathy; by the guiding power of Him that is greater than all that can be against him, by the Spirit that reveals to his own spirit more and more the unfailing love of Christ; secure in the highest guarantee, that "He who spared not his Son, but delivered him up for us all, shall surely with him freely give us all things," and the positive pledge "all things shall work together for good to them that love God."

He can harbor the hope, that — however weak and unworthy — he shall not utterly fall nor fail of his eternal portion; and in his intercourse with the world show himself A MAN in the fullest and highest sense of the word, a man sufficient for the duties and trials of life, who hallows his every act by doing it to the glory of God, who learns to do all things through Christ that strengthens him, and to bear all things which in his service he may encounter.

Surely, Brethren, he that thus believeth "shall not make haste." Tribulation he shall have in this world, but "he is of good cheer — for Christ has overcome the world." Sorrows will fall to his share as to the lot of all men, but "he sorrows not as those who have no hope."

Trials must come, trials and afflictions which checker the life of all; but he remembers, that God "chooseth his people in the furnace of affliction;" and he meets all that life can bring him, of duties or trials or temptations, clad in the impenetrable armor of the Gospel of peace: "As thy day so shall thy strength be;" "My grace is sufficient for thee."

Trials are but God's discipline for our good: "he chastens those whom he loves." He who thus believeth shall not be thrown down from his trust in God, not be robbed of that peace which reposes in his love and faithfulness; he cannot become the plaything of every puff of adversity or prosperity; and — restive under God's providence, impatient of his discipline, forgetful of all the everlasting guarantees he rests on and the manly determination that has marked out his course — be driven to the mad career of presumption, or cast into the slough of despondency.

Such is indeed the steadfastness of the believer. This makes him truly great and manly in the vicissitudes of life: "he shall not make haste"

But, Brethren, who of us will boast of such unfaltering, all-governing faith? Who is there, that should not be moved to self-examination and better resolutions by the words of our text?

To the believer we give it as a *test,* to try his faith, its truth and vitality. The unbeliever we point to it, as the only way to that manliness, without which our life and all its purposes and aims must prove a failure.

Is it not want of faith, which is the root of all that murmuring against God's providence, that impatience at delay and the frustration of our plans, that repining under the pressure of misfortunes and losses and reverses? of that hasty spirit which charges our losses upon others, and finds relief in censure and distrust?

Which acts upon the impulse of the moment and forms its conclusions from the passing events of the day, judges of the favor of God by a success and of his displeasure by a reverse? which allows itself to be tossed about by changes which meet us in our earthly life, and rushes with equal thoughtlessness or recklessness — now into presumption on the crest of a prosperous wave — again into utter despondency, aye sinks down in despair, when the billows rise above us and seem ready to swallow us up.

In all this, Beloved — even humanly speaking — there is no principle except our fickleness and unbelief; there is no firmness, no greatness, no manliness; certainly there is no faith. Submission, meek submission, which looks upon the Divine sufferer on the cross and humbly prays "Thy will, not mine be done."

Patience, which takes its pattern from our long-suffering Saviour, and remembers that he is not slack concerning his promises, but defers them in mercy to us, and to strengthen our faith, to root it more deeply and draw it out in richer fruits. Calmness and self-possession — though all should be dark around and all earthly promises fail; for above the storm that threatens, rules the same Lord at whose word the waves of Gennesareth were smoothed and the winds hushed into silence.

Charity towards all who may have failed and been unfortunate — knowing that it is God's providence, not man's, which shapes the events, and that it is not a noble mind which covets a victim. Steadfast hope when all others lie trembling, because that hope rests on God. And instead of falling into despair, and giving up and sacrificing all in pusillanimity or personal spite, *manly action,* which meets the stern reality with courage and, in reliance on God's help, and trusting to his mercy, begirts itself to the work before him, and redeems the time by using every lawful means and making every reasonable exertion to do his duty and accomplish his purpose.

Such, I say, are the marks of the true man, of the Christian, of the believer; who shall not make haste, but persevere under trials and against difficulties till his work is done; and who can never fail — even though here on earth he should find no other triumph but the martyr's crown.

This is the true lesson of life, the secret of our failure or success, our victory or defeat in the problem of our existence. Without this faith we but hasten to destruction. It is the lesson I would bring you on this day, the meditation most suited as a preparation for the work of the new year, which in God's mercy we have been permitted to see.

Life has brought to us all "labor and sorrow" and demands all our manliness. As we look back and consult the experience of the past, and look forward and fain would ask of the coming year its hopes and fears, its joys and sorrows: we shall not find a more important and useful truth than that of my text.

The lessons of the last year may be humiliating and sad, and we all more or less have been suffering from that haste which is so inconsistent in the true believer; the prospect of the future may be dark — it is all the more necessary that we should arm ourselves for its coming days with that faith which alone enables us "to stand in the evil day, and having done all, to stand."

The assertion of the text applies to *our inner life,* the hidden life of the soul in the sight of God, its growth amidst the many spiritual trials and temptations and disappointments and drawbacks which belong to our training and probation-life. And it applies to *life in all its forms* and *all its demands upon the individual,* in our daily tasks and each one's peculiar sphere.

And oh! as I see so many rushing along wildly, without a steadfast and a godly principle; see them entering the new year, with its unknown events, without the support of faith, without the guide of a heavenly light, hastening on upon the dictates of their own wisdom, throwing aside the alone support for their laboring spirits, yielding to the tyranny of the moment and the power of mere circumstances, to fall into murmuring or impatience, into recklessness to enjoy the present moment and stake their all upon it, *"après nous le déluge,"* because they have no hopes resting upon a sure and lasting foundation; into despondency and despair, because they have lost sight of God's overruling providence and merciful promises — dwindling down in their own puny selves, and shivering in terror at the trials which give strength to the brave,

I would throw myself in the breach, throw myself in their way, and stem their downward course by raising *the banner of faith* and saying, "he that believeth shall not make haste."

But conscience bids me make a further application of my text this day. The year that is passed has brought us untold sorrows and trials as a people. Reverses have followed us in many parts of our country, and the year opens with dark and threatening clouds, which have cast their shadow over every brow. What we need is *a stout heart* and a *firm, settled mind;* and oh! may we AS A NATION remember, "he that believeth shall not make haste."

I trust I'll be forgiven the introduction of this subject. God forbid that I should speak as a mere man and not as the minister of Christ, that I should introduce politics where Religion alone should raise her voice, discuss measures and men where only principles can be laid down. It is as God's messenger that I speak and preach his gospel in the faith, which is the alone principle that can steady our course and raise our hearts in hope.

We preach to men under the circumstances in which we find them placed in God's providence; we bring them the appeals and the comforts of God's word according to their wants, their peculiar duties and trials. That most godly man, than whom no one was further removed from desecrating the pulpit with politics, that most uncompromising preacher of the gospel in its purity and holiness, the apostolic Bishop Meade — with his prophetic eye upon the struggle in which he knew the very existence of his beloved State would be involved.

In which he foresaw the trials that would befall us and how the faith of many would wax cold in the hour of danger, who anticipated what all combatants for truth and liberty have experienced in their struggle, reverses and despondency, and perhaps defection; but whose faith never wavered as to the justice of our cause and the ultimate victory of truth and right. —

He foretold his ministers that the time might come when it would be their duty to encourage the timid, and by their proclamation of God's truth, uphold the cause and strengthen the hands of the faithful; and on his dying bed besought us to do our duty and boldly proclaim our message.

In his spirit, and in obedience to my heavenly Master's call, I would raise my voice in this the darkest day of our struggle, and — in the only way in which I can do my duty as a Christian patriot — speak to all, people and rulers, administration and legislation, soldiers and citizens, to all whom God has called into this fearful conflict, to all upon whose faithfulness and manly course our cause under God depends, and beseech them to *rally on that faith* which alone can bear us through, and steady our hearts, and nerve our arms, and give us souls patient and enduring and loyal, and lift us from our danger and despondency to nobler resolutions and brighter hopes. "He that believeth shall not make haste."

What is it that makes the present crisis so painful?

Our reverses? NO, BRETHREN. For great as they have been, (and no honest man would hide their extent,) we have had reverses before, and God always has blessed them to us, made them the source of greater harmony among ourselves, roused us to new and greater exertions, and taught us to bear them and repair them as men.

What makes the present crisis so painful and so perilous lies not in what the enemy has done to us with his armies, but in *what our own coward, faithless, selfish hearts may do.* The all but general despondency, the lack of faith in ourselves and in God's assistance, the haste with which, from want of faith.

Many would rush to this or that wild expedient, though at the sacrifice of all that first armed us to the battle, some perhaps at the sacrifice of honor and truth;[1] the mutual recrimination which charges our reverses here or there, and with unyielding prejudice sows discord.

When our very existence is in danger; the hopelessness of many, which is ready to give up and sink into sullen despair, and withholds the needful help at the most critical time, and spreads the spirit of dissatisfaction and despondency, and would not shrink even from poisoning the minds of those who are the great bulwark between ourselves and destruction.

It is this, the fear that we may not be true to ourselves because we are faltering in our faith in God, which presents the dangerous aspect of our present crisis. Oh! if we could take with us into the new year the lesson of our text; if we could stop every croaker and nerve every patriot.

If we could allay every impatience and rouse all to bear what others have borne before, and drive away their unmanly fears by trust in God, by truly, prayerfully committing themselves and the country into His hands from whom alone cometh our help, and urge them on, TO DO AND BEAR, to brave their dangers and endure their privations, to be true men and act as such: the threatening dangers with which the year opens upon us would in God's mercy be changed into blessings.

And this year witness the growth of our national strength and our training for the final victory! "He that believeth shall not make haste." If this sentiment was realized by all — rulers and people alike — and followed up in a God fearing spirit, submitting to his chastisements and learning the lessons of adversity in patience and calm courageous resolution, in mutual bearing and forbearing.

In that manliness which yields where the good of the country requires it, and subordinates self to the high and holy cause in which we are engaged, in that devotion which consecrates all and sacrifices all to the will of God and the common good. —

If our prayers could effect this, there would be no cause left for fear; but from our reverses we would rise in new strength, and — against whatever dangers and by however slow degrees — enter upon that course which must bring victory and peace!

It would give us *that true courage* which shines most conspicuously when all looks threatening, which becomes calm in danger and perseveres to the last, faithful to principle; which rests impregnably upon the rock of faith, and there finds strength to do all things and bear all things in the discharge of duty.

(1.) "He that believeth shall not make haste." This does not exclude work; it includes it. Haste is opposed to proper speed, to the conscientious and judicious use of the proper means, opposed to the faithful discharge of duty.

It is true "not by might, nor by power, but by my Spirit, saith the Lord;" but this excludes only a reliance on a might and a power which is not sanctioned by God — a might and power of their own, which the faithless in their haste substitute for that might and power of God's Spirit which shall accomplish his work in his own good time by the legitimate means of man's activity and faithful, persevering labor.

Here we have the true principles: the conscientious, diligent use of means, but of means which God has sanctioned, and which his Spirit blesses.

When we speak of trust in God, we do not advocate superstition or fanaticism. The day of miracles is passed. No legions from above shall descend, and, as in the legends of old, lead our armies. No miraculous interposition can be looked for to terminate our struggle or give us by a sudden supernatural visitation the victory, which we were not faithful enough to achieve by the judicious and honest use of the means placed in our hands, the power entrusted us.

God everywhere works by means; he blesses them, he gives them success, but only when they are used in accordance with his design; and only upon their use can we count on his blessing. God helps those who help themselves, who through faith in him rise with their work and to their work.

Just as every Christian *trusts* as if God did everything and he nothing, but he also *works* as if the whole success rested upon that, and *he can work,* for he knows "it is God that worketh in him to will and to do."

Yes, Brethren, here must be our strength. We took an estimate of our means and our strength when we entered upon this war. Let us take a new census for this year, honestly, conscientiously. Let us count all that can be and ought to be in the army; all the resources we have the command of, we can husband and increase.

All the wealth with which in God's mercy we yet are blessed, and which no less than our lives and our children's lives are due to the service of the country, which others have often sacrificed on its altars, and which it would be folly to attempt to save at the risk of the ruin of the country which alone can shield us in its possession; which we must part with when we part with our liberty and independence.

Let us add every motive of honor and solemn pledges and patriotism; the prospect of the alternate issue of success or defeat; and then throw into the scale that faith in God which those should have who fight in a just cause, who defend their altars and their homes, the lives and honor of their wives and children; who would be craven could they shrink from any sacrifice to save all that man holds dear and sacred.

Those who indeed would humble themselves before God and acknowledge the justice of their chastisement, yet who trust to his overruling providence, and put themselves under his protection, and commit their all to Him in whose hands are the issues of life and death and the destinies of nations, "who can save by many or by few:" and who are resolved in His name, and by His help, to do their whole duty and never weary in its discharge, and endure to the end, faithful unto death:

And Brethren, is it for such to make haste and through unbelief deny their every premise and give up their every hope, and turn from their lofty goal in selfish fear, in weak despair? Away with faintheartedness! "Heart within and God o'erhead!" Let us do our duty, be faithful in our work, and we can safely leave results with God!

The might and power which our enemies bring against us, are not the might and power of God's Spirit, we may be sure — except so far as they are permitted to chasten us for our sins and train us for the hardships of a godly warfare.

Trust in his Spirit and in his might and gracious promises; and that trust shall buoy us up to do our part in the work of our deliverance and independence. Oh! when I recollect what others have done in the struggle for their liberty and existence, the sacrifices they have brought,[2] the gigantic energy which even the aggressor and the conqueror develops, must I not say, here is our path and here our duty?

(2.) Yes, Brethren, "he that believeth shall not make haste;" for his faith will teach him not only to act and do the necessary work and make the requisite exertions, it will also nerve him *to endure and bear all that must be borne*. Really I am the last person that would underrate our sufferings and the sacrifices that have been brought; yet let us remember we are not the only ones that have thus been called on to suffer.

How true are the words of the present Governor of South Carolina, when in his Inaugural he said: "Other nations, for lesser purposes, have striven longer, endured more than we have, and won for themselves imperishable honor. Let us not hesitate in our purpose, or falter in its execution."

Aye, Brethren, no nation ever gained its freedom without suffering; and had we time to refer to the facts of history, we could easily show how true it is that others have suffered more and struggled longer.[3]

And shall we lack the faith to bear us out in our struggle? in our struggle for liberty and honor, and wealth and independence, and a glorious future? for wife and children and home, and all we hold dear and sacred? for truth and our altars? for our lives and very existence?

Ah, he who here can make haste, and rush either into submission or despair, and give up when such is the stake — he who can make haste in the foolish hope of saving himself when the country is perishing, God have mercy upon his poor, miserable soul; but let him be as a beacon-light to warn off every honest son of his country, and teach us to seek that steadfastness and loyalty which true faith ensures.

Let us confess it, brethren, there has been no nation which has started upon her career of freedom with such boastfulness, and looked upon her struggles as so transient, her victory as so easily achieved, as ours. Shall we be found boasters indeed, vain boasters?

There have been many whose great stimulant was not the principle of national freedom and the sacred cause of constitutional and inalienable rights, but the aspiration for wealth and power and a great new empire. But "pride goeth before a fall" — can we wonder that such a fall should overtake us?

But shall we be cast down and not rather take it as a solemn, painful lesson to profit by, and be led to the true and only foundation of all right and hope and prosperity? Shall it be said of us, that "we begun to build and were not able to finish?"

The question resolves itself into this: Shall we be of the number of those who, in the crucible of affliction, were found wanting, and proved themselves unworthy of the prize they fought for? or, shall we be of those who, through trials and fiery persecution, endured and glorified God, and honored themselves and blessed their country by remaining faithful, and in every danger proved themselves true men, brave men, Christian heroes?

Yes, *Christian heroes!* For however the worldling, the infidel, and all "who make haste," may sneer at it, the only true basis, the only perfect guarantee for loyalty and faithfulness in our earthly relations and earthly duties, is FAITH IN GOD.

This is as true as the word of God is true. Let us be Christians, let us acknowledge our relation to God, let us realize him as our covenant God and Father; let us do our duty as in His sight and to His glory, in His faith and His strength, and in obedience to His will, *and we cannot, we shall never fail!* "Some trust in chariots and some in horses; but we will remember the name of the Lord our God. They are brought down and fallen: but we are risen and stand upright."

Can we take these promises — which in their fullest sense belong to the Church of God — can we take them to ourselves? Can we apply them to our cause and country? Brethren, the answer to this question rests with YOU.

Oh! if we individually place ourselves under his protection and his guidance; if we individually try to do our duty, and our whole duty — do it wherever we may be placed, because we fear to sin against God; if his servants, watching for souls, can on their rounds from house to house and town to town, from post to post and corps to corps, call out to each other "all is well," we need not fear; and the more this spirit spreads, the safer our condition.

The new year has opened upon us. What shall it bring?

The horoscope is easily cast. There are but two alternatives. If, indeed, we give up our faith, and with it our strength, and every high motive and soul-elevating hope, our ruin is certain — we would be hastening to it. Nor would such a nation be worth saving; they would not be fit to use their success to God's glory and their own good.

But if we stand in His faith, and, dependent upon His help, continue to labor and to work, and having done all, commit ourselves and our cause to Him, then, whatever the temporal issues may be, we cannot perish; we can still say, in the fullest assurance of faith, "The Lord of hosts is with us, the God of Jacob is our refuge."

Dear Brethren, I look for brighter days in the new year. I trust in God's mercy, and hope he will send us his blessing.

I cannot despair of our cause, which in my heart of hearts I believe to be the cause of right and truth. I will not believe that our people are so craven, so lost to all that ever has distinguished them, as to forget and betray their pledge of wealth and life and sacred honor to their country's cause.[4]

I do believe, that under God's blessing the right means will be used, and used conscientiously, zealously and quickly; that the people are sufficiently determined to endure and to persevere; that both our administrative and our legislative authorities will so act as to restore and increase confidence.

Errors have been committed, failures have been made — where in the history of the world has this not been the case? Who is exempt from them? But it is not a generous spirit which hunts down its victims.

When C. Terrentius Varro had by his imprudence and bad generalship lost the fatal battle of Cannae and brought the Republic to the verge of ruin, after he had delivered the fugitives he had rallied at Venusia and Casilinum into the hands of his successor, himself set out to Rome to make a personal report of his conduct.

With what feelings he approached the city may be imagined. But as he drew near, the Senate and people went out to meet him, and publicly thanked him "for that he had not despaired of the Republic." Saith the Roman historian: "History presents no nobler spectacle than this. Had he been a Carthaginian general, he would have been crucified." Which code shall Christian nations adopt?

Errors, grave errors have been committed, no doubt. Only let us acknowledge the hand of God even there, even in our failures; and let us remember that the great error, the great difficulty is *in us,* in ourselves, in our own faithless hearts, and sinful lives, and selfish fears, and hasty judgments; and oh! I do pray and hope that God will have mercy upon us, and give us better minds and stout hearts and unfailing faith, that shall not make haste, that shall win the prize.

But if we fall, let us fall with our faces upward, our hearts turned to God, our hands in the work, our wounds in the breast, with blessings — not curses — upon our lips; and all is not lost! We have retained our honor, we have done our duty to the last, and lived and died as the servants of God, lived in faith and died in the hope of glory.

But this bright new year's sun, this glorious Sabbath-morn which ushers it in amidst the prayers and praises of God's people — it does not augur failure or defeat. It rises like a star of hope upon the dark clouds in which the last year has set.

And I do believe that our present reverses are tokens, not of God's anger and his abandonment of our cause, but a merciful discipline, a fatherly chastisement for our sins, to make us more humble before him and dependent on his alone saving grace, more earnest and single-hearted in the duties of our life; to call forth the latent energies that still sleep within us and shall wake at the touch of his Omnipotent hand, and arm our souls with unconquerable strength by faith in his promises, and by the prayers which shall ascend to the throne of grace and bring down his blessing upon us

Beloved Brethren, let us devote ourselves, our souls and body, to his service, and bring to his altar the sacrifice of all we have and all we are. Let this be the resolution with which we enter the new year, that His we will be, and His shall be our heart and strength and time and wealth and life. Let us bear our present trials as His dispensation, and therefore "quit us as men and be strong," and "not make haste!"

Let us make it our sacred duty to uphold and increase — not to shake or undermine, public confidence; but forgetting all enmities and jealousies, surrendering all prejudices and selfish aims, join hand and heart, and as a band of brothers, enlisted in Christ's service, let us seal our vows of loyalty to God and man, our country, and our every duty, in the holy sacrament to which the day invites us! And may God smile upon us and give us his blessing, and crown the year with his mercy and goodness, and beautify us with his salvation!

NOTES:

[1] After the terrible defeat of the Roman legions at Heraclea in their first decisive encounter with Pyrrhus, Rome was thrown into the greatest alarm, and Pyrrhus desired to avail himself of this to secure the fruits of his victory. His shrewd minister, the diplomatic Cineas, "whose tongue had won him more battles than his own sword," was sent there, and by his address gained the most dangerous influence.

Although the terms he had to offer were stringent and ruinous to Rome's position, yet he so played upon their fears, and won upon them by his insinuating ways, that he would have persuaded the Senate to submit to these terms if it had not been for one man. "This was Appius Claudius, the Censor. He was now in extreme old age; he had been blind for many years, and had long ceased to take part in public affairs.

But now, when he heard of the proposed surrender, he caused himself to be conducted to the Senate-house by his four sons and his five sons-in-law, and there, with the authoritative eloquence of an oracle, he confirmed the wavering spirits of the fathers, and dictated the only answer worthy of Rome — that *she would not treat of peace with Pyrrhus till he had quitted the shores of Italy.*" The dying patriotism of Appius saved Rome. May his spirit descend upon our Senate, our rulers, our people! "Cineas returned to Pyrrhus baffled and without hope." He told his master that "to fight with the Roman people was like fighting with the Hydra;" he declared that "the city was as a temple of the Gods, and the Senate an assembly of kings." And the people upheld them, and Pyrrhus read his doom in the firmness of the Romans under defeat.

[2] I would once more, by way of illustration, refer to the history of Rome. Her stern and unyielding patriotism in the best days of the Republic, and when struggling for her existence, has never been surpassed. The invasion of Hannibal reduced her to straits similar to those which form our present crisis. What was her course? The campaigns of

218, 217, and 216, with the defeats on the Trebia, the Lake Trasimene, and the crushing blow at Cannae, where her legions were all but annihilated, the defection of all Southern Italy, and the dread of *"Hannibal ante portas"* had reduced her to the last extremities.

In that terrible battle 40,000 Romans (at the lowest calculation) had fallen, and 3000 horse, involving the death of some of the wealthiest and most distinguished citizens, with one Consul, both the Proconsuls, both the Quaestors, 21 out of 48 Tribunes, and not less than 80 Senators among the slain. History does not record any defeat more complete, and very few more murderous.

The first step was to guard against the results of a general panic. "The Senate instantly met, and at the motion of Fabius each Senator was invested with the power of a magistrate: they were to prevent all public lamentations; to hinder the people from meeting in the Forum, lest they should pass resolutions in favor of peace; to keep the gates well guarded, suffering no one to pass in or out without a special order" — for fear of the approach of Hannibal, &c., &c.

Then came their resolute course towards the enemy. Hannibal, too wise to lead his insufficient force at once against Rome itself, opened negotiations and "sent ten of the chief men among his prisoners with offers to hold all whom he had taken to ransom. The Senate, on motion of T. Manlius Torquatus, a man who had inherited the stern decision of his ancestor, refused to admit the messengers to the audience, and ordered all to return, as they had bound themselves, to Hannibal's camp."

No compromise there; and this uncompromising spirit was accompanied by commensurate acts. Fabius, with the coolness of age and experience, directed their measures, and M. Claudius Marcellus, "the sword of Rome," was sent to the command of the fugitives and stragglers, whom Varro — the unfortunate leader at Cannæ — was trying to rally, with young Scipio and other Tribunes. Levies were ordered in Rome and Latium; and as owing to the terrible losses of the last three campaigns, (at least 80,000 Romans and allies,) the regular levies were proceeding slowly, the Dictator, M. Junius, proposed to buy 8000 slaves from their masters to serve as light troops; and also to enroll debtors, prisoners and other persons, by law uncapable of serving in the Roman legions.

The Senate was replenished by the bravest and the worthiest citizens, and a new army was put in the field for the next campaign, under the Consuls T. Sempronius Gracchus and L. Posthumius, (and afterwards Fabius Maximus,) Marcellus and Varro retaining a command as Proconsuls.

But the vast expenses demanded extraordinary exertions; and no means was spared during this and the succeeding years to call out the full strength of the country, its wealth and resources.

Early in the war the Senate had merely doubled all existing imposts, and the commanders in Sicily, Sardinia and Spain, were ordered to subsist their troops from the resources of those countries. But in the year after Cannæ, their commanders reported that they were destitute of all things — money, food and clothing.

It is curious and instructive to see how the exigency was met. We quote from Liddell's admirable compendium of Roman history: "Upon this the Senate proposed to the contractors to supply the required stores and wait for payment till the end of the war, it being understood that whatever was shipped from Italy was to be paid for, whether the vessels reached their destination or not.

This offer was readily accepted; but some of the contractors were guilty of a fraud, disgraceful enough at any time, but at a time when the State was struggling for very existence, utterly detestable. These wretched men put a quantity of worthless stores on board crazy vessels, which were purposely lost on their passage, and then claimed payment in full, according to their contract." ["*Mutato nomine,*" &c. — HORACE Sat. I, 1, 70.]

"The fraud, however, was discovered, and these unworthy citizens were obliged to seek refuge in dishonorable exile.

Contracts taken on such terms were, in fact, a loan to the State. The contractors advanced their property for the service of the State, and received in exchange a ticket promising them payment at some future time. Till then they lent their goods and held her promissory note as a security. In the same manner, the owners of the 8000 slaves who were enlisted by Gracchus, gave up their slaves to the State, and waited for payment till the Treasury was replenished."

"In the following year (214) the Senate was obliged to borrow money in a more direct form. The fortunes of minors and widows, which were in the hands of guardians or trustees, were now advanced to the State, all the expenses incurred on the part of the owners being discharged by orders upon the Treasury. These treasury bills (as they may be called) were probably taken in payment by the tradesmen and others, who did not press to have them exchanged for the coin, till it was convenient for the Treasury to do so. In these loans, it does not appear that the State allowed any interest upon the goods or money advanced. It is probable that the bills or orders upon the Treasury continued in use as money, as our Bank-notes."

"In the same year an extraordinary measure had been taken for manning the fleets. All citizens, except the poor, were required to furnish one or more seamen, with six months' pay and their full accoutrements. Senators were called upon to equip eight, and the rest in proportion to their rated property. Such was the Roman ship-money.' "

But the war continued and the necessities increased. The coinage was lowered in value; but of course this only raised the price of all articles to meet the change, and public credit was shaken. New taxes seemed impossible. "The Senate met to deliberate, and the Consul Laevinus proposed (210 B. C.) that the great Council should set an example of patriotic devotion.

"Let us," said he, "contribute all our treasure for the service of the State. Let us reserve — of gold, only our rings, the bullae worn by our sons, and for the ornaments of our wives and daughters one ounce apiece, — of silver, the trappings of our horses, the family salt-cellar, and a small vessel for the service of the gods, — of copper, five thousand pounds for the necessity of each family."

This proposal was carried by acclamation, and the noble example followed emulously by all the people. So eager was the throng which pressed to the Treasury, that the clerks were unable to make a full register of the names. This patriotic loan saved the State; and it was even more valuable in the spirit which it called forth, than for the actual relief which it afforded to the Treasury."

Thus people act when they are in earnest, and such earnestness ensures success. In 204 B.C. the State was able to repay all and cancel every obligation.

[3] See the preceding note. Remember how Athens gave up her city for the salvation of Greece, transported her women and children to Aegina and Troezene, and sent her men to man "the wooden walls" which the Oracle had pronounced their safety, and in which they gained the battle of Salamis.

Remember the siege of Tyre and Sidon and other cities, and their heroic defense — the like of which this war has not yet seen; the retreat of the French from Moscow, the crossing of the Berezina; the rear-guard under Ney, whose heroic endurance yet stands unrivalled.

Think of the long, long, bloody resistance, hoping against hope, and nursed only amidst reverses and sufferings and persecutions with fire and sword, of the Netherlands; of the unequal struggle for seven years of our forefathers, without means and resources but their own stout hearts, their fixed determination, and their trust in God. Can we forget such lessons? such lessons above all as are read us in Hebrews 11th chap. v. 35-38?

[4] I think the literature given to our people chiefly in the daily newspapers should be of an encouraging and inspiring, not a depressing and often demoralizing tendency; of a character to unite them in the great cause, and not to excite and spread disaffection. This applies especially to our armies.

Our soldiers are different from all others; they are no mercenaries, no mere machines. They are our equals, and will think and judge for themselves. What a solemn responsibility to guide that judgment aright! In numbers we will always be inferior — no matter; for it is minorities which always have achieved the greatest triumphs. But in their spirit, their patriotic convictions and motives and hopes, we have an overbalancing superiority. Let that spirit be to all a sacred thing; for if once this foundation of our strength were sapped, the issue would be fearful.

Thank God for the religious life which has spread in our army, for the blessing of His grace which has ennobled so many of our soldiers. As long as men are faithful soldiers and servants of the Lord Jesus against sin, the world and the devil; so long they will be faithful to their country, faithful in every duty, "they shall not make haste."

Various Books Published By
CONFEDERATE STATES PRINTING OFFICE[5]

You can find these fine books and others by C.S. Publishing Office at your favorite Bookseller, or at www.lulu.com

The Confederate States of America in Prophecy, by Rev. W.H. Seat, a Southern Methodist Minister, and is edited by Dr. William G. Peters. This work examines Daniel's prophecy of the of the Five Governments; with the United States as the Fifth Government and the Confederate States as the little stone cut from the mountain, as a revived Government of Judah.

The Eschatology of the United States as Restored Israel, and the Confederate States as a Restored Judah, is a secular prophecy of the people of North America as God's special chosen people.

In the heady days of Southern victories over Northern armies, Rev. Seat posits the future history of the Confederate States based upon the Prophet Daniel.

Sermons of the Confederacy 1861-1862, edited by Dr. William G. Peters, is a collection of sermons by Southern ministers, bishops, and priests, from 1861-1862.

These ministers cover, in their sermons and discourses, a wide range of subjects, from the cause of the War, differences between Yankees and Southerners, Negroes and their purpose among Southerners, the life and death of Confederate heroes, service to God, military service and Christian Faith, etc.

This is an excellent book for those who want to understand our Confederate ancestors, the C.S.A., and the South's Faith in God and victory in the face of implacable Northern invasion.

Sermons of the Confederacy 1863-1865, edited by Dr. William G. Peters, is a collection of sermons by Southern ministers, bishops, priests, and rabbi from 1863-1865, and a continuation from "Sermons of the Confederacy 1861-1862."

These men of God cover a wide range of subjects, from the cause of the War, differences between Yankees and Southerners, Negroes and their purpose among Southerners, the life and death of Confederate heroes, service to God, military service and Christian Faith, etc.

This is an excellent book for those who want to understand our Confederate ancestors, the C.S.A., and the South's Faith in God and victory in the face of death and destruction from Federal invasion.

---

[5] Also designated as C.S. Printing Office. A division of Confederate States of America, Inc.

The True Church Indicated to the Inquirer, by Bishop John McGill. Confederate Bishop of Richmond, Virginia, edited by Dr. William G. Peters.

Bp. McGill examines the claims of various and sundry groups to be the true Church. He examines these claims in the light of scripture, history, tradition and reason. Then he contrasts them against the claims of the Catholic Church to be the One, True Church, showing how the claims of all other groups fall short.

The Confederate Army Navy Prayer Book is the Episcopal Prayer Book for the Armed Services of the Confederacy, edited by Dr. William G. Peters. The Prayer Book went through annual editions from 1861-1865, and was the official military prayer book of the Confederate States.

Additional prayers have been included, including national calls to prayer by President Jefferson Davis throughout the War, and a sermon by Bp. Stephen Elliot delivered upon the Day of National Humiliation, Fasting and Prayer in 1861.

The Catholic Devotional for Confederate Soldiers was written by Bishop McGill for the Confederate soldiers to carry with them into battle, and for their encampments.

The work was published and registered by Bp. McGill in the Confederate States of America in 1861, and is edited by Dr. William G. Peters.

The Devotional contains many Catholic prayers, novenas, selections from the Mass, etc., which are appropriate to daily devotions, for Catholics and other Christians.

Faith The Victory by Bishop John McGill, Confederate Bishop of Richmond, Virginia, edited by Dr. William G. Peters.

Bp. McGill presents an explanation of Catholic doctrine for Catholics and non-Catholics who hold to the old orthodox Protestant beliefs and traditions, and want to know more about the development and meaning of Christian doctrine.

A non-polemical work, the Bishop provides a rational explanation of sometimes difficult subjects. It is a clear concise summary of doctrinal points of interest to all Christians, without being either too brief, or tedious.

www.ingramcontent.com/pod-product-compliance
Lightning Source LLC
Chambersburg PA
CBHW030133170426
43199CB00008B/55